# MIKHAIL GORBACHEV AND THE END OF SOVIET POWER

*Also by John Miller*

GORBACHEV AT THE HELM: A New Era in Soviet Politics?
(*edited with R. F. Miller and T. H. Rigby*)

# Mikhail Gorbachev and the End of Soviet Power

John Miller
*Senior Lecturer in Communist Politics*
*La Trobe University, Melbourne*

**St. Martin's Press**

First published in Great Britain 1993 by
THE MACMILLAN PRESS LTD
Houndmills, Basingstoke, Hampshire RG21 2XS
and London
Companies and representatives
throughout the world

The author and publishers gratefully acknowledge the support of the
Publications Committee of La Trobe University, Victoria, in the
production of this book.

A catalogue record for this book is available
from the British Library.

ISBN 0–333–54615–6

Printed in Great Britain by
Antony Rowe Ltd
Chippenham, Wiltshire

Reprinted 1994

---

First published in the United States of America 1993 by
Scholarly and Reference Division,
ST. MARTIN'S PRESS, INC.,
175 Fifth Avenue,
New York, N.Y. 10010

ISBN 0–312–09080–3

Library of Congress Cataloging-in-Publication Data
Miller, John, 1940 Feb. 4–
Mikhail Gorbachev and the end of Soviet power / John Miller.
p.   cm.
Includes bibliographical references and index.
ISBN 0–312–09080–3
1. Soviet Union—Politics and government—1985–1991.   2. Soviet
Union—Politics and government—1953–1985.   3. Gorbachev, Mikhail
Sergeevich, 1931–   .   I. Title.
DK288.M55   1993
947.085'4—dc20                                        92–29615
                                                        CIP

To Sue, Mary and Harold

# Contents

# Preface

This book is about the dramatic changes that brought an end to the Soviet Union and its ruling Communist Party in 1991, and about the leader who presided over this process between 1985 and 1991, Mikhail Gorbachev. Its structure is as follows. Chapters 1 to 3 set the scene, with treatment of Russia's long-term history and culture and the Soviet system; the problems that set in after Stalin's death; and a chronological framework for the Gorbachev period. Chapters 4 and 5 discuss Gorbachev, first as a person and then as a political leader. There follow three chapters on the principal aspects of his reforms, in the order in which they became prominent: the media and interest groups; political institutions; and the problem of the Communist Party. Chapters 9 and 10 survey Soviet society and politics in the last two years of the Union's existence, and Chapter 11 analyses the failed attempt to preserve it in a federal form. I seek to draw some conclusions in Chapter 12.

My aim has been to provide a common sense interpretation of the subject for the non-specialist and non-Soviet reader. It is not easy to analyse and discern trends in events as they are happening, and next to impossible to combine this task with that of capturing the chaos, flux and sheer unpleasantness of revolutionary times, and I have not attempted the latter. Rather I have tried to analyse and interpret, in the hope that readers may be helped to make sense of a confusion of reports and impressions. There is a risk in this of reducing people's painful experience to insensitive and abstract formulae; if I seem guilty of this, I ask the reader's forgiveness.

The book's focus is first on the domestic affairs and second on the politics of the Soviet Union's final years. I have given little direct treatment to foreign affairs or economic policy, for two reasons. Although they are important, I do not think they are central to an understanding of the Gorbachev experiment; and I am not at ease in economic or international analysis. The focus on politics means inevitably that a good deal of attention is paid to processes and personalities 'at the top' and perhaps too little to social processes; this is not an easy balance to strike, since social processes clearly affect politics. Some readers may be sceptical of my emphasis on the figure of M. S. Gorbachev, and when I embarked on the study I had not expected it to turn out like this. But Gorbachev set his stamp on events, more so than most western prime ministers or presidents and more than his immediate Soviet predecessors: no interpretation can avoid tackling his role, and it presents considerable intellectual puzzles. Others may be curious that I have said little explicitly about Gorbachev's or the Soviet 'ideology': I think the nature and function of ideology in Soviet affairs have been badly misunderstood by outsiders, and I hope I have provided some corrective to this throughout the book, by suggesting some purposes it really served.

Studying the Soviet Union was like trying to describe icebergs or Arctic nunataks from what one could see above the surface. Information from inside the country was fragmentary and deliberately distorted and to make sense of things the student had to become a detective. Several of my readers have suggested I over-use phrases like 'must have'; indeed I do, and it illustrates the way in which circumstantial evidence and backing one's hunches assumed heightened importance in this kind of work. The figure of A. A. Nikonov in Chapter 4 provides an example. In my card index of personnel I had three cards for persons of this name; I suspected they represented one and the same person at different stages of his career, but I could not demonstrate this until 1988.

The book is based mainly on primary Soviet material and I have made relatively little use of secondary sources; I must confess that I find it difficult to work out a personal synthesis when others' opinions are too fresh in my mind. There is a price to be paid for this of course; I owe apologies to those I have unwittingly echoed without acknowledgment, and to those whose analysis was sharper than mine. The primary sources are the main Soviet newspapers and journals, and to some extent Soviet television; a vote of thanks goes to Australia's Special Broadcasting Service for relaying the Soviet news programme 'Vremya' in 1990–1. There is a limit to one man's reading, however, and I should have been lost without two sources of summary and comment on the rest of the Soviet media. Radio Free Europe/Radio Liberty in their research materials rose magnificently to the challenge of analysing the last seven years; and the international computer network SOVSET' (managed by the Center for Strategic and International Studies in Washington, DC) has brought up-to-date information and comment to an otherwise isolated writer.

I should like to thank many people, but in particular Robin Jeffrey, Ross Martin, Angus McIntyre, Kate Mustafa, Rudolf Plehwe, Talis Polis, Harry Rigby and Vil'yam Smirnov for their generous comments

on my drafts; and Archie Brown, Hans-Joachim Fliedner, John
Gooding, Marko Pavlyshyn, Peter Reddaway and David Wells for
discussion of particular arguments or the supply of material. I am
indebted to the Australian National University for a study visit to the
Soviet Union in 1991 and to La Trobe University for a publication
subsidy and the sabbatical in which I did most of the writing.

*Melbourne*                                    JOHN MILLER


*Note*:   The author and publishers gratefully acknowledge the support
of the Publications Committee of La Trobe University, Victoria, in the
production of this book.

# Glossary

| | |
|---|---|
| All-Union | adjective for the Union or Federal echelon of Soviet government |
| *apparat* | administrative organisation, especially of the Communist Party |
| *apparatchik* | official |
| ASSR | see Autonomous Republic |
| Autonomous *oblast'* | subdivision of a province inhabited by ethnic minority |
| Autonomous Republic | subdivision of a union-republic inhabited by ethnic minority |
| Ban on Faction | ban on internal lobbying in the CPSU introduced in 1921 |
| Central Committee | CPSU 'parliament' of some 300 members and 150 candidates |
| Chekist | sentimental name for state security agent |
| CPSU | Communist Party of the Soviet Union |
| democratic centralism | label for the principles of internal organisation of the CPSU |
| enterprise | factory, farm or any unit of the economy |
| *glasnost'* | openness |
| *gorkom* | city committee of the CPSU |
| Gosplan | State Planning Committee |
| intelligentsia | intellectuals; professionals; educated people (see Chapter 2) |
| *ispolkom* | executive committee of a soviet |
| KGB | Committee of State Security; before 1953 also called Cheka, GPU, OGPU, NKVD, MVD or MGB |
| *kolkhoz* | collective farm, hence *kolkhoznik*, farm worker |
| Komsomol | Communist Youth League |
| *krai* | territorial subdivision of a union-republic; province |
| *kraikom* | provincial committee of the CPSU |
| *limitchik* | migrant labourer obliged to live outside city limits |

| | |
|---|---|
| MPA | Main Political Administration of the Soviet Army and Navy |
| MVD | Ministry of Internal Affairs |
| *neformaly* | unregistered ('informal') organisations |
| NEP | New Economic Policy (in the period 1921–29) |
| NKVD | see KGB |
| *nomenklatura* | CPSU register of posts or persons to fill them |
| *obkom* | provincial committee of the CPSU |
| *oblast'* | territorial subdivision of a union-republic; province |
| *oprichnina* | administrative corps under Ivan the Terrible |
| Party | with capital letter, shorthand for the CPSU |
| *perestroika* | reconstruction |
| *podmena* | intervention, usurpation (usually of others' functions by the CPSU) |
| Plenum | meeting of a full assembly, usually of the Central Committee |
| Politburo | central cabinet ('political bureau') of the CPSU |
| political organs | CPSU organisations in the armed forces and police |
| *raikom* | county or ward committee of the CPSU |
| *raion* | subdivision of a province or city; county or ward |
| republic | shorthand for Union-Republic or Autonomous Republic |
| RSFSR | the Russian union-republic; Russian Soviet Federal Socialist Republic |
| *samizdat* | unregistered ('do-it-yourself') publication |
| soviet | council |
| specialist | employee with complete secondary or tertiary education (see chapter two) |
| Union-Republic | one of the fifteen states that made up the USSR |
| USSR | Union of Soviet Socialist Republics |

---

Russian words and names have been transliterated according to the *Soviet Studies* system, except where another usage has become familiar in English; thus 'Yeltsin', not 'El'tsin'.

# Chronology

## Principal Events 1982–1991

### 1982

| | |
|---|---|
| 25 January | Death of Suslov |
| 24 May | Andropov moves from KGB to Secretariat |
| 10 November | Death of Brezhnev |
| 12 November | Andropov becomes General Secretary |

### 1984

| | |
|---|---|
| 9 February | Death of Andropov |
| 13 February | Chernenko becomes General Secretary |

### 1985

| | |
|---|---|
| 10 March | Death of Chernenko |
| 11 March | Gorbachev becomes General Secretary |
| 23 April | 'April Plenum' of Central Committee |
| 1–2 July | Shevardnadze replaces Gromyko as Foreign Minister; Gromyko becomes Head of State |
| 27 September | Ryzhkov becomes Chairman of Council of Ministers |
| 18–21 September | Geneva Summit |
| 24 December | Yeltsin becomes Moscow first secretary. |

### 1986

| | |
|---|---|
| 25 Feb–6 March | XXVII Party Congress |
| March–August 1986 | Major changes to media and foreign affairs personnel |
| 26 April | Chernobyl' disaster |
| 10 August | Appointment of first non-communist editor |
| 16 December | Fall of Kunaev |
| 19 December | Release of Academician Sakharov from exile |

**1987**

| | |
|---|---|
| 28 January | 'January Plenum' of Central Committee |
| 26 May | Law on Cooperatives |
| 28 May | Flight of Mathias Rust; purge of Defence Ministry |
| 21 June | Local soviet elections |
| 1 July | Law on State Enterprise |
| 10 July | Term 'socialist pluralism' first used by Gorbachev |
| 16 July | First group rehabilitation (of economists) |
| 21 October | Quarrel between Ligachev and Yeltsin |
| 11 November | Dismissal of Yeltsin as Moscow first secretary |

**1988**

| | |
|---|---|
| 5 February | First group rehabilitation of politicians (Bukharin) |
| 20 February | Unrest begins in Nagorno-Karabakh |
| 13 March | 'Andreeva letter' (Pravda reply 5 April) |
| 14 April | Agreement signed to withdraw from Afghanistan |
| 13 May | Publicity for leases in agriculture |
| 28 June–1 July | XIX Party Conference |
| 30 September | Reorganisation of Secretariat and Central Committee *apparat* begins |
| 1 October | Retirement of Gromyko; Gorbachev becomes Head of State |
| 1 December | Constitutional amendments passed |

**1989**

| | |
|---|---|
| 26 March | Elections begin to Congress of People's Deputies |
| 9 April | Army kills demonstrators in Georgia |
| 25 April | Mass 'resignation' from Central Committee |
| 15 May | Withdrawal begins from Afghanistan |
| 25 May | Congress of People's Deputies opens Gorbachev elected Speaker of Supreme Soviet |
| 10 July | Miners' strikes begin |
| 4 August | New Council of Ministers formed |

| | |
|---|---|
| 19 September | Central Committee Plenum on nationalities policy |
| 14 October | Party moves to withdraw from *nomenklatura* |
| 26 November | Gorbachev publishes *The Socialist Idea and Revolutionary Perestroika* |
| 25 December | Establishment of Committee of Constitutional Supervision |

**1990**

| | |
|---|---|
| 19 January | Army operation in Azerbaidzhan |
| 7 February | Central Committee accepts withdrawal from political monopoly |
| 11 March | Lithuanian Declaration of Independence |
| 14 March | Amendment of Article six of the Constitution |
| 15 March | Gorbachev elected President |
| 3 April | Law on Secession passed |
| 29 May | Yeltsin elected Speaker of RSFSR Supreme Soviet |
| 19–25 June | Inaugural Congress of Communist Party of the RSFSR |
| 2–13 July | XXVIII Party Congress |
| 1 August | Law *On the Press* . . . comes into effect. |
| 9 October | Law *On Public Organisations* passed |
| 17 November | Gorbachev forced to accept new programme in Supreme Soviet |
| 20 December | Resignation of Shevardnadze; retirement of Ryzhkov |

**1991**

| | |
|---|---|
| 13 January | Army killings in Lithuania |
| 23 April | 'Novo-Ogarevo Agreement' |
| 12 June | Yeltsin elected President in RSFSR |
| 20 July | Yeltsin bans party activity in workplace |
| 19 August | Gorbachev ousted by 'State Committee for the Emergency' |
| 21 August | Collapse of coup |
| 24 August | Gorbachev resigns as General Secretary |
| 28 August | Government dismissed |
| 6 November | Yeltsin bans Communist Party in Russia |

# 1 An Outline of the Soviet System

'Imagine an autonomous *Gulag* in which the commandant resolves to carry out radical reforms, with the aim of making the camp system, well, if not exactly civilised, then at least capable of dealings with civilised society.'

(Yu. Shreider)[1]

## INTRODUCTION

In August 1986 a conservative Soviet newspaper published a vicious attack on Soviet religious believers, on religious organisations in Britain and on named British students who had attended a certain Soviet university.[2] The author made no secret of using material supplied by the Soviet Committee of State Security (KGB); the article's purpose seemed to be to intimidate people in the groups mentioned. A fortnight later the Moscow correspondent of an American magazine was arrested by the KGB and charged with espionage.[3] Some western journalists doubtless have been spies, but there seemed little doubt in this case that it was a piece of simple hostage-taking – to gain a pawn to swap against a serious spy arrested in New York, or perhaps to jeopardise the planned summit between the US President and the Soviet leader, M. S. Gorbachev, who had been in office eighteen months.

Both these incidents could have occurred at almost any time since the Soviet experiment began in 1917, and they tell us a great deal about the atmosphere of Soviet life. They were also among the last of their kind. In mid-September a bold author was to advocate multiple candidacies in Soviet elections; a fortnight later foreign journalists were given a conducted tour of the Soviet nuclear test site in Semipalatinsk – yet photographing an aviation factory had figured large in the attack on the students![4]

Less than three years later Gorbachev opened a freely elected Soviet parliament, many of whose members had defeated Communist Party officials in the ballot. He called as first speaker Academician A. D.

1

Sakharov, the physicist and human rights campaigner who had been in exile in 1986. A deputy whose father had perished in the Great Purge denounced the KGB in parliament,[5] and its members voted to strike the notion of 'anti-Soviet agitation and propaganda' off the list of 'crimes against the state'. The chief victims of the Purge had already been rehabilitated, and peasants permitted to leave the notorious collective farms. The Soviet publication of Solzhenitsyn's *Gulag Archipelago* and the Soviet Army's evacuation of Afghanistan were both in preparation. Two and a half years after **that** the Communist Party had been banned and the KGB (if only for a time) broken up. When Gorbachev summoned the leaders of the constituent republics of the Soviet 'Union' to initial a treaty designed to turn the Union into a federation like the United States, half did not turn up and those who did refused to sign. Five days later the Russian leader, B. N. Yeltsin, announced that his Russian administration (of about half the Union's inhabitants) would take over the crippled Union budget. At the end of 1991 a handful of the deputies elected with such hope in 1989 voted the Supreme Soviet – and the world's second 'superpower' – out of existence.

What happened between 1986 and 1989, and between 1989 and 1991? What went wrong with the seemingly formidable communist system, indeed what **was** this 'communism' whose last defenders were army officers, factory managers and peasants? What went wrong with the Union, and why do so many of its people seem ready to sacrifice prosperity, perhaps democracy also, to live in separate states? And what was Gorbachev's role in the drama: playwright, midwife or prisoner, or all three? This book is an attempt to tackle these questions.

One common misconception should be raised straight away. It was easy to think of the Soviet Union as a modern, industrialised, European superpower, and of Gorbachev as a parliamentary democrat. These opinions had their truth, but were also misleading unless we realise that the Soviet Union and Gorbachev came to be what they were along routes very different from those familiar to Europeans. A hundred years ago Russian society was as inscrutable to most Europeans as Indian or Chinese, and, because of its superficial familiarities, more easily misconstrued. Russian politics never had an equivalent of Magna Carta and since the thirteenth century developed in a quite different direction from those of Western Europe. Gorbachev came intellectually from a tradition that was deeply hostile to most of what Europeans consider the successes of their civilisation. All of which underlines the extraordinary nature of recent events, but suggests we are liable to misunderstand them, unless they are placed in historical context. This is the purpose of the present chapter.

## THE RUSSIAN HERITAGE

Russian and then Soviet history and politics have been shaped by Russia's northern latitude and severe environment.[6] Sheer distance and climatic obstacles to travel meant that, until the advent of the telegraph and railway, it took as much as two years to communicate with the capital from remoter parts of the country. Agriculture is impossible over half of Siberia, and elsewhere is marginal and confined to a short growing season; it has remained by world standards unproductive and technologically unsophisticated. Primitive agriculture and communications hindered the development of markets, trade and a cash economy – and underdevelopment helped in turn to keep agriculture and communications backward. Longer than anywhere else in Europe, large parts of rural Russia kept up a subsistence, non-monetary, nearly self-sufficient economy.

This had profound effects on society and government. Russian society – still four-fifths rural and illiterate at the beginning of this century – lacked the knowledge, interest and stimulus that could have fuelled social and economic change. It did not experience that differentiation of economic power and interests, and the consequent competition, first economic, then political, among self-interested 'classes' which became the hallmark of West European history. Peasants stayed unspecialised in techniques and relatively homogeneous and equal in their internal structure. The few obligations they recognised beyond the village took the form of personalised bonds to lord or patron, or symbolic bonds to Tsar or Church. After the 1917 revolution many peasants simply refused to grow or sell for the towns and thereby opted out of organised economic and political life – and in 1929 were forcibly reincorporated into it at grievous cost. So little did they feel themselves, so little were they treated as members of Soviet state or society! This was indeed not a true society in the sociological sense of *Gesellschaft*, but in many respects still an assembly of traditional communities (*Gemeinschaften*).

In particular people were unfamiliar with things our industrialised, interdependent society takes for granted: the routine, discipline and rule-adherence that is part of cooperation in any large enterprise or organisation; acceptance of such impersonal, secular, regulatory devices as law and contract; division of labour and competition among interest groups; accommodation and adjudication among the latter, and the accumulation of such trade-offs that comes to be called 'social contract'. Such middle class or bourgeoisie as emerged was feeble and lacking in confidence, hardly equipped to challenge the rulers, to press for the security of trade within a predictable and accessible framework of laws, or to promote the skills and values of negotiation and compromise; it was not in fact a middle class that could hold the balance, in Aristotle's sense,[7] between rich and poor.

Rulers thought they faced tasks more daunting than in countries to the west, and with fewer resources. Not surprisingly they sought to increase state power and to dismantle natural and man-made obstacles to it. They made harshness, arbitrariness and the use of secret police matters of deliberate policy and pride; and they went out of their way to block social mobility and initiative, and to oppose the growth of towns, commerce, law or interest groups – anything that might set limits on government, as it had come to do in Europe. It was society that needed limiting, they thought, not government. By the nineteenth century their power was in a sense greater than in the fourteenth – but it was the personalised power of a court, the object of unremitting struggle and intrigue, easily captured by usurpers. At the same time society was kept, by European standards, inert, immobile, and unstructured. There is a vicious circle here: society is robbed of coherence and infrastructure, and confirms the state in the role of isolated predator. Analysis in terms of a 'weak society' confronting a 'strong state' became the norm.

The polarisation was exacerbated by the fact that the Russian state had come to include a large number of non-Russians also, speaking many languages, and many of them not adherents of the Russian Orthodox faith. Ethnic diversity is notoriously something which increases the pressure on a political system: government becomes more difficult because fewer decisions can be standard or routine, and resources must be devoted to their reliable transmission and execution. At the time of the Empire's collapse in 1917 its population had an ethnic make-up among the most complex in the world, of which Russians were no more than 44 per cent. Besides their number and diversity, the distribution of non-Russians, predominantly along the western and southern borders, affected politics. Russian rulers developed a perception of their own border regions as populated by untrustworthy, potentially treacherous heretics, and hence controls were strengthened or programmes of Russification adopted. The message again was that society is precarious and turbulent unless held together by a ruler with unlimited powers.

The political thinking that reflected experience of this sort – and in turn served to rationalise it – was predictable. Among ordinary people self-sufficiency was combined with a narrow-minded, parochial conservatism, opposed to change for which neither information nor incentive had been offered. The outside world was a frightening place, something against which one could only seek protective authority, or put up barriers of non-compliance, evasion and trickery; if these failed it was often only a short step to violence. Yet people dreaded social breakdown, what Pushkin called 'senseless and merciless Russian revolt'.[8] They dreaded weak or divided councils on high, such as had produced the Time of Troubles, the chaotic interregnum that preceded the Romanov dynasty in 1613. Harsh and unlimited government was often welcomed.

The counterpart of this on the rulers' side blended autocracy – the unlimited, divinely ordained, personal power of the monarch – with a conservative opposition to social and economic change, and to processes or institutions that might seem to foster it. Because the regulatory role of law, institutions or self-interest was so weak, other ways of ordering people were cultivated: controls and coercion; patron-client alliances; the idolisation of leaders that came to be called the 'cult of personality'. They were quick to adopt the Byzantine notion that society gained in cohesion by being unanimously orthodox; the twentieth century version of this was the 'state ideology' and state monopoly of education and public relations.

The vicious circles linking environment with social structure, and social structure with social perceptions, seemed tighter and more intractable than in the West. Nineteenth century Russian intellectuals, calling them the 'Accursed Questions' (*proklyatye voprosy*), came to see them as the driving force behind Russia's divergence from the path taken by the rest of Europe. It was common to discern an element of the ineluctable (which could be rationalised into 'destiny') in the way Russia had developed. From this was to evolve 'Slavophilism', the notion of the special mission of the Slavs, and particularly of their largest nation, the Russians. Slavophilism was opposed in the nineteenth century by 'Westernists', who emphasised instead that all societies followed a similar path of development, but that some might be further along that path than others. In both camps the sense that Russia was the prisoner of elemental forces contributed to an urgent and desperate approach to politics in which considerations of popular consent were easily brushed aside.

Common to everyone's thinking, it seemed, was fear of the elements and fear of change, and more than a suspicion that change was assumed to be not gradual but elemental in its workings. This fear of the elemental was taken over into the perceptions of post-revolutionary Russia: the word 'elemental' (*stikhiinyi*, more often translated 'spontaneous') was the word chosen by Lenin to label the sort of unregulated mass politics he opposed. In consequence the notion of control as one of the primary functions of the state was common to both imperial Russian and Soviet communist politics: control to ward off elemental change, and control **of** change.

It is the classical Hobbesian position: that an absolute ruler is the only alternative to mutual butchery.[9] And mention of the Englishman Hobbes serves to remind us that there is nothing peculiarly Russian about the views I am exploring. On the contrary, it was Western Europe which diverged from what used to be world-wide perceptions, with its suggestion that the 'war of every man against every man' is not **too** costly, the self-discipline of cooperation not **too** burdensome, and that society can cope with a good deal of competition and dissension before it breaks up.

The discussion so far has been about **political culture**, that medium of assumptions, perceptions and expectations about organised life that permeates all policy and politics. A political culture is by no means immutable; it evolves with its society, as the contrast between English views today and those of Hobbes illustrates, but only very slowly – over generations not years, at society's own free pace rather than that of its leaders or thinkers. Politicians cannot change a political culture by *fiat* – though they can encourage social change and its articulation in ideas. Shock and trauma from outside – tyranny, revolution, military defeat – tend to fossilise a political culture in exhausted conservatism.

Russia's political culture was in one respect more complex than simple Hobbesianism, even in Hobbes' own time. Russia had been overrun by Mongol/Tatar invaders from Central Asia in the 1230s and it was two centuries before the princes of Muscovy began to roll back Tatar overlordship. This period of the 'Tatar Yoke' was thought to have kept Russian culture frozen for two hundred years and educated Russians have been preoccupied ever since with the notion of Russia's backwardness by comparison with Western Europe. Perceived initially as poverty in general culture and civilisation, it became increasingly identified with economic and technological backwardness. The urge to catch up is inconsistent with fear of the disruption change brings; the two perceptions tended to be voiced by different groups (Westernists and Slavophiles in the nineteenth century) and policy tended to oscillate between modernism and conservatism, emulation and isolation. But the tension between the two generated a type of programme that was characteristically Russian: planned and forced modernisation, imposed from above, using the powers and methods of autocracy to achieve quickly what in Europe had been the outcome of gradual evolution and experiment. Two famous authors of such 'revolutions from above' were Ivan the Terrible (1530–84) and Peter the Great (1672–1725). Particularly interesting for twentieth century observers are the organisational means used by these two to drag an unconsenting society into modernity. Ivan recruited a corps of special agents (called *oprichnina*; nowadays they would have been a secret police) to smash the vested interests of the landed aristocracy. Peter organised a short-lived 'service nobility', one into which talent might be coopted from outside the aristocracy – and which made land ownership conditional on official employment.

Often overlooked – especially in the enthusiasm of a Great Leap Forward – was that such programmes did not leave society any stronger, more confident or more capable of autonomous evolution. Planning, investment, momentum, rewards, all were monopolised by the state; even the newly trained tended to be narrowly specialised and dependent on the state for employment. When momentum waned the 'corps of special agents' turned into a new ruling class. Revolutions from above were not in fact revolutions in a strict sense and left social structure untouched. They simply relaunched society on its cycle of convulsion followed by privilege, stagnation, backwardness, envy and more convulsion.[10] The real task – as a few enlightened politicians like Alexander II (1818–81) or P. A. Stolypin (1862–1911) recognised – was to get spontaneous social evolution started without unleashing chaos.

It was against this background that the Russian **intelligentsia** evolved. It is often forgotten that this word is Russian and was borrowed because there is no exact equivalent to the intelligentsia in English speaking countries. One of Peter the Great's successors waived the rule that land ownership should be conditional on public service, and from 1762 Russian landwners were exempt from taxes and had rights over their serfs and generally comfortable circumstances – but no responsibilities unless they chose to assume them. The prejudice of the regime against urban life, and therefore against professions and interest representation, compounded this disengagement from the problems of modern life. Children of landowning, official and clerical families – in Lenin's phrase, 'the educated representatives of the propertied classes'[11] – became the so-called 'superfluous generation', frequently described in nineteenth century fiction: talented, educated, idealistic and deprived of outlets for their energies. Members of this intelligentsia were easily captivated by 'trendy', foreign social theory (not difficult to contrast with state sponsored orthodoxy) and easily came to assume that the world owed them a living for armchair criticism. It was difficult to indulge in social theory without coming to the attention of the Tsar's censors and secret police, and they were pushed increasingly into alienated radicalism. In time radical views came to be treated as evidence of intellectual independence, and state employment as a surrender that disqualified one from membership of the intelligentsia. A great deal of this tradition survived the Revolution, and indeed was revived by Soviet forms of organisation.

One trend among the intelligentsia blended radicalism with anguish at Russia's backwardness. Modernisation seemed a far more urgent goal than democracy or human rights, and intellectuals of this tradition – important nineteenth century figures are Pestel', Ogarev and Tkachev – opposed the monarchy not for its unfettered powers, but for the conservative use it made of them – coupled with a conviction that their own use of such powers would get results. Their aim was not a democratic or constitutional order but revolution from above, using the state's absolute powers. It is this tradition in Russian radicalism which, for whatever reason, won out; it is hard not to think that it was the more seriously thought-out tradition.

It has come increasingly to be recognised that the native tradition of modernisation from above was every bit as important a contributor to Lenin's thinking and to Soviet communism as were the writings of Marx. If we interpret the Bolsheviks as autocratic modernisers – in the tradition of Tsars Ivan and Peter and the radical intelligentsia – a great deal becomes clear which has been obscured by preoccupation with Marxism and socialism. A small group from the intelligentsia seized power, gripped by a burning sense of mission to overcome Russia's backwardness; Tucker has called this sense of mission 'transformism',[12] borrowing a word of which Stalin was fond. Their task seemed to them so urgent that considerations of popular consent paled into insignificance; the masses would be saved from themselves in their own despite, dragged into the twentieth century whether they willed or understood it or not. This element in Bolshevism struck a

chord in Russian experience and attracted like-minded people, whilst
the recipes of West European socialism looked remote, abstract and,
above all, **slow**. The communist regime emphasised the theme of
modernisation increasingly, and jettisoned aims from Marxism and
social democracy as it sensed that modernisation was what engaged
support. Here we have a clue to one of the appeals of Stalinism.

How to set about realising this mission in terms of programmes and
institutions? The Bolsheviks found the classical powers of the Russian
state (and the passivity of the Russian masses) far too convenient to
give up. It seemed clear to them that there had to be a centralised,
state-run development programme, and that the state's priorities must
be able to override everyone else's. This entailed the ability to control
most aspects of socio-political life, both in order to identify and utilise
resources efficiently, and to minimise opposition and disruption.
'Totalitarian' is the word most often used to describe such a political
programme; it is an appropriate word, but somewhat lacking in
analytical precision. For our purposes the important thing to note is
that the Bolsheviks wanted to subject state and society to a **single
organisation**, so that they might be devoted to a **single purpose**.

The state structure Lenin founded was that of a political party writ
large[13] – and of a small, conspiratorial party at that. If one contrasts
his two best known works, *What is to be Done?* (1902) and *State and
Revolution* (1917), one cannot fail to be struck by the partial scope of
his political aims: by the zeal and meticulous detail he brings to the
organisation of his 'party of a new type' in the former, and in the
latter, where the focus is society, by the disdain for quite elementary
questions of management and morale. There have been such 'mono-
functional' experiments before – the Jesuit state of Paraguay, Geneva
under the Calvinists, Quaker Pennsylvania for more than half a
century – and they have usually been short-lived experiments because
humans vary in their needs and they want to pursue a variety of good
things in life. They are rarely happy (and then not for long) with
subordinating everything else to one overriding goal.

The definition of **politics** in such 'mono-functional' systems differs
crucially from Aristotle's sense of the word as the common affairs of
the small town community. With Aristotle acceptance of diversity and
competition are at the heart of politics; politics are the art of organising
that cooperation or that balance of competition that constitutes a
functioning community. They are not about finding perfect, all-time
solutions; 'in politics there is hardly perfect win' (the brilliant
formulation of a student not yet fluent in English), and this means

that political outcomes are messy, involve compromise, are the least unsatisfactory, least disadvantageous of a bad bunch of options.

The conclusion is inescapable: Lenin was not concerned with **politics** at all, in its familiar sense of the organisation of diverse interests, and this narrowness of his focus diminishes his claims to be a statesman or state-builder. If we bear in mind that communist systems were set up for one overriding purpose only, and hence that they lacked essential features as political systems, a lot that is puzzling about them falls into place. It becomes clearer why Lenin's writings, or Soviet policy or legislation were so serious, exacting and detailed about some things, and apparently so heedless and abstract about others. We see one reason why Stalin captured the system so easily; why a new dispensation had to be worked out after Stalin's death; and why this dispensation collapsed, after little more than thirty years. And it illustrates the daunting nature of the tasks Gorbachev faced: he had not only to seek a new equilibrium but to tackle tasks of state-building that had never been faced in Soviet history.[14]


## THE MONO-ORGANISATIONAL SYSTEM

It was the Communist Party of the Soviet Union[15] (or CPSU) which became the Bolsheviks' chosen instrument for centralised development and control of society, the twentieth century equivalent of Ivan's *oprichnina* and Peter's service nobility. When they came to power the Party already had many of the centralised features that were to make it so effective an instrument for their purposes. In 1917 Lenin already thought in terms of its 'vanguard role', but this described its relationship with the working class only. Under the pressures of Civil War this concept evolved into one of a **single ruling party** that claimed a monopoly on political debate and decisions, and the right to crush organised competition. It seems the Bolsheviks groped their way inarticulately towards this, but by the early 1920s they were willing to make a virtue of it and explore seriously its radical implications for government. Because of these haphazard beginnings the place and functions of the Party in the political system were never clarified in constitution or law – apart from Article six of the 1977 ('Brezhnev') Constitution where it is called – rather unhelpfully – 'the leading and guiding force of Soviet society'.

One-party rule imposes a remorseless logic if it is to survive. Independent political activity is potentially the basis of a rival party and a challenge to the single Party's monopoly. Thus to preserve the monopoly the Party must get and keep a controlling position in a number of spheres of social and political life. It must control public communications (the mass media, education and culture) through **censorship** and an official **state ideology**. It must regulate the formation of spontaneous **public organisations** – clubs, associations etc – and steer their affairs through Party cells formed within them. It must enlist most people in **public service** and **management**: this is why more than half the CPSU was in white-collar employment from the late 1930s. And it is lost if it fails to penetrate the **officer corps** of armed forces and police; almost all officers were Party members.

The need to control administrative and managerial employment, combined with the need to mobilise millions of people for rapid economic development, gave the Party an abiding interest in the selection, training and deployment of personnel; they saw, in Stalin's words, that 'cadres decide everything'. There emerged the system of *nomenklatura* ('list of names'), whereby the Party imposed a central, coordinated policy on millions of appointments and promotions to positions of responsibility.[16] This was achieved by allocating to Party committees lists of jobs which were under their control and in their gift. At the apex of the system the Party's Politburo ('Political Bureau') or its head-quarters staff in the Central Committee Secretariat approved thousands of senior positions throughout the Union.[17] In the exercise of their *nomenklatura* rights Party committees could override the administrative superiors of the nominee or experts in the job's duties, and above all they could override local interests. A university vice-chancellor, for example, would be 'recommended' not by his own institution, nor by local authorities or education bureaucrats, but by a regional Party committee. This committee need not contain any representative of the university or of local or educational interests, and was bound by central policy.

The *nomenklatura* system had two consequences which may not be clear at first sight. It enabled the Party to impose its political priorities in most walks of life, at a time when price fixing and centralised allocation of supplies had deprived money of much of its usefulness for getting what one wanted. As the power of money declined, so the power of appointment increased: **this** became a resource for which people competed, and the Party committees which allocated staff came to be among the most powerful in the land. Second, duty to one's employer was supplemented by other, less tangible loyalties; someone hired by a *nomenklatura* committee owed more to that committee than to his apparent administrative superiors. This soon gave rise to an 'old boy network' with all its implications: patronage, corruption, public perceptions of secrecy and unaccountability. To be successful one-party rule could not confine itself to the elite. It was the function of millions of **ordinary Party members** to represent the Party at the 'grass roots': to popularise policy, mobilise support, sustain morale – and to keep head-quarters informed about popular mood and the real outcome of policy. They formed a reserve of aspiring, upwardly mobile people who cooperated out of ambition for themselves or their children. Their role was like that of squire, parson and schoolteacher in the idealised English village, and, carefully managed, they were a more effective means of social control and channel of communications than police, secret or open.

The Party always insisted on the distinction between its own officials (or *'apparat'*), paid from Party funds to do Party work, and the much larger 'state' bureaucracy.[18] The latter put policy dutifully into practice; the former made and interpreted policy, but was supposed to refrain from **usurpation** (*podmena*) of executive tasks. But this was not a division of labour which could be defined clearly or oberved in practice. We have seen how personnel decisions came to be matters of policy. Security police and censors seem likewise to have taken their orders from the Party rather than from the state. Before 1990 all military units had 'political organs' and 'deputy commanders for politics', set up by and responsible to the Party Central Committee rather than the Ministry of Defence. In these examples we see how a single ruling party takes on direct administration, how it supplants state functions until 'party' and 'state' are merged in one conglomerate state-party or party-state. An important consequence is that Party functionaries may come to have more in common with the state bureaucracy than with the members of their own Party.

The examples suggest also that one-party rule does not stay in stable equilibrium, or not if its purpose is social transformation. There is a tension between the claims of monopoly power and those of mono-functional purpose. How to stop the Party-saturated bureaucracy from representing merely traditional state interests? The Party can try to maintain 'revolutionary' commitment by excluding capable persons who have the wrong ideas, but this exposes the monopoly to external threats (and hence the need for more police). Alternatively it can draw virtually all talented and articulate persons into its ranks, but at cost to its single-mindedness. The CPSU never resolved this dilemma satisfactorily, but we see why, along with protection of its power, it had to put unremitting effort into maintaining **intra**-Party cohesion and discipline.

This meant, first, the selection, testing and training of individual members and the regulation of its overall social profile; in the Party Rules before 1990 the section on admissions and expulsions was the most elaborate and frequently amended part. It was not open to anyone who wanted to join, and new members were usually invited to apply, often on the basis of a central recruitment plan. Once inside, members entered a world of near-military or monastic discipline. 'Democratic centralism', as it was called, was codified under Stalin in 1934 as follows: 'election of all leading Party organs, from the lowest to the highest; periodical reports of Party organs to their Party organisations and to higher organs; strict Party discipline and subordination of the minority to the majority; the decisions of higher organs are obligatory for lower bodies'.[19]

Again there is more here than meets the eye. Political information, discussion and the rights of minorities were severely hampered by the decision of March 1921 (significantly a decision taken when Lenin was at the height of his powers) to punish 'factionalism', defined as group activity organised on the basis of a distinct platform.[20] Penalties were to be imposed by the Party 'organs' (elected officials or their appointed staff), who thus had a splendid weapon against lobbying or 'head-counting' before important decisions, and even more against attempts to reopen decisions of the past. It was part of these officials' job to prepare contingency plans or policy options, and thus the '**ban on faction**' strengthened them at the expense of their competitors. The powers (and career prospects) of officials were further improved by the application of *nomenklatura* procedures to Party elections, so that candidates for office were 'recommended' from above and stood unopposed. Together these measures stripped democratic centralism of any democratic content ('informed centralism' might be more accurate); and they served to transfer power from membership to officials. A vanguard role had been created for the *apparat*.


## FEATURES OF SOVIET POLITICS

For all the partiality of its scope, it is a mark of Lenin's seriousness that he created a logically coherent, almost watertight system. This emerges when we try to draw out some of the salient features of Soviet politics as they appeared in the early 1980s. All flow on, in some sense, from the premise of a mono-organisational, mono-functional system, which in turn has its roots in Russian political culture. And their inter-related nature points to yet another problem for someone like Gorbachev, namely the difficulty of gradual reform: if he removed any brick from this structure, the temple might crash down; the temptation must have been strong, either to retreat to a conservative holding operation, or to mount his own revolution from above. From this Gordian knot let me single out four threads of particular importance. The first two are ancient features of Russian politics which have remained surprisingly potent despite – perhaps because of – seventy years of communist rule; there follow two important ways in which the Soviet period left its mark.

Pride of place must go to the absence of constitutionality and of generally applicable, publicly accessible **law**. At the constitutional level the place of the Party in politics was never defined. Nor had some of the Party's principal weapons – *nomenklatura*, censorship, political organs in the armed forces – any basis in law. Between 1988 and 1990 Gorbachev tried to define, for example, which person or institution was the supreme commander of the Armed Forces, which declared a state of emergency, to which the head of the security police reported – all vital matters of state. We simply do not know how those questions should be answered concerning the Khrushchev and Brezhnev periods. We can guess, and the guesses would name either the head of the Party, the General Secretary, or the Politburo – or perhaps each at different times. Such important relationships, and thousands of others less important, remained complete mysteries to the overwhelming mass of society.

Official disdain for law and institutions was frightening in its pervasiveness. Khrushchev in his 'Secret Speech' against Stalin was simply unconcerned with Stalin's wide and unchecked powers, and with how the Party let him acquire them, and he suggested no safeguards (other than personal vigilance) against a repeat performance; it was fundamentally not a political, but a moralistic critique. Not until 1966 – nearly fifty years after the Revolution! – did the Party Rules lay down how the General Secretary, was to be chosen. Khrushchev's mild attempts to set limits on repeated holding of office were struck down by Brezhnev and not reintroduced until 1990. The Rules before that same date ordained expulsion for Party members who 'commit a **punishable** offence'. The word 'punishable' signalled that Party organisations were free to prejudge matters that had not yet come before the courts. It was suggested – in 1990! – that the clause be replaced with 'sentenced by a court for a criminal offence . . . , after the sentence has come into force'.[21]

The outcome for ordinary people was that they could not consult rules so as to pursue their personal interests within a framework of personal security. Phenomena like secret rules whose content was known only to officials, or the non-justiciable administrative power of officials to send people into exile, survived into our own time:[22] Sakharov was not sent to Gor'kii by a court. Party procedures were likewise hidden from the general public: when the citizen dealt with officials appointed from *nomenklatura* lists he observed that they were not accountable to their visible administrative superiors (who had not appointed them), and he concluded that public complaints or pressure were pointless. This encouraged nepotism and maladministration among officials and strengthened public alienation from the ruling class. Politics came to seem remote and arbitrary, and people either turned away from involvement in – from thinking about – politics and society, or else they turned to self-defensive strategies of evasion and corruption. The behaviour we expect under notions like 'enlightened self-interest', 'social contract' or 'rule of law' remained disturbingly undeveloped. Many communities began to evolve a cellular or neo-feudal social structure, designed to insulate them from the inroads of outsiders and of the central government.

One is bound to infer that the failure to develop law was deliberate: that rules would have constituted an unacceptable check on what zealous leaders might do, and that instinctively they preferred a passive and atomised society. It was easy enough to talk about the 'withering away of the state'; much harder to break out of the mind-set which saw organisation, controls and propaganda as cure-alls.

This suggests a connection between lawlessness and lack of **integration** as a society (the Soviet Union was of course never a nation!). Geographical and demographic diversity might in any case have impeded the transition from communities to society, but twentieth century politics did not help. The vicissitudes of the Soviet period stunted social confidence and threw people back to reliance on near and familiar ties. More important, communist leaders were ambivalent about whether they wanted a modern society with all its implications. On the one hand they were transformists, and through industrialisation created much of the infrastructure and the work skills needed for the transition. But in a deeper sense they were conservative about political methods and ignorant of social dynamics: all but a few seem to have missed the (eminently Marxian!) process whereby the new interest groups engendered by industrialisation rose up to challenge their creators. Such things as the hieratic use of ideology and the leadership cult, the distrust of professionalism and interest diversity, the feudal and patronage tendencies implicit in *nomenklatura*, even the insistence on holding the Tsar's former subjects within one state: all suggest a confused desire to pluck modernity's fruits without paying for them.

Perceptions and behaviour thus stayed remarkably unchanged from those of the nineteenth century. Fear of weak government and social breakdown, and the Hobbesian lessons it suggested for politics, did not dissipate. People did not lose their instinct for self-sufficiency. The Soviet experience – especially endemic economic scarcity – has taught them to trust personal and local loyalties, to look after themselves and their own before anything else. Individuals and groups – families, factories, farms, ministries, regions, Union-Republics – try by hoarding and legal or illegal cornering of supplies to turn themselves into microcosmic states and economies. Urban residents carry string-bags called 'in-case' bags (*avos'ki*), in case they encounter some *defitsitnyi* item, whether they want it immediately or not. Ministries, whatever their task, make sure they have their own supplies of food and fuel, their own transport and construction services, sometimes their own police forces; and they can be every bit as competitive among themselves as capitalist firms. The Party railed for decades against the twin evils of 'localism' and 'departmentalism' (*mestnichestvo* and *vedomstvennost'*) – as if it did not realise that these were natural defence mechanisms. At every level the person-to-person skills of barter, jobbery and racketeering flourished, whilst impartial organisational and managerial skills, those of trade or negotiation, atrophied.

Nowhere was this more the case than in the field of ethnic politics. The 1917 revolution had seemed to promise great things to the non-Russian majority of the old Empire, but these hopes were soon dashed. Disillusion arose partly from the too easy Russian assumption of leadership in the new regime, and from the reassertion of old boundaries for what was basically Russian *raison d'état*. It was compounded by Stalin's mass deportations, which were in some cases simply the pursuit of Caucasian vendettas. But even without such blunders and crimes, the Leninist 'nationalities policy' was counterproductive. Stripped of rhetoric it amounted to two things: an unexamined adherence to the Marxist (and liberal) notion that economic development would simply mitigate ethnic loyalties; and, until this should take effect, competitive activity among ethnic groups

– i.e. ethnic politics in a strict sense – was suppressed. Minority cultures were encouraged, but in isolation from each other; comparisons and contrasts might not be drawn in public. With this went the freezing of the administrative boundaries of the early 1920s. The evidence of the 1980s is overwhelming that ethnic perceptions were not dissipated, but merely relegated to an underground subculture, and that they became more passionate for not getting public airing. Can one wonder that, when mass politics emerged, they were volatile, confused and intolerant, and that people did not behave as if they belonged to one society?

When we turn to the changes effected by the last seventy years, the consequences of **monopoly** and the suppression of competition stand out. The party-political monopoly was extended to the economy in the early 1930s, and here too the implications were radical and far-reaching. If the planned economy was to work, manufacturers and farmers must be made to produce exactly what the state ordered, not what seemed profitable or met demand. A principal solution was to put an end to the market mechanism of prices fluctuating according to demand; if prices were fixed centrally, they could not serve as a stimulus to autonomous economic action. The State Planning Committee (Gosplan) which initiated orders became in effect the only customer with any capacity to influence output. But price fixing also robbed money of its function as a measure of quality, costs or efficiency, replacing it with alternative 'currencies' that were arbitrary and authoritarian. Planners lost useful criteria for deciding between policy options, and as monopolists exempt from competition it was easy for them to lose touch with demand and with the real economic world.

The parallels outside the economy are striking and less familiar. Marxism-Leninism was made the official **state ideology** in the early 1930s;[23] material used in education, the media, culture and science had to follow prescribed, standardised vocabulary and associations of ideas, and censors and Party secretaries for ideology ensured compliance. It is hard to exaggerate the impact of the ideological monopoly on Soviet society; it was as important as, and perhaps more insidious than the impact of simple tyranny. As a state operation Marxism-Leninism took on the features, interests and personnel of state public relations, and by the 1970s it amounted to little else. It elevated technique at the expense of content and reinforced the intolerance of a monopoly with state chauvinism. Its priests had a vested interest in opposing competition among ideas, in preventing ideas being put out to tender. Just as the functions of the market were

rejected in the economy, so were those of the market in ideas: reason
and argument, debate and negotiation all suffered; politics lost criteria
of judgement other than *raison d'état*, survival in power, personal
careerism and suiting political masters. Monopoly thus helped keep
people dependent, intellectually and politically as well as economically.

Popular reactions to the ideology spanned a range from uncritical
parrotry, through imperviousness and boredom, fascination with
forbidden fruit (especially pseudo-science and occultism), to the
generation of a new alienated intelligentsia. The latter faced, not
merely practical difficulties (which they tried to circumvent with 'do-
it-yourself publishing' or *samizdat*), but formidable difficulties in
thinking, articulating and developing ideas outside the official framework. Orwell's notion of 'thought-crime' was close to the truth: people
could be every bit as inhibited about talking politics as we think our
grandparents were about sex. The ideological monopoly not only
divided society; it impoverished non-communist and anti-communist
thinking also.

Behind the urge to monopolise lay an image of society as a
mechanism or machine, and of politics as **social engineering**. The
component parts of a bicycle, or a bridge, or an aircraft have no life
of their own: they function only within the framework of an overall
design; machines can be dismantled and reassembled without damage;
and only certain designs will work at all. It was a model influenced,
first, by military patterns of organisation (always potent in Russia)
and, second, by the Industrial Revolution, perceived from the outside;
computing gave it a new lease of life in the 1960s and 1970s. The
alternative theory, that espoused in this book, and in general taken for
granted in Europe since the Renaissance, is that individuals and
groups have autonomy of action, and that politics is the art of
organising them into society.

Politics thus came to be visualised as the working out and
implementation of a blueprint for society. Party leaders were confident they possessed the correct design. Technical sub-problems
would doubtless arise in the course of construction, but to these, it
was assumed, there existed technically correct solutions; anything
falling short of these would vitiate the entire structure. It was a
model that encouraged a bureaucracy of confident social engineers,
often recruited from engineering proper, and they left their mark on
politics. If society has no more spontaneous life than a machine, then
politics cannot be a matter of bargaining or adjudication among
competing interests. Common assumptions about politics are forgot-

ten: the notion that policy may be refined by challenge or scrutiny; the expectation that the outcome of politics will almost always be an unsatisfactory compromise.

L. I. Brezhnev put some of this into purple prose in 1967:

> Apart from the Communist Party we have not, and cannot have in the Soviet Union any other political organisation which would take account of the interests and particular features of the classes and social groups we have, of all nationalities and peoples and all generations, and combine these interests in its policies. The Party sees to it that each tiniest streamlet of everyday, current concern harmoniously flows together into a single mighty torrent.[24]

In consequence the Party never tolerated spontaneous social organisations. Under Stalin those that survived had to function as 'transmission belts' (another mechanical metaphor!) for state policy. Even after 1953 the bizarre doctrine was maintained that society contained no 'antagonistic' conflicts of interest. Public organisations were licensed and monitored; expert policy advice was by official invitation only; people with experience of common problems – farms growing the same crops, Party cells in the same kind of factory – could not get together to compare notes.

We have noted the tension between the Party's organisational monopoly and its transformist mission. It was the attempt to yoke these two that made the communist experiment unusual; if it had not been for this, communism would have been indistinguishable from 'oriental despotisms' throughout history. It was also what led to its undoing, in two senses. First the obsession with making government effective, and the consequent indifference to abuse of power, made the system an easy target for someone like Stalin. The second cause of instability was a paradoxical one. No previous 'revolution from above' had produced more than a change in the ruling elite. Implicit in the aims of this one was mass literacy in a society whose literacy levels had not been much better than those of ancient Egypt or Mexico. But organisational monopoly was based essentially on pre-modern military and police models and presupposed a social docility which mass literacy was bound to erode. Too late, Stalin's successors began to grope their way out of this dilemma; their solution – hinted at in Brezhnev's words – was quietly to abandon the transformist mission and to deal with society, not as engineers, but like any authoritarian, conservative rulers.

This had natural consequences for the single ruling Party. It was now part of its duty to embrace the concerns of most of society's character types, interest groups and institutions. Increasingly it became a 'broad church' whose discipline served not so much to suppress diversity as to control its outward manifestations. Beneath this crust, it has been said, members of the same Party had less in common than British communists and conservatives. To ask, as is often done, how Party members as far apart as Yu. V. Bondarev and S. S. Shatalin 'reconciled their views with socialism' is about as useful as to ask how the characters in Eco's *The Name of the Rose* reconcile their views with Christianity; both cases are set in a context of the breakdown of an ideological monopoly.

Overall this was a political system dedicated to solving one particular problem, that of industrialisation. Obsession with this at the expense of other problems of politics made it a system, like dinosaurs, well **adapted** to particular conditions, but by the same token not very **adaptable**, and from a stable political system we expect some kind of ability to respond to the unforeseen. Still worse, in pursuit of its obsession the Party kept other forms of social development in cold storage; in this one is reminded of the period of the Tatar Yoke. When its monopoly was broken in 1990 one got an uncanny sense of society taking up where its evolution had been interrupted. But during the seventy years hiatus political skills and capacity to acknowledge others' interests had been damaged; old agenda are pursued with a new intolerance and passion. In both its loss of adaptability and its deskilling effect the Soviet period has resembled previous attempts at revolution from above.

# 2 What went Wrong under Brezhnev?

'You pretend to pay us, and we pretend to work.'

## THE CLIMATE OF THE KHRUSHCHEV REGIME

Khrushchev came to power with the realisation that things could not go on as before. His main motive was not altruistic, but the fear shared by the surviving leaders for their own safety: never again should a single person have the means to destroy his rivals in the way Stalin and Beria had done. He was also shrewd enough to see that government could be more stable if leadership and popular appeal replaced terror and force.[1]

The first step was to scale down Stalin's police state. Army generals were brought into the Politburo chambers in July 1953 to arrest Beria, the head of the secret police; he was subsequently shot with many of his adherents and his vast empire broken up. State security was separated from other police work, the former consigned to a Committee of State Security (or KGB) and the latter going to the Ministry of Internal Affairs or MVD. Police enterprises in gold, rare minerals and lumber – they had run most of the economy of the Siberian North and East – were handed over to ministries for management. And hundreds of thousands of surviving prisoners who had worked these enterprises were quietly released over the next few years – though often without the right to live in big cities. Particularly obnoxious forms of discipline and control were abandoned: factory management no longer held workers' residence permits or allocated their housing; collective punishment, punishment by association and the ban on marriage to foreigners were abandoned. The security police continued to be used as an instrument of politics and was still not subject to law; but its use henceforth became more specific and calculated and less indiscriminate, so that in time people could discern, and therefore observe, the informal 'rules' by which the KGB operated. Their sense of personal security increased, as did their capacity to evade government obtrusion into private life. Without this

21

the dissidents of the 1960s and the independent politics of the 1980s would have been impossible.

Khrushchev's next tasks were to construct a leadership system less vulnerable to hijacking than the Leninist one, and instruments of social control that did not make enemies of the population. Revival of the Communist Party offered many of the answers. Major decisions and appointments were in future to be made by collective Party bodies that met regularly. Chief of these was the Politburo, a dozen or so top Party politicians, continually jostling for priority, but united in the need to keep the General Secretary[2] no more than first among equals and to crush other signs of undue ambition; the head of the KGB was not included. Party officials had their tasks and status increased, and their career structure regularised. At the same time it became much easier to enter the Party. Millions of people were eager to seize this chance of bettering themselves, and they became the 'eyes and ears' of the regime in society. (Brezhnev later had to restrict this avenue of social mobility.)

Both processes accelerated after one of the Soviet Union's few 'constitutional crises', that of the 'Anti-Party Group' in June 1957. A group headed by Malenkov and Molotov and based on the economic ministries sought to depose Khrushchev in the Politburo, and Khrushchev challenged their right to do this. He appealed instead to the Central Committee, in formal terms a Party legislature of some 130 members, and gained its ruling that a General Secretary must be confirmed in office by the Central Committee, on the nomination of the Politburo; it was this procedure that was later used to overthrow Khrushchev.

Beyond the Party, Khrushchev appealed for the support of social groups that had suffered under Stalin: his cultural 'thaw' seems tame nowadays, but educated people showed more appreciation for it than they were later to give to Gorbachev's *glasnost*'; collective farmers were paid more for compulsory purchase of their produce and were brought into social security schemes. And he was a great believer in personal leadership and the virtues of enthusiasm (often orchestrated). In the 'Virgin Lands Scheme' hundreds of thousands of mainly young people were persuaded to move from Europe to Kazakhstan and South Siberia to plough up marginal steppe and grow grain.[3] A similar faith in ordinary people's instincts led him to enrol volunteers as part-time policemen, and to hand over minor court cases to neighbourhood or shop-floor assemblies, empowered to impose penalties up to exile.

This was populism – and it represented a departure in principle from the rigidities of the mono-functional model. There was a recognition here that society could not be controlled like a machine. But it was nowhere near democracy, nor the rule of law. The scope and limitations of Khrushchev's liberalisation are clear in his 'Secret Speech' of February 1956 *On the Cult of Personality and its Consequences*, delivered to a private audience of some 1400 communists and then distributed internally in the Party.[4] Its main message is damnation of Stalin for abuse of power towards Party members and army officers; this was the product of some kind of character degeneration that had set in during 1934. But there was no analysis of his powers as such, or of how to avoid them being acquired by one man. The choice of date allowed selective and licensed condemnation of the Great Purge and the conduct of the War, but left central features of Soviet power and policy – the Party monopoly, the choice of Stalin, collectivisation, the Five Year Plans – still immune to criticism; even when headed by a virtual madman, the Party collectively had remained on the correct path. Here was no encouragement to ordinary people to think aloud about politics.

Nonetheless Khrushchev's populism infuriated the bureaucracy. When it frustrated his gimmicks, he would appeal over his colleagues' heads to society at large. His purpose of keeping bureaucrats on their toes was often patent. From 1961 administrative reorganisation and reshuffling became positively manic; officials not only felt thwarted in their careers but could mount a plausible case that they were being stopped from doing an orderly systematic job. This is why they deposed Khrushchev in October 1964, and put Brezhnev, a predictable bureaucrat, in his place.

## THE CLIMATE OF THE BREZHNEV REGIME

Khrushchev had been overthrown by a palace revolution. A great deal that is distinctive about the politics and policies of the Brezhnev years flowed on from these beginnings.

First, the 1957 and 1964 crises had established the precedent that the Central Committee appointed the General Secretary, and this was written into the Party Rules in 1966. The senior Party officials who made up this committee still owed their positions, under the workings of *nomenklatura*, to the General Secretary (which is why Khrushchev had kept his job in 1957) – but the powers of the General Secretary were no longer absolute and unilinear. Instead a 'circular flow of power' had been created: officials were appointed from above, but leaders were dependent on their support, and officials had some recourse against a boss who forfeited their confidence.[5] For the first time conventions and rules were starting to emerge in Soviet politics, though as yet they affected a tiny elite only.

The impetus for these conventions has been mentioned: the common interest among senior politicians in preventing any of their number treating them as had Stalin and Beria. What had emerged was a self-policing oligarchy. It was an oligarchy which had its own internal differences, and very occasionally – when one side needed to mobilise support – these politics might spill out into the open. Here the media no longer showed quite the same 'monolithic unity' as they had. But if their mild disputes are examined closely, a powerful patron can usually be found behind the more daring bits of journalism. Such politics as were public were carefully orchestrated.

It soon became clear that in becoming the officials' candidate in 1964 Brezhnev must, tacitly or explicitly, have come to terms with them, that is, he must have given them guarantees that he would not repeat Khrushchev's errors. Henceforward we can think of General Secretaries presenting a 'platform' to an 'electorate' of a few hundred and working to retain the confidence of this electorate. What might have been the terms Brezhnev negotiated with the bureaucracy? Assuaging their anxiety about their own careers must clearly have been high on the list. Soon after taking over, Brezhnev began to speak warmly about 'stability of cadres' – signalling that they could expect undisturbed tenure in office unless caught out in gross misconduct, and that organisational structures would remain undisturbed.[6]

Brezhnev's agricultural and pricing policies showed the same underlying purpose as his deal with the bureaucracy. For the thirty years since collectivisation peasants had carried Soviet industrialisation on their backs. Brezhnev continued Khrushchev's policy of increasing state payments for agricultural produce, and probably sometime in the early 1960s the overall subsidisation of town by country came to an end; collective farms began to prosper, and farmers, though still poor, were no longer in a financial world apart from the towns. Khrushchev in 1962 had passed on some of the increased costs of farming to the consumer in the shape of increased retail prices for food; there was a strong reaction, the worst episode of which will be mentioned shortly. Three years later, after another price rise for farmers, Brezhnev let it be known that retail prices would not rise. From this time on (until 1991) urban food prices were virtually static, and the state absorbed the difference between these and the costs of production. By 1975 Alec

Nove was already calling it 'the most gigantic agricultural subsidy known in human history';[7] by the time of Gorbachev the subsidy had become four times larger and exceeded the defence budget (the real defence budget). To understand why the Brezhnev government accepted this constraint on its policies we need to consider social changes in towns after the death of Stalin.

No politician, before or after the Revolution, had ever given urban housing and services priority: the Tsar thought that urban life was a perversion of natural order; Stalin's priorities were production, not services; and the Great Fatherland War destroyed half the urban living accommodation. Millions flocked to live in shanty towns on the fringes of existing cities, and millions more to new foundations that were literally company towns: the industrial enterprise which was the settlement's origin in the 1930s had built its living premises and streets, installed water and sewage, gas and electricity, street lighting and urban transport – and often continued to own and run these services into the 1980s. Because of the priority of output urban services were financed according to the 'residual principle', that is, they were always at the back of the queue for investment. Local soviets (councils) did not have the power to raise funds locally; but in addition many of them had no control over – sometimes not even knowledge of – the infrastructure within 'their' territory that belonged to enterprises and ministries.[8]

Even in cities well established before the Revolution life was grim. Soviet citizens were allotted living premises, supposed to be at least nine square metres per person, by the executive of the city soviet. Many cities in the 1980s did not dispose of this amount of accommodation, and in others up to a third of families were on waiting lists to be moved from 'seriously crowded conditions'; it might take a generation to work one's way up such a list and their management was notoriously corrupt. Immigration into cities was tightly controlled but cities still contained hundreds of thousands of illegal immigrants and semi-legal *limitchiki* (migrant labourers who had to reside outside city limits). About 25 per cent of urban housing was without running hot water and about fifteen per cent without baths. At the same time many aspects of urban life were cheap. Between 1953 and 1991 public transport prices in Moscow remained unchanged (as did much of the rolling stock!), and the city soviet did not have the power to remedy this. Urban premises had no gas meters; the planners of the 1930s apparently never thought of urban services coming to be valuable enough to need measuring! Warehouses carried stocks the equivalent of two to three months retail sales, much of them unwanted; at the same time the average citizen had accumulated bank savings equivalent (in 1988) to eleven months pay. What had emerged was an urban lifestyle in which food and services were cheap but of demoralising quality and rationed by the queue. Inevitably people were bad-tempered, aggressive and on the make; inevitably they turned to the shadow economy and corruption.[9]

By the 1980s urban life was heading for crisis. The long term strain of keeping supplies coming in and immigrants out; increasing pollution from industry not designed to take account of community or environment; ageing dilapidated buildings and machinery; financial parlousness: all coincided with a surge in demand for the goods and services that for most people are the purpose, perhaps the only purpose of urbanity.

We begin to see why the Brezhnev administration was ready to subsidise retail food prices. Without a breakdown of food supplies to towns (they may have remembered) there might never have been a Revolution. Twice under Khrushchev riots about urban supplies had been violently put down, in 1959 in the Kazakhstani city of Temirtau, and in 1962 in the south Russian city of Novocherkassk.[10] Put simply, they needed to buy the docility of the urban population. If there was any doubt in their minds, events in Gdańsk in December 1970 must have removed them. The Polish subsidies policy, modelled on the Soviet one, had become exorbitant more quickly; the riots – which were spiritually the birth of Solidarity – followed steep price rises. Solidarity (rather than, say, the Prague Spring) was the omen in the Soviet Union of what could happen there.


THE SOCIAL COMPACT AND ITS DECLINE

Brezhnev had come to terms not just with the bureaucracy but with farmers and urban consumers. By the late 1970s the situation had come to be perceived as a 'social compact': a tacit understanding between leaders and led about each side's functions and sphere of operation, and the demarcation between them. The compact's slogan might have been 'Welfare, Security, Tolerance'. But more illuminating is the quip at the head of this chapter: 'You pretend to pay us, and we pretend to work . . . '

Notice first that the speaker is no abject prisoner cowering in a labour camp. He is not forced to work at gun-point, and indeed is confident enough, in a wry way, to think in terms of a **relationship** between workers and authorities – a twisted relationship, certainly, but a voluntary one, and one which recognises that each side has interests which the other could damage. The truce between them has led to an undertaking: on the regime's part to refrain from mass deportations, arbitrary arrest, guilt by association, conscription of labour; and on the part of workers to avoid open revolt, lynching or assassination, strikes or occupation of factories, and to deliver social order (but not enthusiasm).

Next, pretend work is being **exchanged** for pretend pay: this is an economic exchange. People who keep the compact will help keep the economy working, even if it works badly. Workers will offer routine, perfunctory work and reasonable self-discipline; the regime will offer nominally full employment and job security at low but reasonably equal rates of pay. Workers undertake to restrain the ambitious and consumerist among their number, to curb social mobility and differentiation – and to stay out of politics. In return the regime offers basic welfare provisions and stable prices – even at the cost of expensive subsidies. The deal is about a stable, quiescent, depoliticised society, with all-round welfare at a low level, and no glittering prizes for either side.

And third, to exchange **pretend** work for **pretend** pay includes a strong element of 'live and let live', of turning a blind eye – rather than putting in the boot. We pretend not to notice your privilege, your secret police, your possessiveness and arrogance about politics (if that's what turns you on) – and in return **you** should turn a blind eye to our absenteeism, drunkenness, ethnic and religious subcultures (provided they stay out of politics), the petty cash we make from things that fall off the back of the Truck of State.

It is an apt picture of the Soviet Union under Brezhnev: authoritarian, inefficient, apathetic, without opportunities; but basically orderly and without gross inequality or violent abuse of power. In 1989 one commentator, L. V. Karpinskii, called it an 'alliance of despotism and parasitism', and showed by his choice of words that it was aimed against the pressures of an emergent middle class.[11] Karpinskii's father had been a communist in 1917 and he himself had been a member of the Bureau of the Communist Youth League (Komsomol) in the early 1960s along with E. A. Shevardnadze, before falling foul of the Party;

this was criticism from an expert source. It points up the essential difference between Brezhnevism and Stalinism: it is accepted that the masses have **some** legitimate interests and rights, and the leadership **some** obligations to society that go beyond their programmes.

No contract can last indefinitely. This one began to break down for two reasons: each side changed its mind to some extent about what it really wanted or was willing to deliver; and there were unexamined assumptions in the original compact which proved wrong and made it difficult to work. To begin with it proved impossible to train people for industrial society without arousing new tastes and expectations. Important groups on society's side of the compact refused to be excluded from the freedom of communications and consumption they had become aware of abroad – but western suburban lifestyles had not been part of the compact. In turn these groups came to view aspects of the regime's foreign policy as ambitious beyond the terms of the agreement: not at first (maybe) the East European empire or the space race, but certainly the resources poured into propping up Cuba and then the invasion of Afghanistan.

Unforeseen flaws in the compact were its assumption of abundant resources, effective planning and economic growth. Resources were not inexhaustible and were becoming scarcer or less accessible in the 1970s. This applied not just to oil, coal, metals and water, but also to cheap labour; the pool was drying up of peasant would-be migrants whose dream was to get a city job. The planning system was predicated on continuity and predictability; it left little in reserve and made poor provision for innovation. Almost any change of circumstances – foreign policy reverses, changes in technology, natural disasters, new popular expectations – would cause a steep decline in performance. But so much in the compact was linked to growth – especially the combination of subsidies with an effective war machine. As growth rates fell in the late 1970s the Soviet Union began to face a classical 'guns versus butter' dilemma.

And once the compact began to break down in any of its terms – say, the ability of the regime to deliver cheap food and welfare, or the willingness of engineers to be content with a blue-collar future – then distrust and suspicion of bad faith were bound to build up; groups on either side began increasingly to explore other means of getting what they wanted – by opting out of the relationship, by forming new alliances, by insulating themselves against unwelcome pressures, and by trickery.

We have seen how one interest group, the officials, began to act on its own behalf under Khrushchev, and how Brezhnev bought off pressure from others. By the 1980s autonomous social evolution had gone much further than was generally realised outside the USSR. Let us examine three cases.

### The Rise of the Professionals

In 1955 2.7 per cent of the workforce had a tertiary degree and a further 3.7 per cent had the qualification called 'secondary specialist' – something like a trade or craft certificate obtained after secondary schooling beyond the legal minimum. In 1985 the comparable figures were eleven and fifteen per cent – a dramatic increase in education levels and one achieved entirely by state investment. Together, people with tertiary and secondary specialist training were labelled '**specialists**', and specialists were the darlings and the main beneficiaries of the Soviet system, much more so than manual workers. Specialists included employees in education, science, health, culture and communications, but the archetypal specialist was a technician, and in particular, an **engineer**. The significance of engineering is symbolised by the fact that under Khrushchev and Brezhnev it was the most common occupational background in the Politburo; the lawyers, farmers, teachers and businessmen familiar in Western parliaments were not in evidence. Specialists came increasingly to be treated – and to see themselves – as a distinct group with interests in common.

Two definitional points should be made here. First we should distinguish specialists firmly from the 'intelligentsia'. After 1917 the Bolsheviks made determined efforts to rid the latter word of its original sense of independent critic, by extending it to cover everyone with above-average qualifications or in white-collar employment; official Soviet parlance always used 'intelligentsia' in this sense, so that it was interchangeable with 'specialists' and included Party and state bureaucracy. At the same time the nineteenth-century usage persisted, and was invigorated when the Purges and Soviet cultural policies created a new generation of educated and alienated critics. For this self-styled intelligentsia membership was defined not by qualifications but by intellectual independence. Such people formed a distinct and significant group, and from now on I shall reserve the word 'intelligentsia' for them. Second, for the intelligentsia the distinction between themselves and the state bureaucracy had been central; but from the 1930s a third and larger group emerged of state employees who earned their living from their qualifications without either belonging to the administrative bureaucracy or fitting readily into the 'intelligentsia'. For these I shall write 'specialists' or 'professionals'. These professionals worked typically in large-scale hierarchical organisations. Their ideals were not those of the self-made or self-employed entrepreneur, but rather were 'based on trained expertise and selection by merit, a selection made not by the open market but by the judgment of similarly educated experts'. This affected their perceptions of success and of the state: they depended less on property in material resources than on social recognition of the services they offered, and thus they 'look[ed] to the state as the ultimate guarantor of professional status'.[12]

Because of their confidence and the nature of their skills it was difficult to keep specialists ignorant of the working conditions and lifestyles of their equivalents in Western Europe and the United States. In 1941 it had been a realistic proposition to confiscate all privately owned radio sets. By the 1980s this was no longer realistic (though similar principles still governed access to photocopying), first because the workings of economy and state had come to depend on widespread understanding of communications technology, and, second, because technology was the specialists' skill – and the regime's pride. Again Poland had provided the warning signs: in 1970 and 1980 it had been impossible to keep events in Gdańsk secret because of widespread private ownership of telephones and cars; and Solidarity, in effect, had dared the regime to bombard workers in their own factories – and called its bluff. (A mere decade earlier, but a world away, it had been possible to cut Novocherkassk off from the outside world, and it took years for the details to filter out.) But who in the 1980s could control, not just cars and telephones, but ham radio transmitters, reception of foreign television, personal computers, video cassette recorders (the list went on and on) – without crippling the country in precisely the areas of which it had boasted? So jamming of foreign radio was abandoned, and the *putsch* of August 1991 did not even try to cut internal or external telecommunications. Soviet professionals, in short, were slowly winning their battle for middle-class lifestyles and opportunities, especially to read, view and travel; they saw these as the appropriate, modern reward for their skill.

Because specialists were held up as models (and also perhaps because the rewards were always just over the horizon), fierce social competition was unleashed – to put the life of peasant or manual worker behind and to join the ranks of professionals. Entry into tertiary training provides illustrations: some institutions received ten applications for every place they offered and bribing one's way into tertiary study became widespread. Further evidence comes from admissions into the CPSU, which, it will be remembered, needed to maintain a dominant influence in the professions and management: 28 per cent of the Party had had tertiary or secondary specialist qualifications in 1956, but 57 per cent had them in 1986. In other words more than half the Party had qualifications that merited 'white-collar' employment; more than half were in white-collar employment, though this was not admitted until 1990. The trend was thought to be disturbing in the Brezhnev period and people who a generation earlier would have walked into membership began to be excluded.[13]

In such a climate it is hardly surprising that the education system turned out too many specialists.[14] Brezhnev was not one to court unpopularity and he may have thought that competition among professionals for scarce jobs would deter them from uniting to press their claims. In 1960 a specialist in industry or construction had earned half as much again as a blue-collar worker. By 1985 this relativity had been whittled away to ten per cent more in industry, whilst in construction specialists were earning slightly less than workers. In the 1980s more than ten per cent of specialists were employed as blue-collar workers, often because the pay or conditions were preferable.[15] Many continued to be trained in obsolescent technologies.

By the 1980s the perception had gained hold that professionals had lost out in relation to workers and were underpaid, underemployed and undervalued by the state. Some sought to renegotiate their special relationship with the regime. There was an increase in the system of 'closed enterprises', descendants of the secret research establishments set up in Stalin's prisons; employees worked under quasi-military discipline and could not change jobs at will – but they got priority supplies, with consequent benefit to bonuses and work morale. Some factories pushed for conversion to closed status with the support of their employees.[16] These pressures were not only disruptive of economic planning (not everyone can be at the front of the queue), but represented a victory for the social differentiation Brezhnev had tried to block.

More generally professionals pressed to have their identity and interests recognised as distinct from those of the bureaucracy and intelligentsia (however defined). They became less willing to follow the lead of intellectuals in matters of taste and opinion, and that of bureaucrats in professional matters. Party discipline had long served to maintain the fiction that professional and bureaucratic interests coincided; but beneath the surface a gulf was widening between an *apparat* increasingly defensive of vested interests, and professionals alarmed at the unresponsiveness of the economy. This alarm was documented in 1983 in Zaslavskaya's *Novosibirsk Report* on the social and organisational preconditions for economic growth. Professionals, in short, are a strong and assertive social group that had begun to feel threatened before the end of the Brezhnev era; they had come to be a force in politics.[17]

### Feudalisation of Administration

Brezhnev's 'stability of cadres' policy may have led for a time to greater efficiency. It was also the start of a more ominous trend.

*Nomenklatura* procedures made officials immune to sanctions from their administrative superiors or to public pressure. The principal means of keeping them obedient and honest had been to move them on after short tours of duty: this prevented them building up local power bases and gave their successors the chance to expose malpractice. 'Stability of cadres' removed this sanction. From the mid-1960s officials were subject to fewer checks as long as they got the results the Centre wanted, and it is not surprising that many became less scrupulous in their methods. Over the same period the public seem to have grasped that the real relationship between officials and their formal bosses was not what it appeared to be. The result was a growing distrust of official channels – and a growing resort to other, trickier but more reliable ways of getting things done. The image of administrative harshness began to be replaced with one of administrative **corruption**.[18]

It was in people's interests to cultivate local officials, and it suited officials to favour, protect – even represent – local interests. Officials – who increasingly were of local origin – could build up local followings and nominate their own successors. In their relationship with the Centre many were coming to look like subcontractors, responsible for plan fulfilment and keeping the peace, rather than obedient executives. In parts of the country the 'shadow economy' was possibly comparable in volume with the legal economy. Centralisation was being replaced by something like feudalism.

These tendencies are graphically illustrated by the 'Uzbek cotton scandal' of the 1980s. This led to the dismissal of most senior officials in Uzbekistan, to the imprisonment in 1988 of Yu. M. Churbanov, Brezhnev's son-in-law and former First Deputy Minister of Internal Affairs, and it was said to implicate members of Gorbachev's Politburo also. Until this case the Soviet media had never used the phrase 'organised crime'.[19]

From the beginning of the Five-Year Plans the Soviet authorities had imposed something close to a monoculture in cotton on the Union-Republics of Central Asia. For a time this brought the local population a prosperity not found in the collective farms of Russia proper, and high birth rates in Central Asia may have owed something to this. The prosperity proved ephemeral. Cotton was promoted at the expense of food crops and livestock. Investment went into irrigation rather than into piped drinking water or sewage, with the result that drinking water was increasingly contaminated by bacteria, fertilisers, pesticides and defoliants. Public health suffered and infant mortality soared. The cotton monoculture kept rural Uzbeks unskilled, and deprived them of diversified employment. What emerged was in fact a colonial plantation system. Medical and educational facilities could not keep pace with the rising population and there was widespread youth unemployment. Knowledge of Russian, Party membership, the suitability of Central Asian youths for conscription all declined – and this weakened the Union's principal means of integrating Central Asians into Soviet ways and of keeping them in the Union.[20]

One cannot wonder that schemes were devised in Uzbekistan and elsewhere for deflecting the Centre's pressure, which meant one way or another reducing cotton production. The commonest was to return false production figures to Moscow, pay off accountants, inspectors and police to cover this up, and compensate textile management for what it should have received. It was an operation on a grand scale: it penetrated beyond Uzbekistan to the highest echelons of the MVD and it permeated every level of Uzbekistani society. One of the most flamboyant of those arrested in the late 1980s had built himself an estate out of several neighbouring state farms which he ruled from his castle using a private police force and a private prison.[21] He had become a feudal lord. Feudalism involves gaining rights in exchange for duties to protect; and that is what many Uzbek leaders were seen as doing for their own people. On the larger scale the All-Union leadership was willing (or persuaded) to give Central Asian leaders a free hand, provided they made no trouble; this relationship too was turning into a feudal one.

In Uzbekistan the slackening of controls from above combined with social pressures from below not just to corrupt Soviet institutions but to generate the organisational fabric for indigenous Uzbek politics – should they be called for.

## Nationalism

Brezhnev's new responsiveness to interest groups would never (in his mind) have extended to ethnic or religious interests, yet even here cautious concessions were made: during the mid-1960s a variety of Societies for the Preservation of Monuments of Culture were set up, and it was an open secret that their membership drew on those who might otherwise have been attracted to organised religion or nationalism. The trends were reinforced by deeper and more potent factors.

First was a general effect of industrialisation from which the Soviet Union was not exempt. Industrial revolutions are not just productivity but communications revolutions; they introduce mass-circulation newspapers, trains, automobiles and films, and later transistor radios, televisions, video-cassettes and jet travel. In conditions of mass literacy and widespread travel people compare and contrast their own group identity with that of others – and may be pushed into articulating and defending this identity. More important, industrialisation generates the modern public service and white-collar occupations. Their indispensable currency is written memoranda, forms, invoices and inventories, and hence the language of government and management assumes an importance it has not had before. People like Russians (or English, Serbs or Malays) who are brought up knowing such an 'official' language have a congenital advantage in entering desirable jobs; those who are not must find ways of coming to terms with, or overcoming, this disadvantage. Soviet development promoted an indigenous, bilingual, white-collar elite in the non-Russian Union-Republics that was excluded from political decision making, but not from occupational ambitions.

Soviet nationalities policy had a paradoxical effect on ethnic aspirations. It had depoliticised ethnic cultures, and young people grew up into a sentimentalised and emotionalised group identity. Non-Russian elites, except for a tiny minority, were excluded from high politics, but they formed the local bureaucracies that implemented central policy; this served to concentrate their attention on local issues.

They had little experience in political debate – the deployment of their interests in rational terms, the persuasion of outsiders – and this fostered an affective, symbolic, zero-sum approach to politics. All this was fermenting beneath the crust of Brezhnevian society.

The Union-Republic of Georgia offered a sign of what was to come in 1978. During the revision of its constitution the draftsmen do not seem to have thought twice about an amendment that dropped Georgian as the 'state' language. (Russian language is notoriously weak in Georgia, and perhaps it was thought that the future of the Georgian language needed no legalistic support.) Instead a hostile crowd gathered outside the Supreme Soviet in Tbilisi, and the Party first secretary, E. A. Shevardnadze, could placate it only by promising to restore the deleted clause. In response, a few weeks later, the Abkhazians, a minority related to the North Caucasian peoples who have long chafed against Georgian rule, began an agitation to secede from Georgia and join the RSFSR. The events were a milestone in Soviet development in several ways. They showed the strength of ethnic perceptions among ordinary people – something the leadership had been denying for fifty years – and the connection between ethnic politics and language. Second, they constituted the first case of successful mass politics since the 1920s, and thus illustrate growing social confidence – all the more remarkable because rioters had been shot down in Tbilisi in 1956. And Shevardnadze, unlike the officials in Novocherkassk sixteen years earlier, was not dismissed for 'letting things get out of hand'. The implications will not have been lost on M. S. Gorbachev, first secretary in the neighbouring Stavropol' province; subordination to Stavropol' would have been one of the options if Abkhazia had been allowed to leave Georgia.[22]

These implications became blatant with the eruption of the Nagorno-Karabakh dispute in February 1988. The Nagorno-Karabakh Autonomous *Oblast'* is a mainly Armenian enclave of some 190,000 people, subordinate to and wholly within Azerbaidzhan, though at one point its distance from Armenia is less than a mile. The trouble started in public on 20 February 1988, when the majority Armenian soviet of the *oblast'* voted to cut its ties with Azerbaidzhan and unite with Armenia.[23] At this time divided votes and votes to overturn established policy were still unheard of. The mechanism for preventing them was the Party group which must be formed in all public bodies and whose tasks included preliminary, private arbitration of controversial issues. Under Brezhnev the vote – which was outside the competence of the *oblast'* soviet – would either never have reached the public agenda, or only when an unexciting compromise formula had been agreed. Why did the mechanism fail?

In the next few days Armenian activists in Nagorno-Karabakh and in Armenia proper were able, virtually overnight, to muster crowds of hundreds of thousands, and to count on an organisation (communications, funds, premises) apparently in every workplace. And Party members, who should have been reporting and resisting this in every workplace, seem either to have stood aside or to have joined in. It is most unlikely that either the cohesiveness of the protest movement or the incoherence of the Party came about overnight. What emerged in 1988 reflected the real but suppressed interests and sympathies, the invested energy of many people over many years. The grievances, which go back to the early 1920s and beyond, are so anchored in popular consciousness that it had become impossible to select Party members who did not share them; indeed the latter seem to have been only dimly aware of the way they diverged from central policy.

Here we see similar processes at work to those in Uzbekistan, with the difference that the outcome was not corruption but overt resistance. In both cases political interests were denied expression and driven underground; and they returned to cannibalise public organisations, making them real outlets for local demand, and destroying them as instruments of central policy. In all three illustrations we see portions of society cutting loose from the mono-organisational system, and in some cases fending quite successfully for themselves.

## WHAT WAS HAPPENING TO SOVIET SOCIETY

Not long after his accession Gorbachev spoke of a 'pre-crisis situation' – words which were not at all mealy-mouthed in the Soviet Union, as Marxism-Leninism had held that crises were a capitalist phenomenon. During 1987–8 he abandoned the genuflection to orthodoxy and began to portray a state of crisis which only a **new revolution** could solve. These would be strong words from any politician and they were extraordinary from a Soviet leader. What was it about Soviet problems that prompted him to speak with such urgency and alarm?

It was easy enough to say that the planned economy had lost its dynamism, and that ordinary people were alienated from Party and bureaucracy. If that had been all there was to it, there might not have been cause for alarm. But the leadership was surely alarmed by something else: the increasing autonomy of large areas of life, the tendency of things to happen quite outside the scope of planning or Party leadership. Besides the shadow-economy and the counter-culture – problems that had engaged attention under Brezhnev – there had developed a parallel system of **politics**. These 'para-politics' tended to be autarkic and isolationist. In some places they had wrested initiative away from the Party leaving the Centre powerless.[24]

A Western liberal might have analysed this as follows. The 1917 Revolution had obviously been a mistake, because it did not embody the interests of those in whose name it was made, but rather those of their self-appointed spokesmen. Now however elements in that society were demonstrating something truly revolutionary and unstoppable: their mature capacity to take charge of and manage their own affairs. Curiously, one form of Marxism – but not the Marxism-Leninism promoted in the Soviet Union – would have said something very similar. Industrialisation and the education and social mobility that accompanied it had engendered new needs and interests; these were quite clearly breaking the bonds of unchanged 'production relations' and of course the situation looked revolutionary, because that was what it **was**. Few people inside the Soviet Union will have interpreted it in these terms. Fewer still – but possibly isolated individuals[25] – will have perceived that what was happening was not just the routine degeneration of a 'revolution from above', but the revolutionary situation that had been lacking in 1917.

But for Marxist-Leninists of the traditional mould, those who treated the Party as the bearer of an irrevocable commission to be the vanguard, to represent people's real interests, the situation could not have been more threatening. For 'true believers' it struck at the core of their beliefs. Even if they were not believers – something that had come increasingly to be thought about the Brezhnevite elite – it still struck at their vital interests: because politics that had cut loose from the Party must, in the long run, become politics that would compete with the Party for power.

# 3 Events since Brezhnev

'The people whose votes were decisive in choosing the successor to
Konstantin Chernenko . . . could not have envisaged even in a
nightmare that they were charging him with the . . . demolition of
the world socialist system and of Soviet socialism.'

(A. Strelyanyi)[1]

THE INTERREGNUM (January 1982 to March 1985)

The last survivor of Stalin's Politburo, M. A. Suslov, died in January
1982 and, as if he had been the kingmaker, his death seemed to
unleash the struggle for the succession to Brezhnev.[2] General Secretaries chaired two important committees, the Politburo and the
Central Committee Secretariat, and to become General Secretary, it
was assumed, a politician should already be a member of both
committees. In 1982 besides the senile Brezhnev there were three
others in this position: K. U. Chernenko, who had been something
like a chief of staff to Brezhnev and was treated by him as heir
apparent; A. P. Kirilenko, older still than Brezhnev and regarded as a
spent force; and M. S. Gorbachev, at 51 by far the youngest in the
leadership and perhaps too young for the top job. There were already
indications that Gorbachev was an ally of the Chairman of the KGB,
Yu. V. Andropov. In May Andropov resigned from the KGB and
became a Central Committee Secretary; he was already in the
Politburo and the move signalled his bid for power.

When Brezhnev died in November 1982 it was Andropov who was
nominated by the Politburo and confirmed by the Central Committee
to succeed him. His secret police background, his political independence and his record in leadership posts all contrasted with the career
of Chernenko; the choice suggests that a majority in the Politburo
thought there were problems requiring energetic solutions. What they
apparently did **not** know (and a KGB chief would certainly have been
in a position to keep it quiet!) is that Andropov was already seriously
ill with kidney disease when he came to power. He achieved very little
in his fifteen month term of office and was being treated as a lame
duck leader by August 1983.

But the general thrust of his policy is clear enough. For a centralised and authoritarian system like the Soviet one energetic, reliable and honest administrators were vital, and corruption, especially official corruption, was a symptom of terminal illness. One scholar has labelled his programme 'Discipline **and** Reform'.[3] In his pursuit of a new brand of leadership he brought together, often from outside Moscow, many of the important figures of the late 1980s, people like Ryzhkov, Ligachev, Vorotnikov or A. N. Yakovlev; in fact he picked the first *perestroika* team, with Gorbachev clearly a principal figure in it. It was later claimed (by a Gorbachev supporter) that Andropov tried to designate Gorbachev as his successor, and was thwarted.[4] True or not, Andropov's illness had the effect of bringing people like Gorbachev close to the centre of decision making.

Yet after Andropov's death in February 1984, Chernenko was chosen to succeed him, another old and sick man. It was an extraordinary decision, all the more if we remember that for many of those involved Andropov's true state of health must have come as a shock, and a recent one. How we interpret it makes quite a difference to our picture of subsequent politics. One interpretation of the puzzle would be like this. The gerontocracy had been frightened by Andropov's initiatives, and especially (remember 1964) by the threat to their own positions. So they revised their earlier opinion about the need for change, and chose someone who was clearly conservative and manipulable, a figure-head; and they chose merely to drift. This **could** be correct; but it involves postulating a major change of mind within the Politburo three times in three years – over the successive choices of Andropov, Chernenko and then Gorbachev.

The alternative possibility is that a majority of the Politburo still backed reform in 1984 and was shocked by its own apparent negligence in choosing a terminally ill leader. (Surely it must have occurred to them to ask, whose finger would have been on the button if a serious confrontation had come out of the KAL disaster of September 1983?) But at the same time they did not wish to alarm or dishonour the generation that was relinquishing power. They therefore chose a General Secretary who was clearly a transitional figure-head, **and** at the same time reached an understanding concerning an effective second-in-command who could be expected to take over from him on his departure.

The second line of interpretation is surely more cogent. It explains Gorbachev's prominent role under Chernenko: it was he who nominated Chernenko for the position of Head of State in April 1984;

according to A. A. Gromyko, he chaired the Politburo when Chernenko was ill, and may have been deputed to run the Central Committee Secretariat.[5] And it helps explain the unusual speed with which Gorbachev was chosen in March 1985, in the absence of the Politburo's longest serving member, V. V. Shcherbitskii.[6] If the interpretation is correct, there was an understanding, going back at least to early 1984, that Gorbachev was being groomed for the leadership, and it is reasonable to think of him as *de facto* second-in-command and heir presumptive to Chernenko. This would imply that the evolution of rules in Soviet politics had moved to a new stage, one where provisions were made in advance for a smooth transfer of power.

And that is really about all that can be said about Chernenko's term in office. There were virtually no significant policy initiatives in this period, nor significant changes in personnel. Enter M. S. Gorbachev, chosen very quickly to succeed Chernenko on 11 March 1985, at the age of 54 the youngest General Secretary since Stalin.

## GORBACHEV'S FIRST YEAR: CONSOLIDATION OF POWER
(March 1985 to February 1986)

We should not be surprised that Gorbachev did little during his first year in office to mark him out as unusual. All political leaders have to consolidate their position but a new General Secretary faced a task more difficult than most. He had no 'honeymoon' in office. He could not pick his own cabinet but rather had to work with the Politburo which had nominated **him** as its chair. Before he could begin to impose his own stamp on the political agenda he must surround himself with reliable assistants and colleagues and establish his authority among senior figures from the previous administration. The emphasis in the early stages of a new Soviet regime had to be on personnel politics. Gorbachev had the advantage that he had been close to policy-making since 1983, but he had two handicaps: as a relative newcomer to Moscow he lacked a strong clientele; and the bureaucracy was already suspicious of his patron, Andropov's approach.

Six weeks after he came to power a further Plenum of the Central Committee was convened to endorse some of the new team. N. I. Ryzhkov (the future Chairman of the Council of Ministers), V. M. Chebrikov (Chairman of the KGB), and E. K. Ligachev were made members of the Politburo. Ligachev had been Party leader in the

Siberian province of Tomsk, and in April 1983 became Head of the Central Committee Department of Organisational-Party Work (the heart of the *nomenklatura* system); this he combined with the post of Central Committee Secretary (one of Andropov's last decisions) in December 1983. To bring the *nomenklatura* Secretary into the Politburo was a clear signal that he was being made Gorbachev's second-in-command. Ligachev soon came to be seen as the representative of Party officials and Party interests in Gorbachev's team, and these tended increasingly to be identified with a cautious approach to reform.

Soviet public relations laid great stress on this 'April Plenum' of the Central Committee, as if it, rather than the choice of Gorbachev in March, marked the new start. It is not easy to see the significance of this. Such speeches as were published from the April Plenum are unremarkable[7] and do little to gainsay Gorbachev's repeated claim that the major policy decisions for reform came later. If the April Plenum **was** important, this importance should probably be sought in two things: a mandate for reform given to Gorbachev, though it would seem to have been a qualified mandate; and the new distribution of powers and functions among the senior leaders and especially, for Party officials, the designation of Ligachev as bulwark against undue radicalism. One can detect, in other words, even at this date, hints of Party caution towards Gorbachev.

For the rest of 1985 there was systematic replacement of senior personnel: in the Council of Ministers, of which Ryzhkov became Chairman in September; among the heads of the Central Committee departments; and among Party first secretaries in the provinces. By the time of the XXVII Party Congress in February 1986 about 40 per cent of the most senior jobs in the country had changed hands.[8] Three things are noticeable about the 'new broom' officials who came to the top at this time. First they were young and energetic. Few of them were much older than Gorbachev and they tended to share with him the features of his generation: a good education, a smooth career untroubled by war or political violence, and a relatively confident approach to government and the Soviet past. The choice of E. A. Shevardnadze to be Minister of Foreign Affairs in July 1985 was characteristic. He was a man very much in the Gorbachev mould, energetic and pragmatic, with a reputation in his native Georgia for skilful manoeuvring and tough action against corruption. They had known each other since the early 1960s when each was Komsomol leader in his home province, and by the 1980s they shared a common alarm at what was happening to the country.

Second, appointments paid a new attention to education and expertise. Andropov had begun this tendency, and it had led him to cultivate some of the political 'casualties' of the Brezhnev regime. A good example of both is A. N. Yakovlev. Yakovlev had been acting head of the Central Committee Department of Propaganda in the early 1970s and had quarrelled with the leadership over attempts to develop a cult of Brezhnev; in 1973 he was 'exiled' to Canada as Soviet ambassador, where he became an influential writer on international relations. Gorbachev met Yakovlev in May 1983 in Ottawa, almost certainly for the first time, and almost certainly to arrange Yakovlev's return to head the prestigious Institute of World Economics and International Relations. Yakovlev became a Central Committee Secretary in 1986, Politburo member in 1987 and in 1990 a member of the Presidential Council – one of Gorbachev's closest allies. He was also one of the most distinctive characters in the new leadership. Interviews reveal him as sympathetic to the underdog (he has been seriously ill for long periods of his life) and tolerant of social and philosophical diversity; he seems to have been the driving force behind *glasnost'* and the new policies on association, rehabilitation, nationality and religion. Very unusually in the Soviet Union he was a Marxist who knew the early writings of Karl Marx and applied Marxism to interpretation of his own country; yet he was also one of the first there to criticise Marxism, rather than simply drop out of such discourse. His contribution to the theoretical framework and coherence of policy under Gorbachev was immense.[9]

Note finally how many of the new appointments came from the home regions of the top three politicians: from Stavropol' and the North Caucasus where Gorbachev had spent most of his career; from the Urals and especially Sverdlovsk where Ryzhkov had worked until 1975 as director of one of the largest heavy engineering combines; and from West Siberia, the political base of Ligachev.[10] The traditional practice of stacking politics with reliable former associates had not changed, and indeed in the absence of an impartial public service it is hard to see how new leaders could have done otherwise. Nevertheless, despite the importance such personal alliances had in Soviet politics, one should not get them out of proportion. People have their own ideals and purposes, and they can be loyal to institutions as well as to patrons. The coalitions associated with Gorbachev, Ryzhkov and Ligachev were at the same time regional and occupational lobbies. The North Caucasus is the best grain growing area in Russia; alliance with the Urals group brought in people from heavy and defence industry and planning; and Ligachev's group included oil and coal mining interests and scientists from the important research centre of Novosibirsk. It would be difficult in most circumstances for such disparate groups to combine policy-making with maintenance of their own cohesion; and Gorbachev, by soliciting wider input into policy, made 'faction discipline' harder to preserve. So it is not surprising that differences soon became discernible among the three regional groups, and among individuals **within** them. B. N. Yeltsin, apparently a protégé of Ryzhkov, is a good example.

A housing construction engineer by profession, Yeltsin led the Sverdlovsk Party organisation until he was made a Central Committee Secretary in July 1985. He soon showed himself a passionate campaigner against bureaucracy and privilege, and this seemed to make him an appropriate choice to head the corrupt Moscow Party organisation in December 1985. But in October 1987 he resigned from the Politburo, claiming that the reforms lacked drive and coherence, and was dismissed, vindictively, by the Moscow *gorkom*.[11] The episode suggested an impulsiveness and populism that was not to the taste of the Gorbachev leadership. But it appealed to the population: in the general election of 1989 he won overwhelming endorsement from Moscow voters, in 1990 he was elected Speaker of the RSFSR Supreme Soviet and resigned from the CPSU, in June 1991 he became the first popularly elected President in Russia. It was an unprecedented comeback for Soviet politics.

We can visualise Gorbachev's political support in early 1986 in the form of concentric circles. The 'outer coalition', formed under and by Andropov, was a tactical alliance of senior politicians agreed only on the impossibility of continuing with a Brezhnevite course; by 1987–8 major differences in their policies had become apparent. Gorbachev's 'inner coalition' consisted of people whom he trusted, often because he had known them for a long time, or because they shared his diagnosis and priorities. Within this group we may distinguish political colleagues from personal staff. Important among the former were E. A. Shevardnadze, A. N. Yakovlev, G. P. Razumovskii and A. I. Luk'yanov. Personal staff were less prominent but often important, both in their own right and because they provided the crucial link between General Secretary and the Party *apparat* through which the earliest reform measures were introduced; names we shall meet again are G. Kh. Shakhnazarov and V. I. Boldin. In contrast to all previous Soviet leaders it was noticeable that Gorbachev had no particular links with the military.

THE *GLASNOST'* PROGRAMME (February 1986 to January 1987)

Policy as distinct from personnel began to change in the first half of 1986, for two distinct reasons. First, the administration itself was undoubtedly planning something; how else to explain this unprecedented sentence that appeared in *Pravda* in early February 1986:[12]

> The idea has taken shape . . . that it is the immobile, inert and tenacious 'party-administrative stratum' which does not want radical changes, and in fact stands between the Central Committee and the working class.

This was political dynamite, and it was shortly after this, and before the Party Congress at the end of February, that the words *glasnost'* and *perestroika* ('openness' and 'reconstruction') began to be used in the media with greater frequency. Alert people could already infer that the regime was announcing the headlines for its new policies. But what policies? The XXVII Party Congress hinted at liberalisation of culture,[13] but was in general cautious, disappointing and easily forgotten.

Whatever was intended, it was overshadowed completely by the Chernobyl' disaster on 26 April 1986 and the monstrous attempt at a media cover-up that followed.[14] One of the most serious disasters in history had happened not far outside the Ukrainian capital, Kiev. Millions of people soon knew they had been lied to about the worst event of their lives, to say nothing of the contempt with which states across the western border had been treated. The poet A. A. Voznesenskii revived memories of Pushkin's king who confiscated arrow poison to sow destruction on his neighbours![15] After Chernobyl' relations between leadership and society could not be the same again. A mild foretaste came on May 15: members of the Cinematographers' Union took the unheard-of step of deposing their first secretary; in his place they elected E. G. Klimov, a popular director and not a Party member, many of whose films had been refused showing. Over the ensuing months public anger was reinforced by the realisation that the disaster had been caused, not by accident, design flaws or subversion, but by a stupidity and irresponsibility promoted by the system itself.

There was need for quick and bold action, directed in particular at public opinion, and it seems Gorbachev took it with two initiatives.[16] Before May 1986 *glasnost'* may have been no more than an experimental slogan, one among several; Chernobyl' virtually dictated change at least to public relations policy. Some time in May or June (it is difficult to establish a precise date) a major revision of censorship practices (though not of the institution of censorship) was conducted under a new chief censor. In June Gorbachev is said to have asked a private meeting of writers for help against 'an administrative layer – the ministerial and Party apparatus – that does not want changes'.[17] By August four of the most influential journals had passed to new liberal editors, one of them, *Novyi mir* (the journal which had once published Solzhenitsyn) to a non-communist, the first such since the 1920s. The effects were dramatic: by the end of 1987 Soviet newspapers, films, books and television were publishing a variety of material and opinion unknown since before Stalin.

Less conspicuous but no less significant in its impact was a relaxation of controls on the spontaneous groups, clubs and associations that had come to be called 'informal organisations' and then *neformaly* ('informals') for short. During 1986 new directives seem to have been issued to state officials not to be zealous in banning or suppressing *neformaly*, and to Party organisations to relax the way in which they steered and coordinated the business of non-Party groups. The result was an explosive increase in spontaneous organisations, including a minority of overtly political 'ginger groups' which were to play a major role in the future.

Let us note three things about these initiatives. First, neither *glasnost'* nor the encouragement of the *neformaly* involved changes to law, but rather to official practice as controlled by the covert and extra-legal activity of the Party. They were initiatives of Gorbachev and his supporters utilising their control of the Party *apparat*, and this is important for our interpretation of reform. They were, second, of particular interest and benefit to the educated middle class, and amounted to an offer of coalition with it and the adoption of part of its agenda. Finally they started social processes whose outcome – if the experience of the Prague Spring was any guide – could not be clearly foreseen.

Two events in mid December 1986 illustrate this. The first was the dismissal at Central orders of D. A. Kunaev, the Party first secretary for Kazakhstan. Kunaev was a Kazakh and an old friend of Brezhnev, whilst his replacement, G. V. Kolbin, was a Russian associate of Gorbachev. Kazakhstan has a large Russian population and had had Russian first secretaries before, of whom Brezhnev had been one. But on this occasion the Kazakh population of the capital, Alma-Ata, rioted, and, they made it clear, felt freer to express anti-Russian sentiments because of *glasnost'*. Three days later Academician Sakharov was released from exile, and his release was followed by that of over a hundred other high-profile dissidents. The year 1986 had brought Gorbachev into contact with scientists and intellectuals who supported Sakharov; they must have shown him that there were (or might soon be) people in prison for saying things that were being printed and advocated openly. Sakharov gave no undertakings of 'good' behaviour but made it clear that he would resume political activism. Nothing could illustrate better both the 'opening to professionals' and the uncharted waters into which Gorbachev was steering.

THE STRUGGLE FOR RECONSTRUCTION (January 1987 to May 1988)

The Communist Party was the crucial political institution. It followed that reform – or change of any kind – must have the Party among its targets; yet (at the same time) that reform could hardly be conducted except by and through Party organs. We have already seen Gorbachev using them to this purpose. How could the Party be both the agent and the object of reform? The answer is that different parts of this colossal organisation (19.25 million in 1987) could play different roles, but the contradiction was bound to strain Party unity, and especially once the new freedom of self-expression turned into pressure for institutional change, literally from *glasnost'* to *perestroika*. This is the background to the politics of the next eighteen months.

In autumn 1986 it was reported several times that a Central Committee Plenum had been postponed. When it was convened in January 1987, Gorbachev raised for the first time in public the idea that reform entailed internal renewal, including competitive elections, in the **Party**, and he proposed holding a Party Conference on the matter.[18] The Central Committee resolution which concluded the Plenum did not react to either of these proposals.[19] It seemed that he had encountered high level resistance, and it is plausible to surmise that the January speech had touched on matters thought to go beyond his April 1985 mandate.

Gorbachev's response was an increasing radicalisation of his public stance and more overt appeals beyond the ruling circle. In a major speech in July 1987 he began to present reform as a **social** process, generated by social pressures apparently independent of the Party and capable of leaving the Party behind. This was an astonishing reversal of Lenin's distrust of spontaneity and it had far-reaching implications for the vanguard role of the Party. On the same occasion he introduced the phrase 'socialist pluralism'. It was to be a 'pluralism of opinions' only and the suggestion of institutional pluralism was carefully avoided (until 1990). Nevertheless the phrase alarmed traditionally minded communists and they did not fail to notice its borrowing from Western social science.[20] In the spring of 1988, under the slogan 'socialist constitutional state', the proposal was floated to subject all parts of society, including the Party, to the rule of law.

He was also bidding for allies by calling for a fresh look at some of the most controversial episodes of the Soviet period. He initiated a drive for peasants to negotiate individual or group leaseholds from collective farms – giving in effect the go-ahead to those who wished to opt out of collectivisation.[21] Stalin's purges and collectivisation were condemned more explicitly and coherently than ever before, and the public rehabilitation of Stalin's victims began. A group of distinguished economists and sociologists (of whom the best known names are A. V. Chayanov and N. D. Kondrat'ev) had their convictions annulled in July 1987.[22] In October a Politburo commission was set up to examine the cases of Stalin's political opponents. Beginning with Bukharin in February 1988, and in time extending to all except Trotsky, these were exonerated and their Party membership posthumously restored.

These were still initiatives of the Party leadership, realised through its control of the Party bureaucracy. A cautious beginning was also made to reform measures introduced through legislation. An important Law *On the State Enterprise* was passed in July 1987, along with legislation permitting citizens in certain circumstances to sue officials for abuse of their powers.[23] In May 1988 many of the legal restrictions were removed on economic cooperatives, spontaneous profit-sharing arrangements outside the state plan; this seems to have been the first occasion on which a Supreme Soviet made serious amendments to a government bill.[24]

Yet two things could not escape notice. The pioneering radicalism was confined to the General Secretary himself, to a tiny group of like-minded associates, and to a wider but still small circle of supporters among professionals and the media. And little came of it in terms of substantive change; it remained at a programmatic or 'consciousness raising' level. The reason was half-heartedness, confusion and downright obstructionism in the application of policy. Local government elections were held in June 1987, allowing in some constituencies more candidates than seats; but on closer examination the competitive element proved illusory – defeated candidates were declared 'reserve deputies', scheduled to take over if anything happened to the winners![25] The law on abuse of official power foresaw proceedings only against individuals, not groups (eg committees), and then only after the failure of complaints to the individuals' administrative superiors. Enterprise managers found they could use their new freedom under the Law *On the State Enterprise* to raise prices unrelated to demand or performance, and the result was inflation. Middle-level state and Party officials turned out very effective at obstructing the emergence of cooperatives and private leases. In short, vested interests were disabling policy in its making and after it came into force, and it was not hard to see which vested interests: a draft law on the status of *neformaly*, leaked in early 1988, was astonishing in what it revealed of bureaucratic narrow-mindedness and delusions of grandeur.[26]

Increasingly people identified obstructionism and intrigue with the bureaucracy and the big economic ministries, and increasingly those threatened by change looked to Ligachev as the champion in the Politburo of continuity, vested interests and job security. And when Yeltsin tried to resign from the Politburo in October 1987, claiming that reforms were too slow and too incoherent, it was clear that the leadership was not united, and an open secret that he had had a brawl with Ligachev. In December Ligachev told *Le Monde* that he, not the General Secretary, chaired meetings of the Central Committee Secretariat.[27] Suspicion that high politics were retreating again into orchestrated charade was strengthened in March 1988 by the long neo-Stalinist letter of an obscure Leningrad chemistry teacher, Nina Andreeva, in the chief newspaper of the RSFSR.[28]

It is not surprising that ordinary people began to sense both confidence and confusion. Informal groups with political interests began to adopt titles like 'Society for the Defence of *Perestroika*'. In the first half of 1988 some of these in the Baltic and in the cities of Russia formed themselves into federations, often called Popular Fronts, and began to challenge local Party organs. The disorder and violence over Nagorno-Karabakh in February showed the dangerous side of this upsurge of popular feeling. For radicals it proved the need for legal and defined channels of self-expression; for conservatives, the irresponsibility of relaxing a firm hand.

In this period Gorbachev failed to surmount resistance to his policies, and both sides began to muster support outside the ruling class. Supporters of reform still understood it largely in terms of extending self-expression and interest representation, and saw the Party and state bureaucracy as their opponents, but not yet the Party itself. Indeed Party members (though often disaffected ones) played a leading role in the consolidation of the Popular Fronts. Only a few far-sighted people (on both sides) could perhaps look beyond to a competitive politics that might challenge the Party's role.

## PERESTROIKA (June 1988 to March 1990)

Gorbachev got his way about a Party conference and the XIX Party Conference was held at the end of June 1988.[29] He persuaded its delegates to approve, if only in outline, a wide programme of change to institutions, law and procedures which began to be realised from September 1988; *perestroika*, restructuring in a real sense, can be dated from this time. Its achievements included competitive elections of state and Party officials with limitations on their terms; in May 1989 a freely elected, full-time legislature that passed laws freely and held the government to account; and certain elements of the separation of powers between Party and state. This meant a limited system of competitive politics.[30] The Conference also accepted internal Party reform, and from 1988 Gorbachev could claim a mandate to recon-struct the Party as well as other institutions.

Competitive politics were inseparable from spontaneous, unorche-strated social participation. By mid-1989 Popular Fronts existed in most Russian and Ukrainian cities and in most of the non-Russian Union-Republics. They had become wildly successful in the Union-Republics of the Baltic and Transcaucasia, where they had shouldered aside the local communist parties and were setting the political agenda. Not yet parties in name, they were, *de facto*, opposition parties and poised to take government, which they generally did during 1990.

None of this could occur except at the expense of the CPSU, in the role it had played hitherto. Although the Party had underwritten *perestroika* at the Conference, it is plain that many of its members did not understand or did not support the Conference line. This brought into the open the struggle between the General Secretary and Party conservatives, for Gorbachev a struggle to get the Party to accept new realities and reform itself, but for many Party functionaries a battle for survival. At Central Committee Plenums in September 1988 and September 1989 nine members or candidates of the Politburo retired or were removed, five of whom had joined it under Brezhnev; in April

1989 no less than 110 people 'resigned' from the Central Committee –
about a fifth of its membership.[31] The proceedings of this last Plenum
and of a similar meeting in July were published and revealed harsh,
sometimes vicious criticism of the General Secretary. Nevertheless in
October 1989 G. P. Razumovskii, since 1986 the *nomenklatura* Secretary, recommended that the Party withdraw from control of non-Party
personnel.[32] In November Gorbachev presented his reappraisal of
socialism and of a reformed Party's role in an essay entitled *The
Socialist Idea and Revolutionary Perestroika.*[33]

The intra-Party conflict and the freedom of the new legislatures
combined to focus attention on the anomalous position of the CPSU:
politics might have become competitive but the competition was still
far from equal. By January 1990 Gorbachev had been persuaded to
recommend that the clause guaranteeing the Party's role be dropped
from Article six of the Constitution, and in February he in turn
persuaded a reluctant Central Committee to endorse this. Article six
was duly amended in March. To declare that the CPSU was no longer
the exclusive source of policy and political personnel meant ousting its
Politburo and Central Committee staff from the role they had played,
virtually since the Revolution.[34]

It also meant that new central institutions must be set up that were
independent of Party or parties: the post of President of the Soviet
Union, with a Presidential Council to replace the Politburo. When the
Congress of People's Deputies elected Gorbachev President on March
15 1990 he had at last secured a political base away from the CPSU
and was at the height of his formal powers.

COLLAPSE (March 1990 to December 1991)

The formal powers were illusory and virtually confined to the upper-
most reaches of politics. Two processes contributed to this and to the
final collapse of the Soviet Union over the next eighteen months: the
residual influence of the CPSU, now alienated from the President; and
deepening social turmoil and hostility to the Union government.[35]

CPSU organisation remained intact, including its permeation of the
bureaucracy and officer corps, and with it immense informal influence.
In many provinces the local power structure did not change. But its
formal displacement from the 'leading and guiding' role meant that
this influence was no longer coordinated. Humiliated and frustrated
Party committees regressed easily into ancient conspiratorial habits,

and at the same time the initiative in conservative and reactionary politics was passing to other groups, often imitating the Party's style but not under its control. Nothing illustrates this decline better than that the leaders of the August coup – though of course all CPSU members – included only one full-time official of the Party, and seemingly had no plans for its restoration.

Gorbachev was still the Party's General Secretary as well as state President, and at the XXVIII CPSU Congress in July 1990 he pressed ahead with Party reform and beat off moves to depose him; it was a virtuoso performance at a task by now irrelevant. Dissociation from the Party had deprived the Presidency of an experienced executive and Gorbachev personally of his political base, and powerful interests now set out to fill the gap vacated by the CPSU. Far more important than Party reform were two acts of omission: Gorbachev did not set up a system of Presidential agents in the provinces, one that could have replaced and mirrored CPSU organisation; and he did not seek to rally political support, for instance from the Party's reformist wing.

Politicians were in any case running before the storm. In many places, when the flow of Party directives ceased, officials and local soviets lacked the experience and authority, sometimes the will, to put anything in their place. Coordinated planning faltered, exacerbated by aspects of the 1987 Law *On the Enterprise* and then in July 1989 by the serious miners' strikes. As supply networks began to break down, inflation and 'under the counter' deals stripped urban shops bare, and regions began to put up trade barriers against their neighbours. Crime rates soared, especially crimes of violence and against property. Society was dissolving into its traditional communities, as it had done in 1917–18.

Worse still were serious outbreaks of ethnic violence in most of the southern republics during 1989 and 1990;[36] demonstrators were killed by the regular army in the Georgian capital in April 1989; guerilla fighting on the borders between Armenia and Azerbaidzhan had rarely died down since 1988. Where local leaders managed to keep things running and retain popular loyalty – most notably in the Baltic – it was in their interests to keep the rest of the Union at arm's length, indeed to flout Union and Presidential legislation. In March 1990 an elected Supreme Soviet dominated by the Lithuanian Popular Front (or *Sajūdis*) declared Lithuanian independence from the Union and was subjected to economic blockade until July. The example spread quickly to other republics. By September most of them had declared 'sovereignty', with the intention in some cases of leaving the Union as soon as feasible, and in others of reducing it to the loosest of alliances.

The CPSU had based a great deal (too much!) on the proposition that Russian, Soviet and communist interests coincided. As long as Russians accepted this, Russian nationalism would continue to bolster up Party and Empire, and in June 1990 Russian *apparatchiki* sought to preserve the tradition by founding the Communist Party of the RSFSR. But Russia's national revival was already putting Russian interests firmly ahead of those of the Centre. It was this that brought Yeltsin to the leadership of the RSFSR Supreme Soviet in May 1990 and to the Presidency of Russia in June 1991, and Gorbachev made the fatal mistake of trying to stop his rise.[37] Relations between the Union administration and the now anti-communist administration of the largest Union-Republic never recovered.

During 1990 two major alliances coalesced out of post-monopoly politics. The first was a coalition of CPSU and state bureaucrats, military and security officers, economic planners and defence industry managers – all groups whose power, status and livelihood were linked with the old order. Towards the end of 1990 it was figures from this coalition – possibly by threatening military intervention – who pressured Gorbachev into a major retreat from *perestroika*. The same forces were responsible for killing civilians in an attempt to overthrow the government of Lithuania in January 1991. The second grouping aligned urban democrats of Yeltsin's Russian regime with the emergent elites of the Union-Republics. In April 1991 Gorbachev broke with the conservatives and signed an agreement (called the 'Novo-Ogarevo' or '9 + 1 Agreement') with this latter group, and Union politics became more liberal again.[38]

Central to these manoeuvres was the Union Treaty: an attempt by Gorbachev to replace the pseudo-federal centralism that hampered reform with arrangements of genuine federalism.[39] Negotiation of this with the Union-Republics began in August 1990 and it became clear as it progressed that no bargain could have united all sides. Most republics sought the loosest of confederal arrangements – which the conservatives saw as a fatal concession. It was when Gorbachev consented in August 1991 to a formula that sided, marginally, with confederalism, that conservatives from the armed forces, the KGB and the Party decided to take matters into their own hands. In the coup of 19–21 August they deposed Gorbachev and were in turn overthrown by the people of Moscow, rallied by Yeltsin. The coup exposed the fatal weakness of the reformed Union: the CPSU was abolished in November and the Soviet Union dissolved in December 1991.

# 4 The Making of Gorbachev

'This "moulting" of mine . . . touched upon the very fundamentals of Marxism. Up to two years ago I tried, by stretching Marxist teachings, to bring them into accord with practical realities . . . I fully realised the impossibility of such tactics when I gave a lecture at the Fabian Society on the subject, "What Marx really taught" . . . I still have the manuscript of that talk; it is a frightening example of a well-meaning rescue attempt. I wanted to save Marx; I wanted to show that he had predicted everything that had and had not happened. When I got through with my "artistic performance" . . . the thought flashed through my head: You are doing Marx an injustice.'

(Eduard Bernstein, 1898)[1]


## QUESTIONS ABOUT A HUMDRUM CAREER

Mikhail Sergeevich Gorbachev was born in March 1931 in the village of Privol'noe, Stavropol' province, south Russia.[2] Stavropol', north of the Caucasus and between the Black and Caspian Seas, is part of the rich agricultural region known as the Kuban'. His parents worked at the time on the collective farm in Privol'noe, a farm that had been set up and was headed by Gorbachev's maternal grandfather, a 'middle peasant' of Ukrainian ancestry; among his relations it was this man whom Gorbachev mentioned most often. As a teenager he was, at least seasonally, a farmworker and in 1950 was accepted (without doing military service) into the prestigious Moscow State University, where he studied law (1950–5) and joined the Communist Party (1952). Three people should be noted among those he met as a student: Raisa Maksimovna Titarenko, whom he married in 1953; Zdeněk Mlynář, later Secretary of the Czechoslovak Communist Party during the Prague Spring; and A. I. Luk'yanov, a fellow law student and later Speaker of the Supreme Soviet until he was dismissed after the August 1991 coup.

After graduating Gorbachev returned to Stavropol' and worked as an official for 23 years, first of the Youth League (Komsomol) and then of the Party. He headed the Stavropol' Komsomol organisation in 1961–2 in which capacity he must have met E. A. Shevardnadze who held the same job in Georgia. He was second secretary of the Stavropol' Party organisation from 1968 to 1970, and its first secretary – in effect the provincial prefect – from 1970 to 1978. In November 1978 he was promoted Central Committee Secretary for Agriculture and moved to Moscow. This post was soon combined with a place in the Politburo (the Soviet Cabinet) as a candidate member (November 1979) and then as a full voting member (October 1980).

Two things strike us about this career. Gorbachev's advancement, though not unique, was rapid; he clearly had qualities that caught the attention of the *nomenklatura* authorities. And compared with that of many other officials, the career seems narrow and lacking in variety: no experience, say, of the army, of industry or of the non-Russian half of the Soviet Union. Given what we know now about his policies and actions, we ask where he got his ideas from, and how such a person could have risen to supreme power? Did his superiors see his potential, were they deceived, or did Gorbachev evolve? It is to analysis of his character and to the origins and development of this character that the present chapter is devoted.


## TEMPERAMENT AND PERSONALITY

Gorbachev was clearly an unusually energetic, almost hyperactive person. He worked tirelessly, and his impatience with people who did not was often made plain. When faced with tasks involving unfamiliar material, he studied the facts personally until he had mastered his brief. And he enjoyed work; the gusto and sense of excitement he brought to politics singled him out from previous Soviet leaders and contributed greatly to his appeal. This combination of energy and enjoyment seemed to give him a psychological resilience, a capacity to rise to challenges and to bounce back fighting from setbacks.

These characteristics were publicly displayed. He was an outgoing, gregarious person, one who loved talking and arguing, and who was articulate and incisive on his feet. He was a great performer, had a good sense of theatre and knew how to improvise and how to play his audience. One could picture him (even from the printed page) ringing the changes between preaching, inspiring, haggling, teasing, and bullying. On television one could see him trying to penetrate the defences of poker-faced and calculating audiences. Whilst his preferred style was face-to-face interaction with a defined and familiar audience and he lacked the charisma that swayed large crowds, there was nevertheless a major contrast here with his predecessors as General Secretary (Khrushchev being the partial exception). Soviet leaders usually felt they had to be stiff, dignified and pompous in public; they could supplement the force of their own personalities with the use or threat of other kinds of force and they were anxious to cultivate a remote, icon-like image of themselves. In seeking to humanise his image, Gorbachev used the authority of an actor, rather than that of a soldier, policeman or hierophant. In his book he quoted a letter thanking him for bringing into leadership 'people with human faces instead of stone-faced sphinxes'.[3]

Set alongside this extroversion, qualities of patience, reasonableness and fairness towards the interests of others. People who were critical judges and had no initial reason to trust him (like Margaret Thatcher) portrayed him as a straight talker, more rational than his predecessors, prepared to take criticism as well as to dish it out. Straightness and avoidance of intrigue were qualities he praised in Sakharov after the latter's death. He was ready (indeed eager) to bargain and compromise, and was not afraid to change his mind or learn from experience. This again made a change from previous Soviet politicians, who were generally characterised by rigidity, intolerance, inarticulateness and deviousness.

The recognition that adversaries had their own interests shows an insight into morale that marked him out from the run of Russian and Leninist leaders; the latter tended so easily to treat the masses as malleable clay and to regard organisation and control as cure-alls. His remark will be quoted below to the effect that overcentralisation engendered **both** the shadow-economy **and** the counter-culture. Public acknowledgement of a connection between these two would have been extraordinary even from academicians under Brezhnev; the analysis of 'deviance', indeed all sociology, was still encumbered by obligatory mumbo-jumbo about 'survivals of the past' and 'subversive foreign influences'. Gorbachev knocked some simple common sense into Soviet sociology: it is human to seek to express one's perceptions and interests; it is natural for social groups to share such self-expression; and if self-expression is systematically denied, the outcome is at best passivity and dependence, and, more likely, tricky, corrupt or subversive forms of self-expression.

He set great store by personal drive, initiative and self-help, and had a particular, personalised contempt for laziness and passivity, for the *oblomovshchina* that Russians so often decry in themselves. Alcohol seemed to be a symbol for him of what had kept Russian society dependent, authoritarian and backward. The word 'dependence' (*izhdivenchestvo*) – it might variously be translated as 'sponging', 'bludging', 'parasitism', 'hand-out mentality' etc – was one of his favourites and surely represented something fundamental in his thinking. He applied it to individuals; to occupations or institutions, including CPSU committees that asked for central direction instead of posing and solving problems for themselves; to whole regions thought to take more out of the budget than they put in. One thinks of the independence of his grandfather who organised the collective farm, or of his mother (the farm chairman's daughter) in having him baptised. In villages in the 1920s it was often a matter of chance whether personal independence led on to leadership or to scapegoating as a *kulak*.

The preoccupation with dependence invites questions: what was its imagined opposite, what would he have wished to see in its place? One answer is the phrase *khozyain svoego doma* ('master in one's own house'), an old phrase from agricultural propaganda, but one which Gorbachev seemed to use as if he meant it. When he attacked 'dependence' he seemed to be suggesting that it was weak and reprehensible not to stand on one's own feet, not to pay one's way, to **depend** on orders from above. He must have said dozens of times that there would be no miracles, no ready-made solutions handed down from on high. There was an implied critique here of authoritarianism and centralisation that was far-reaching: the effect of centralised power had been to foster people who were **dependent** on government handouts, literally unfitted for **independence**.

Personal drive and self-help should be directed above all towards achievement. Cracking specific problems, getting tangible results in politics seemed to count more for him than the pursuit of popularity, of a consistent plan or philosophy, or of power for its own sake. To bear this in mind helps us keep a sense of proportion about his relationship both to political opportunism and to Marxism-Leninism. His style and methods were flexible and eclectic, and he was ready to discard dogmas where they stood in the way of problem-solving; yet his dwelling on the critique of dependence suggests that here was a coherent, long-term priority. Such a relationship between theory and practice, or between the implicit and the programmatic, may sound unusual for a Soviet communist, but it would not be at all remarkable in a Western politician.


## POLITICAL EXPERIENCE

Gorbachev's formative years as an official spanned the Khrushchev period and the consolidation of Brezhnev's regime, and we should think of him as absorbing the lessons of those times. The tyrant was dead and denounced; the USSR had earned itself a place as a superpower; with the first sputniks and manned space-flights it was demonstrating its technical prowess. To young professionals of this generation the lessons were of unfolding opportunities, of confidence in the system, of the need to confront problems boldly.

At the same time he was in a better position than most to see what was spurious or fragile in this optimism. The bloody riots in Tbilisi in 1956 or in Novocherkassk in 1962 both happened in regions bordering on Stavropol'; in the latter case most leading officials of Rostov province lost their jobs, including, apparently, the Komsomol first secretary whom Gorbachev must have known. In 1957 the Karachai, one of the national groups deported under Stalin, began to return to their old homelands in the southern part of Stavropol'; Gorbachev must have been involved, if only because thousands of Karachai children had to be brought into the Stavropol' Komsomol, often, one may guess, in the face of parental hostility. Conventional minds could dismiss such episodes as the legacy of Stalinism; but about some of them – the Novocherkassk rising, the difficulty of controlling Khrushchev's eccentricities – it would have been hard to think clearly without confronting essential features of the system.

Could he have had any assistance in such an effort? We know of two possibilities, and these deserve exploration.

The first concerns the influence of an agriculturalist called A. A. Nikonov. Like many Party officials Gorbachev worked part-time for an additional qualification, which he completed in 1967 at Stavropol's Institute of Agriculture; he is unlikely not to have known Nikonov who headed this institute. Though a Russian, Nikonov had lived and been educated in independent Latvia before its annexation by the USSR, and he rose to become Minister of Agriculture in Soviet Latvia from 1951 to 1961. Party discipline does not seem to have stopped him

studying the works of A. V. Chayanov, the distinguished rural
sociologist who had perished in the 1930s and become virtually
unknown in his homeland. Nikonov was one of the casualties when
the administration of Latvia was purged (for 'nationalism') under
Khrushchev – his own punishment being 'exile' to a research institute
in provincial Russia. He staged a remarkable come-back in association
with Gorbachev: in 1978 he moved to a position in the Academy of
Agricultural Sciences in Moscow, and from 1984 was its President. We
remember that the first group rehabilitation under Gorbachev was
that of Chayanov's group; Nikonov's influence lay behind this and
was probably significant in the overall reappraisal of collectivisation.[4]

The second case is that of Zdeněk Mlynář who had known
Gorbachev as a student, and who visited him in Stavropol' in 1967.
Mlynář records that Gorbachev was critical of the impact of
Khrushchev's administrative confusion on agriculture; but it is hard
to imagine that the two did not also discuss Mlynář's current work for
the Czechoslovak Institute of State and Law, which involved leading a
research project on options for political reform of communist systems,
nor his preliminary conclusions: that competition among interest
groups had a legitimate place in communist politics. This work was
an important precursor of the Prague Spring, during which Mlynář
held leading Party posts, and the collapse of which led to his
emigration.[5] On the cases of Nikonov and Mlynář let us simply
comment that it would be a rare Soviet official who had never
encountered one of the regime's victims; but few provincial officials
can have been as familiar as Gorbachev with the purposes of the
Czechoslovak reformers.

What seems to have left a particular mark on officials of the
Gorbachev generation was the contrast between the leadership styles
of Khrushchev and Brezhnev. Their response was to seek a synthesis
that combined the best of both. Khrushchev had tried to get his way
by arousing enthusiasm rather than ordering people about – and his
campaigns were often impulsive gimmicks and led to administrative
chaos. Brezhnev's team reacted by announcing 'stability of cadres' and
emphasising routine, hierarchy and official consensus; this increased
efficiency for a time, but it degenerated into inertia and corruption.
The younger generation learned from Khrushchev that good leaders
need to elicit popular confidence and morale, by establishing for
example a personal bond between leaders and led. From Brezhnev
they derived the benefits to leadership of continuity and impersonal
organisation, of defined and specialised career structures, of technol-

ogy and professional expertise. The message in the fall of Khrushchev was to carry your colleagues with you and not to appeal over their heads to the populace.

Policy should never of course be simply a reflection of spontaneous social interests and pressures: there had to be leadership. Officials of this emerging school sought efficient government through **personal leadership**, leadership which emphasised earned authority and was therefore distinct both from Stalinist tyranny and from impersonal planning. The personal element was later to be encapsulated in the slogan of 1985–6 'the human factor' (*chelovecheskii faktor*). To repeat: their concern was leadership, not democracy or law. But to say that administration needs a predictable framework is to embark on a path that may lead to impartial rules and ultimately to the rule of law. Consultative leadership is by no means representative or participatory democracy, still less competitive pluralism; but it implies a possibility that a good leader may have to defend popular needs against a Centre that has lost touch.[6]

For officials in this mould few things could have been more dangerous than official corruption; it represented utter abnegation of leadership and surrender to social spontaneity at its worst. Gorbachev claims that as first secretary in the winter of 1973–4 he had to sack most of Stavropol's senior policemen for corruption, and thereby made an enemy of 'Shchelokov and his crew', who continued afterwards to try to compromise him. N. A. Shchelokov was Minister of Internal Affairs (MVD) and a close friend of Brezhnev; he was to kill himself in December 1984 when corruption investigations, started by Brezhnev's successor (and former KGB head) Yu. V. Andropov, got too close to him.[7] But in 1974 Gorbachev was taking a considerable risk in crossing such a political favourite, the more so as his démarche became known elsewhere and was copied, so he says, in the distant Urals province of Sverdlovsk – to the redoubled fury of the MVD. One is bound to speculate whether this incident forged a link between Gorbachev and the KGB (ancient rivals of the MVD) and specifically with Andropov (himself from Stavropol') – or whether such a link already existed.

It was an incident with considerable implications for the future, and Gorbachev's account is a careful one. But we see here, first, an early stage in the alliance between Kuban' and Urals officials that was to be a feature of the politics of the 1980s. In Sverdlovsk in 1973 G. V. Kolbin was Party second secretary and the one most likely to have handled a personnel case; we have encountered him as Gorbachev's nominee to head the Party in Kazakhstan in 1986. And it is highly likely that corruption in Stavropol' had connections in Krasnodar, Stavropol's western neighbour and rival in the Kuban'. Krasnodar has almost twice the population, a more diverse economy – including resort towns on the Black Sea coast – and its officials have usually gone further in politics. In the 1970s the first secretary there was S. F. Medunov, whilst G. P. Razumovskii was head of the executive. Gorbachev is likely to have known in 1973 that Medunov was involved in racketeering in the tourist trade. In 1981, when Gorbachev was in charge of agriculture in Moscow, one of his appointments was of Razumovskii to a post in the central agricultural bureaucracy apparently created for him, as if the latter needed a haven. And in 1983, when Andropov moved against official corruption, Medunov was one of the first senior figures to be disgraced. Taking such circumstantial details together, it is a plausible inference that Gorbachev was linked with Andropov during the 1970s in opposition to corruption, and that Razumovskii helped them against Medunov.

## GORBACHEV'S RISE TO POWER

Two politicians, Kulakov and Andropov, assisted Gorbachev's rise to power. Let us consider their roles.

F. D. Kulakov was Party first secretary in Stavropol' in the early 1960s and he must of course have known the local Komsomol leader. That he approved of him is shown by Gorbachev's first full-time Party post, to which he moved in late 1962, that of head of the Department of Party Organs for the Party's provincial committee; it was an important staff position in which any first secretary would want to see his own man. After the fall of Khrushchev, Kulakov moved to Moscow to be Central Committee Secretary for Agriculture; so now Gorbachev had a patron at the Centre. Kulakov's support must have been influential when Gorbachev became Stavropol's second secretary (1968) and then first secretary in 1970. Appointments like this were not determined in the province itself but were on the *nomenklatura* of the Central Committee in Moscow, and a patron like Kulakov was in a position to get the name of a promising candidate placed on the short list.

In July 1978 Kulakov died, and after a four month interval Gorbachev was appointed to his job of Central Committee Secretary for Agriculture, becoming, at the age of forty seven, the youngest member of the Soviet leadership at the time. A promotion such as this, directly from the provinces into the Secretariat, was unusual, though not unprecedented. It was clearly a move of the first importance for Gorbachev and we should probe the background to the appointment.

The first possibility is that Kulakov had named him – 'in his will' as it were – as a possible successor. We know that *nomenklatura* lists were supposed to include the names of 'reserve' candidates who could replace the current incumbents if necessary, and Kulakov would have supervised the list of reserves for his own post. But Kulakov was not present to argue the appointment! Indeed there is evidence that he had been perceived as a threat by Brezhnev and Chernenko,[8] and the four month interval before Gorbachev's appointment suggests controversy. And whatever might be rumoured about Medunov in private, he headed one of the largest agricultural provinces; it would have been difficult to exclude that name from the short list.

A second relevant factor is the high profile that Stavropol' officials had with the central leadership, because the best health spas are located in its Caucasian foothills. Whenever someone from the Politburo or the High Command came to take the waters, the Stavropol' first secretary had to be on hand to give them a formal welcome – and, perhaps more important, was likely to have been consulted by security before the visitation. We remember that Gorbachev's links with Andropov seem to go back to the early 1970s. Andropov's influence could certainly have been a factor that led to Gorbachev's preferment over Medunov.

The first public evidence that Gorbachev was aligned with Andropov came in typical 'Kremlinological' style from the signatures to the obituary of the first deputy head of the KGB, General S. K. Tsvigun, at the end of January 1982.[9] Protocol dictated that the entire Politburo and Secretariat should register condolences at the death of someone of this rank. Instead the signatures from the top leadership were five only: Andropov, Chernenko, Ustinov, Aliev – all of whom had institutional reasons for signing – and Gorbachev. There were precedents for this happening when someone died in disgrace, and rumours were rife that Tsvigun had killed himself after a quarrel with M. A. Suslov (who died himself a week later) about the pursuit of corruption among the elite. Whether or not Tsvigun was conducting corruption inquiries, and whether or not he clashed with Suslov, the signatures to his obituary suggest that Gorbachev was allied with Andropov on some issue of interest to the KGB. Once Brezhnev died his position as Andropov's second-in-command and preferred heir soon became clear.

It would be mistaken to see this merely as a personal alliance. We have seen that Gorbachev represented a leadership type that was coming increasingly to look at odds with the Brezhnev group – extrovert, conscientious, 'trouble-shooting' administrators with more than a chance resemblance to the ideal type of army officer. Examples from Gorbachev's circle in the mid-1980s are Kolbin, Shevardnadze, Yeltsin or A. I. Vol'skii. We can see the way in which they tried to mark themselves off from the bad leaders they had encountered: corrupt ones like Medunov, lifelong *apparatchiki* like Chernenko, or the worshippers of technology whose fetishism led ultimately to Chernobyl'. Andropov at the same time was becoming prominent among politicians alarmed at the implications of 'stability of cadres'. As head of the KGB he had professional cause to pay attention to corruption (as to anything that alienated society from the regime), and there were thus good reasons why he should look to more inspiring leadership and be attracted by young officials of the 'trouble-shooting' type. But such politicians – even Andropov! – had to be discreet: they would not be looking for idealists, firebrands or orators, but for incrementalists and realists who would work through existing institutions, whilst being independent enough not to become their prisoners.[10] Even if Andropov and Gorbachev had never met there were pressures working in favour of people like Gorbachev.

Alliance with the head of the secret police will have brought Gorbachev major benefits in terms of political support and information, but it does not sound a plausible background for political reform. Here Soviet experience is very foreign to us, and we should pause to consider the role of the secret police and especially of Andropov. Russian and Soviet 'secret police' were traditionally used for purposes well beyond espionage and counter-espionage, and in particular as guardians of the internal social and political order. To this end it was in the interests of secret policemen to be better informed even than the rulers about social structures and attitudes, and to develop manipulative rather than coercive techniques of control, 'Machiavellian' rather than despotic methods. They did not need to be told what happened to secret policemen in Budapest in 1956 or in Romania in 1989.

Andropov was a secret policeman in this mould. Although not a career security officer, his career had included administration of non-Russian nationalities and dealings with the Soviet dependencies in

Eastern Europe – both connected with upholding the political order. In October 1956 he was Soviet ambassador in Budapest, and must bear some of the responsibility for the betrayal under truce of Nagy, Maleter and other Hungarian leaders. No closet liberalism here. After the Hungarian revolt Andropov was commissioned to found a Central Committee 'Department for Liaison with Communist and Workers' Parties of Socialist Countries', one that handled a distinct foreign policy towards these countries. In this job he built up a clientele of trusted, well-informed assistants, and when a decade later he became head of the KGB, he took many of them with him; some, like V. A. Kryuchkov, head of the KGB in 1988–91, had been with him in Budapest. Andropov was dedicated to securing an empire abroad and an authoritarian order at home, but – it is shown by his methods against dissidents – he preferred to avoid bloodshed and his use of coercion and intimidation was specific and calculated. He could well have learnt from the Hungarian revolt the sort of lesson some British administrators learned from the Indian Mutiny.

A corollary of this approach to security was that the importance of intelligence increased as that of coercion declined. Andropov needed to 'know his enemy' and he encouraged professional research and analysis, especially of international relations, the West, and threats to the Soviet order. Under such auspices serious work on foreign social thought, even on revisionist Marxism, could be undertaken. People who were familiar (and often radical) public figures in the 1980s: G. A. Arbatov of the Institute for the USA and Canada; Gorbachev's personal aide G. Kh. Shakhnazarov; F. M. Burlatskii, once Khrushchev's speech writer and in 1990–1 chief editor of *Literaturnaya gazeta*; or A. E. Bovin, chief political correspondent of *Izvestiya* – all worked for Andropov in the early 1960s.[11] These were shrewd, knowledgeable and pragmatic men, worlds away from the identikit ideologues who had preceded them.

Most Soviet research was conducted not in universities but in institutes of the Academy of Sciences; such institutes had often preserved nineteenth-century traditions of intellectual independence and offered a refuge to thinking people on the fringe of dissidence or to political casualties (like Nikonov or Burlatskii). In fostering a research backing to policy Andropov was contributing (whether he knew it or not) to the emergence of a new intellectual milieu that was better informed about political issues than the nineteenth century intelligentsia, and more willing to be engaged in them. It was an environment in which the ideas of near-dissident radicals such as B. P.

Kurashvili or T. I. Zaslavskaya, even of former political prisoners like Academicians Sakharov or D. S. Likhachev, could seep through to policy advisers – some of whom, like A. N. Yakovlev or E. M. Primakov, were soon to become politicians.

This was the origin of the 'New Thinking' (*novoe myshlenie*) of the late 1980s, and it was an important legacy of Gorbachev's alliance with Andropov; it brought his confident and restless mind into touch with a sophisticated body of thought and an experienced group of policy advisers, and he put both to excellent use, in a way difficult to imagine from a Romanov or a Grishin, let alone from Brezhnev or Chernenko. At the same time we should be mistaken in portraying Gorbachev as an intellectual; he had an unusual ability to absorb academic analysis and apply it to policy, but he lacked Yakovlev's urge to revise old thinking systematically.

### THE IMPACT OF OFFICE

The discussion so far has revealed Gorbachev as a one of a group of impatient 'Young Turk' officials; an interesting and unusual man in the context of Brezhnev's court, but nonetheless a representative of the Soviet ruling class, and sharing many of its limitations. One gets little sense that his law degree or the ethnic diversity of the Soviet Union had had much impact on his thinking; he was conventional in his use of patronage to gain advancement and muster political support. Neither the ideas of Nikonov, nor contact with the 'think-tank' researchers, nor the in-house analysis of Polish Solidarity (in which Gorbachev as a full Politburo member must have taken part) left any noticeable mark on his conduct of the agriculture portfolio before Brezhnev's death. How was this Gorbachev turned into a reformer, and then into a radical who challenged the system? Was he always a nonconformist in private, waiting to throw off his conventional mask, or did his nonconformism develop?

The *prima facie* evidence is that he did not change until after the 1986 Party Congress. His earliest policies after he became General Secretary were standard Soviet policies, piecemeal and reactive. The merging of ministries to create a giant State Agro-Industrial Committee showed a traditional belief in reorganisation as a panacea. The campaign against alcohol addressed symptoms but not the cause. The new versions of the Party Programme and Rules and his speeches to the April Plenum and XXVII Congress were cautious and unadven-

turous. In the Ukrainian capital in June 1985 he could talk about
'Russia – the Soviet Union, I mean . . . '; in February 1986 Stalinism
was 'a concept thought up by the enemies of communism and widely
used to discredit the Soviet Union and socialism as a whole'.[12]

It was only some time after this that an evolution in his public
statements began to be noticed. Contrast the above attitude to Stalin
with the following, from June 1986, July 1987 and December 1989
respectively:[13]

> If we start trying to deal with the past, we'll lose all our energy. It
> would be like hitting the people over the head. And we have to go
> forward. We'll sort out the past. We'll put everything in its place.
> But right now we have to direct our energy forward.

> [W]e can never and should never forgive or justify what happened in
> 1937–38. Never.

> Certainly the Leader's rule was harsh and repressive. But, really, not
> strong in a political sense. Strong rule is not afraid of its own citizens,
> does not create an atmosphere of general suspicion and denuncia-
> tion, does not eliminate every free expression of thought by means of
> total terror. In general terror in any form is the simplest and crudest,
> but also the most ineffective and short-term means of regulating
> public life; in the last analysis it is a manifestation of weakness.

Gorbachev's critique of dependence evolved too. Before 1986 this
had taken the form of a preoccupation with 'parasitism', usually
exemplified by illicit earnings, and his animus had been directed
against the aggressive anti-social features of economic individualism.[14] During 1986 the focus shifted towards undue passivity and
reliance on others; in a speech given in Khabarovsk in August it
referred to people who whined and blamed everyone except themselves; this usage – on the **side** of individualism – was the one that set
in.[15] It was a remarkable evolution given the Party's cult of obedience.

Yet care is needed in evaluating public utterances like these.
Politicians adapt what they say to audiences and circumstances; and
during the succession struggle and then while he consolidated power
Gorbachev had reason to be careful. How can we know that he did not
keep his real views private until it was safe or advantageous to express
them? It has been argued that his December 1984 speech 'The Living
Creativity of the People', which was not published in full at the time,
reveals the radical behind the mask.[16] This speech is without doubt the
product of a livelier and bolder mind than any other in the leadership

at the time; it betrays the influence of the New Thinking, especially of the *Novosibirsk Report*; and many of the slogans he was to make famous (including *glasnost'* and *perestroika*) are there. Yet there is also a 'catch-all' quality about the speech (it was a 'campaign speech' three months before Chernenko's death!), and some themes in it sit uneasily with coherent concepts of reform. The word *uskorenie* ('acceleration') is used; in 1985 this was to be the new leadership's favourite slogan, and then for a short time it was coequal with *glasnost'* and *perestroika*; but one cannot speed up the production line if it is being reconstructed at the same time! People who live on unearned incomes 'throw down a challenge to honest workers', and investigators should have the power to identify their sources of income. This is the disciplinarian approach of Andropov and it shows a mind not essentially different from Gorbachev's public persona in 1982–5.

I would argue that the evolution apparent in his public statements after 1985 represents a real evolution in thinking, for several reasons. We know first (we hardly needed the August 1991 coup to confirm it) that threats to Gorbachev's position did not diminish after 1985, but increasingly he did things that ran counter to his short-term convenience or interests: Sakharov was released whilst making it clear that he intended to be a loyal oppositionist; the Eastern European revolutions were triggered when Gorbachev let it be understood that there would be no Soviet intervention. To phase out 'acceleration' from the reform trinity involved a similar risk; even in the 1990s there were conservatives who said that **that** was the reform they had really wanted.[17] None of this sounds like a time-server or someone playing for safety.

Second, we should take note of evolution in assumptions or preoccupations that are not essential to his political position, especially where they are off the record. Gorbachev's changing notion of 'dependence' offers the outsider a framework for understanding his development; but he had no **need** to offer it, and none of his predecessors ever did. The June 1986 comments on Stalin were made in private to intellectuals and come to us through *samizdat*; if he had thought it important, this would have been an ideal occasion to acknowledge the burden of history on the present – but apparently he did not.

Overall one has the impression of a person thinking aloud, needing to think aloud in order to progress, and not afraid of sounding unconvincing. One can see him returning repeatedly to some theme which preoccupies him, and one can see that theme developing. It was not until February 1991 that he called himself a 'centrist' – long after it had become obvious to the world! During autumn 1989 he was preoccupied with the question of the Party's role (the question that was to lead to the amendment of Article 6). His thinking aloud on this subject was distinctly weak, and contrasted with his normal intellectual impressiveness. On one occasion, an interview before a large and critical audience of students, his questioners were plainly dissatisfied and pressed him – and he did develop his unsatisfactory response a bit, but not very much further. Now unsatisfactory responses seem to me very revealing: whether he had not thought the issue through, or not thought through its public presentation, is immaterial; the point is that one can witness a case developing, and not always smoothly.[18] This does not have the mark of someone matching his words to his audience.

Instead it suggests someone probing and clarifying his thinking in response to challenge, a process not unlike the 'moulting' described by Bernstein. I think it would be a mistake to treat the knowledge and ideas he might have had from Mlynář or Nikonov, or later from the Moscow think-tanks, as having direct or immediate influence. What he gained from them was dormant, unorganised experience – capable of easing the transition to coherent radicalism, but only if activated, and in a person with the appropriate energy, temperament and skills. What Gorbachev himself said was that he and close colleagues (in particular Shevardnadze) felt that things were rotten and could not go on as they had, but that he had no predetermined plan for *perestroika*.[19] But he clearly had the personality to learn and apply lessons from experience in late middle age, and I believe he learned intensively on the job, acquiring by 1987–8 a qualitatively different, and much more impressive grasp of the tasks he faced and of the implications and interrelatedness of their solutions. We should ask, what kind of catalyst might have stimulated this learning?

If we compare 1986 with the period from October 1989 to April 1990, another time of vigorous policy reappraisal, the common element is pressure to respond to challenge or crisis; in 1986 the nuclear disaster at Chernobyl' stands out as the most likely challenge.

The first reaction of the administration to Chernobyl' was to impose a traditional cover-up. We know next to nothing of the high politics of the next eighteen days. Did Gorbachev or others take time to realise the seriousness of the accident and its implications, or was there a struggle about its public handling? In either case he was a changed politician after this period: his television statement of 14 May, though not in itself impressive, marked a turning point not only in the handling of this crisis, but for *glasnost'* and indeed the whole reform process.[20] It is as if he crossed a personal Rubicon sometime in early May. From his point of view, one can surmise, considerations both of elementary responsibility during a disaster of historic proportions, and of the survival of his young regime, would have combined to dictate clear and rapid action – to repudiate the contemptible public relations of the past fortnight and to seek to restore some credibility to the media and the administration.

The television speech showed him in a curiously transitional light, as if he were still working out Chernobyl's full implications. On the one hand he discarded (for the first time, seemingly, among Soviet leaders) the insistence on man's mastery over nature – and implicitly substituted a need for personal responsibility. On the other hand his attack on Western reactions to the disaster showed a willingness to cast the Soviet Union as the victim and blame the world, something that had been a familiar theme throughout the Soviet period, but which was uncharacteristic of Gorbachev personally. The text was possibly one agreed beforehand; I cannot think of an instance when he tried to shift blame in this way after May 1986 (though other politicians did, especially in 1991). His reaction to the Urals gas pipeline disaster in June 1989 is more characteristic in its focus on domestic faults and on the traditional political culture:[21]

> Once again it seems it could have been avoided . . . Once again it seems to come back to incompetence, irresponsibility, indiscipline, *bezobrazie*. Our affairs will never pick up if slovenliness is going to generate such human tragedies.

Immediately after Chernobyl' it was easy to blame others: the criminal negligence of the power station engineers who conducted the experiment, the cowardice of the Party members who simply ran away, or the arrogant contempt of the politicians who imposed the cover-up. But consideration would reveal that the engineers were acting under orders (even if they broke rules to carry them out), and that everyone was acting under pressure. Soviet power stations had been beset with scandals for years, all with the same cause: central pressure to produce more electricity than equipment allowed. The experiments were criminally negligent, but (as anyone who had lived in the Soviet Union knew) bending and breaking the rules like this happened all the time; it was **systemic** and utterly predictable as long as central bureaucrats had the power they had, and as long as a controlled press protected them in the way it did. The system not only encouraged acts of rule-breaking; it rewarded and promoted obedient, uncritical and passive behaviour – towards superiors and towards technology.

I believe this touched Gorbachev's central anxiety about dependence. We have seen that he was preoccupied with this as a feature of what was wrong with the Soviet Union he inherited, and that the focus of his preoccupation shifted in the second half of 1986. I think Chernobyl' provided the trigger for this: it had been a brutal demonstration of the links between dependence and centralised, authoritarian rule – of how it fostered dependence and of how dependence could turn round and cripple the system.

The critique of dependence brought a new and sophisticated note into Gorbachev's thinking. He began increasingly to draw connections among the notions of dependence, centralisation, corruption and dissent, and to link this with the value he placed on personal leadership and individual initiative:[22]

> The urge to envelop every corner of life . . . in detailed control literally swaddled society. It generated . . . both the 'shadow' economy and the [counter]-culture, parasitic on the incapacity of state organs to meet needs. . . .

Corruption and dissent came to be treated less as deviations (and still less as the outcome of external subversion), and more as the natural defence mechanisms of those who still had some capacity to resist. His harshness faded towards those who would manipulate the state to their own advantage, to be replaced by condemnation of those who simply sucked it dry. His focus thus began to shift from a bland assumption of people's 'living creativity' towards the organisational and cultural forces that frustrated or distorted that creativity – above all towards the role of the paternalist state in maintaining dependence. The critique of dependence was the framework for his developing critique of bureaucracy, monopoly, centralism – and implicitly of 'revolution from above', of the single ruling Party and of Leninist leadership. In their place he began to explore a vision of *razgosudarstvlenie* ('emancipation from the state'), competitive politics and evolutionary development. Gooding has observed that his elevation of individual above collective or state interests was something new for Soviet socialism.[23] This was no egalitarian vision, but a competitive, meritocratic one, one aiming at an elite of the talents. We recall the variety of temperaments and perceptions that had found a home in the CPSU – in this case there was more than a hint of *kulak* individualism and private enterprise!

Three further observations: Gorbachev's vision was an extraordinarily ambitious one, probably over-ambitious. Yet his focus on the social costs of the Soviet period gave him an awareness his predecessors lacked of the limits to what politics or politicians could achieve. Note, second, how the New Thinking had grown away from its origins in the preservation of imperial greatness and become focused on internal renewal, with foreign policy subordinated to domestic priorities. Finally it is difficult to think of any source for these views in the educational materials of Gorbachev's time; the views would seem to have been home-made and to have derived from experience. It argues his personal independence and the poverty of abstract indoctrination when it cuts across such experience.

## POLITICAL CHARACTER

Gorbachev differed from his predecessors in being a product of the new Soviet middle classes – specifically of the new professional class – and in his aspirations, assumptions, style and methods he was representative of these classes.[24] He took the Soviet system and way of life for granted and his initial aim was its success – pursued for its own sake, rather than as a means to national greatness, world revolution or social control, and pursued with the professional's accent on efficiency, the application of organised and cooperative expertise, and hence on the emancipation and utilisation of talent. His social world, the people to whom he addressed himself, was one of self-motivating professionals, people who needed the state to guarantee order and stability but not to tell them how to do their jobs. Like middle classes throughout history they distrusted both dictatorship and mass democracy: natural centrists.

His approach to politics was one of rational problem-solving, and he assumed rationality and the pursuit of enlightened self-interest in others; he also assumed (as professionals do in large, functionally differentiated organisations) that the interplay of rational interests was constructive not divisive, that his fellow human beings were cooperative and socially conscious, and that society cohered naturally. His greatest triumphs were in structured environments – the Party Congress, the Congress of People's Deputies, the summit meeting – where a basis of common purposes and rules could be taken for granted; outside such environments, and especially after March 1990, he was often awkward and his failures were often associated with a mistaken assumption of common purpose. Style and methods too were those of the professional in a structured environment: persuasion and argument, negotiation and accommodation. Notions like competition, conflict of interest, bargaining or compromise had been taboo in Soviet politics until Gorbachev made them political virtues; but he made it possible to speak approvingly of politics as 'the art of the possible'.[25] He was impatient with Brezhnevite clichés and, for all his intellectual vigour, not much interested in putting any systematic world view in their place; so a new flexibility and pragmatism entered policy and public speaking.

The picture so far might seem to be one of a mere technician or 'organisation man'. It was Gorbachev's combination of **energy** and **enjoyment** of his job that allowed him to be effective beyond the merely professional world. A writer on the Presidency of the USA, J. D. Barber, distinguishes four character types among Presidents, and one of these, the type to which he allocates F. D. Roosevelt, Truman and Kennedy, is defined precisely by this combination of two very basic features of human experience. Traits he associates with this type of leader are the elevation of results above the pursuit of power for its own sake and above other rewards of power; a stress on bringing rationality to bear on problem-solving; and flexibility in style and methods and lack of interest in systematic philosophy.[26]

This could well have been written about Gorbachev. Many of his characteristics fall into place if one thinks of their basis in energy combined with enjoyment. This helped him achieve something that many radicals have found elusive – an overhaul of his own thinking in his late fifties – and it gave him the confidence to move easily and boldly from ideas to practical application, where many intellectuals are content simply to have analysed. He loved political activity for its own sake, breaking out of pre-set programmes and revelling in improvisation or 'planful opportunism';[27] like Napoleon '*on s'engage, et puis l'on voit*'. Like many politicians he was prepared to take risks, and impatient with those who could not live with risk-taking. He told the Central Committee: 'Some comrades are treating [change] as amounting to the collapse of the universe. Even if one concedes it's a collapse, then it's the collapse of a **warped** universe!'.[28] If one took a chance and it failed, it might still have been the right one to take.

At the same time the elevation of achievement above other rewards was the background to the 'political methods' of which he was so proud, to his tactical flexibility and impatience with grand theory. A Soviet essayist noted that he was the only Soviet leader to come to office with integrity intact, and the only one to be changed by office.[29] Someone whose personal rewards were independent of others' approval could be relatively uninhibited about redefining the eternal verities of past generations. But the human contact entailed in practical politics helped keep ordinary human interests and limitations in mind so that his vision did not harden into a plan, dogma or crusade; it strengthened his instinct to hold on to the middle ground and not to proceed faster than most people's pace.

The comparison between Roosevelt and Gorbachev suggests something else: each was thought of as vigorous, confident, ebullient, but hardly as radical before coming to power, and in each, coming to power at a time of national crisis was a shock that released hidden capacities; each rose to a challenge in a manner unpredicted from knowledge of his earlier life. In Gorbachev it liberated a vision of the emancipation of individual talent, and one in which a renewed Communist Party, transcending its sclerosis and obscurantism, could play a part. It was a partial vision, one which highlighted middle-class professionals like himself and left others in the shadows, and that was part of its tragedy. But it was a rare attempt to confront the crisis, and not a wholly unrealistic one.

Soviet people had never had a leader like this before. For many his fascination with tactics and accommodation, especially when linked to an *apparatchik* past, suggested basic lack of principle and purpose beyond staying in power, whilst his lack of the common touch suggested authoritarianism. The charge of lack of principle, or (Yeltsin's variant) of half-heartedness, has a certain plausibility – and in the case of the Vilnius killings[30] – more than this, but (as I hope to show) it does not get to the heart of the matter. More revealing is the role that he reserved for himself in relation to other democrats. In the late 1980s he talked often of the need for a 'school of democracy', making it plain who the headmaster was and seemingly untroubled by the prospect of a single individual 'schooling' a whole country. After six years in office he was still playing a lone hand, whilst numerous close allies – Kolbin, Razumovskii, Bakatin, Ryzhkov, Shevardnadze, Yakovlev – had fallen by the wayside, hinting in some cases at lack of support from their boss. As President he dismissed (in effect) a Politburo whose composition he could not control fully and substituted for it a Presidential Council, wholly appointed by himself – yet he did as good as nothing to build up his political support in place of the CPSU he had abandoned. He deprecated those who 'claimed the role of messiah',[31] yet there was an impatience of teamwork here, a deliberate self-isolation that suggests delusions of irreplaceability, if not invulnerability.

In such light one cannot acquit Gorbachev of a kind of authoritarianism. Like Lenin he was confident of his superior judgement and determined to get his own way, and he could be crushing to people less energetic, clear-minded or articulate than himself.[32] We suspect that he suffered fools only at cost of much mental effort. The logic of his policies was to promote the spontaneity Lenin had deplored – but we suspect that deep down he welcomed only certain types of spontaneity: disciplined and cooperative, sensible and rational spontaneity, spontaneity that showed a proper sense of gratitude for years of protective guidance. Gorbachev might have been a convert to democracy but he was not temperamentally a democrat.[33]

Yet his authoritarianism was something he displayed quite openly (*glasno*); he did not try to mystify it or let others do his dirty work. He stuck to the verbal weapons of debate and law, and did not resort, when he lost a vote for instance, to threats or to extra-legal means of getting his own way. And his combativeness was not directed especially at equals and possible rivals, but more often at people who in his view were out of their depth or could not stand the heat of the kitchen. In Academician Sakharov and some other politicians who emerged from the 1989 Supreme Soviet (the lawyer A. A. Sobchak for example) he seemed to respect worthy adversaries. It was the behaviour of an aggressively competitive man, a meritocrat and something of a snob; it was not always gentle behaviour, but it was not that of a power-hungry or solipsistic tyrant.

Gorbachev's greatest weaknesses were related directly to his strengths. Commenting on the failings of the Rooseveltian politician, Barber suggests 'he may fail to take account of the irrational in politics. Not everyone he deals with sees things his way and he may find it hard to understand why.'[34] Gorbachev's assumption of rationality and cooperativeness, his stress on negotiation and compromise marked a breakthrough in the behaviour of Soviet leaders, but, important as 'political methods' were, he sometimes got them out of proportion.[35] Outside the familiar structured environments, his judgements of persons and situations were often badly flawed.

The contrast between Gorbachev and Yeltsin provides illustrations. After November 1987 Gorbachev treated Yeltsin as an 'ambitious' politician, meaning by this not simply a rival, but an obstreperous rival, one who rocked the boat or bucked what reasonable men accepted as the rules. But there was much more than this to Yeltsin's emergence as RSFSR leader: Gorbachev's preoccupation with his personality seemed to blind him to the institutional pressures driving the All-Union and Russian administrations apart;[36] he seems similarly to have overlooked the possibility that Yazov, Kryuchkov or Luk'yanov might actually come to represent the institutions they headed. Unlike Yeltsin, Gorbachev never fought a mass election and had no gift for gestures that captured popular imagination; his embarrassed retreat from a mocking crowd on May Day 1990 was characteristic. His policies were aimed at the politically informed middle class and assumed 'working class deference', and as regards organised politics this assumption turned out generally correct; but the effects of the law *On the Enterprise*, or the later inflation and collapse of retail trade suggest a more general and dangerous misreading of mass attitudes.

Nowhere is this narrowness of focus clearer than in the sphere of ethnic politics ('irrational' politics *par excellence*). He often gave the impression of thinking in predominantly Russian terms, or of addressing himself to a mainly Russian (or pro-Russian) audience; for Russians, he said, cooperating in a multinational state was 'in our genes'. The man who came to accept dissent and private enterprise as manifestations of human initiative had difficulty seeing national self-assertion in the same way. In February 1988 he told Armenian spokesmen that the Armenians had 'stabbed his policies in the back' with their mass support for self-determination. In Lithuania in January 1990 his arguments centred on people's rational economic interest in staying in the Union and he seemed reluctant to face the moral grievance ('No divorce, because it was a rape, not a marriage') which was at the heart of the Lithuanian case.[37]

A complex man who reflected the pressures of a complex society and complex times. In Gorbachev aggressive self-affirmation struggled with recognition that others had a rightful place in the elite of the talents. He was torn between running a school of democracy and accepting social spontaneity; between letting people grow up, and exercising a leadership at which he was good – and arguably better than any visible alternative – and which society and tradition demanded. And as a leader he was uneasy in dealing with mass politics, with emotional or symbolic politics, or (as the August coup showed) with the intrigue of court politics. Though an able strategist and tactician he was nevertheless a 'set-piece general'; he may have been the best man available, but the choice was not ideal for a time of revolution.

# 5 Objectives, Agenda, Strategy

'For the human character is such that men wish to be governed in a human fashion, rather led than dragged, rather persuaded than compelled, for man was created in the image of God, a reasoning, free and independent being. The art of government is thus based upon wisdom and not upon force, upon caution and foresight and not upon trickery.'

(Jan Amos Komenský [Comenius], 1668)[1]

## THE INITIAL SITUATION AND ITS IMPLICATIONS

We have seen something of what was going wrong with the Soviet system and something of the abilities and experience the new General Secretary could bring to bear on the crisis. We need next to reconstruct how the leadership responded to it, what it sought to achieve, and how it planned to realise this: the **objectives**, **agenda** and **strategy** of the new administration.[2]

Even the casual observer could see that the economy was in decline; that people had lost confidence in the economy and administration; and that these processes were reinforcing each other. If one probed beneath the surface something more alarming could be discerned: not just loss of confidence but a tendency for society to opt out of the Soviet order and develop alternative ways of doing things. The Andropov regime seems not to have probed far beneath the surface; its prescription of 'discipline **and** reform' could probably have held back rising social pressure for a while longer. But such discipline – especially the former policeman's discipline that was not law – would in the end have compounded the problem; it would simply have turned still more people to their own devices.

Gorbachev was Andropov's choice for successor, and more than most incoming leaders he needed to demonstrate his fidelity to Party tradition. It is not surprising that he presented his earliest policies as an evolution from those of Andropov. For the first year his emphasis

75

was on two things. Improved leadership and organisation should combine responsiveness to social needs with consistent discipline, directed both at ordinary people and at corrupt and self-serving officials. Pay should be related strictly to inputs – which he defended by recalling that socialism meant ' . . . to each according to his work'. He derided the Brezhnevian social compact by attacking the 'psychology of mutual forgiveness' among management and workers. Second, this coordinated and disciplined effort should be harnessed to economic modernisation; the key-words were **'acceleration'** (*uskorenie*), 'intensification', 'scientific-technical revolution', 'mobilisation of reserves' etc; planning was still 'the heart of administration'.[3] Psychologically revealing is the hostility to 'unearned' incomes: their individualism challenged a state programme, directed from above in the state's interests.[4]

At the same time one can also catch glimpses of the later Gorbachev in the speeches of his first year: social interests had a right to be heard, good leadership should solicit feedback, hard work and talent were entitled to reward. Where Andropov had seen only insubordination, Gorbachev seemed to see misguided or demoralised initiative, and his responses were less in terms of discipline, and more in terms of reclaiming such activity and enterprise for the common cause. But even this minor shift in emphasis – the palest of glosses on Andropov's policies – might have disturbing implications. Might not Gorbachev be a bit too ready to recognise interests and initiative wherever they arose in society, a bit too perfunctory about the Party's role in shaping and coopting them? Orthodox minds in the Party might have recalled that Khrushchev had tried to use social mobilisation against the *apparat* – and look how that had ended in 1964. Gorbachev must have realised very early – we know he was conscious of it by mid-1986[5] – that to be head of the CPSU was in its own way a constrained and vulnerable position.

And the *apparat* was arguably more powerful than in 1964. Brezhnev's political coalition was still well organised, well placed and well equipped – an alliance of Party officials with the armed forces and police, the heavy industrial ministries, the technicians and specialists who were essential to defence and heavy industry, and, finally, the urban population whose good behaviour was bought with consumer goods subsidies. Some, but only some of these – technicians and urban consumers perhaps – might be detached from the coalition. Others, army and heavy industry, could mount formidable opposition if their interests were threatened. By contrast the most restive of the 'outgroups' – peasants, professionals, non-Russian nationalities – lacked organisational coherence and resources. But these were not the only components in the situation. Many Soviet people were troubled by what was happening to the country and more receptive to change than they had been in 1964; if a shake-up was needed, who better to head it than a young and dynamic Party leader? The Party's quasi-military structure and traditions made it an effective and durable instrument in the hands of such a leader. It still produced officials who could serve a transformist cause with energy and selfless loyalty. It contained millions of others who would doggedly carry out orders even if they did not fully understand them – indeed who would accept surgery on the Party provided it was administered by one of their own. These were factors working in Gorbachev's favour.

Two major lessons, and two minor ones, emerge from this cursory survey of the initial situation. What stands out is the centrality of the Party to both problem and solution. The CPSU was the country's major political resource and agent of change; yet it also stood in the way of change, the most obstinate of the vested interests. Facing a somewhat similar choice, Stalin and Mao Zedong had simply called up external forces and battered the Party into submission. It did not require great insight or knowledge of Party history to see that these forces – secret police or mob terror – could be used only for certain purposes. Were these purposes Gorbachev's? We can be sure that Gorbachev did not seriously entertain this option. He was ambitious and confident that he could inspire willing service from an institution he knew well. And a variety of factors – recent history and society's mood, his own experience and temperament – dictated that what he undertook must command consent and build on the resources to hand: his purposes were those of reform, not revolution. He is likely to have pondered two other cases in recent communist history, the Czechoslovak and Polish ones. No-one in Gorbachev's position would have wanted to get into the mess of the Polish communists in 1980, and this could have inclined him to a Party-led renewal movement like that of Dubček.

There was thus no question of replacing the Party and its *apparat*.[6] He must work with them and through them, whilst at the same time, quite literally, 're-forming' them through leadership, inspiration and challenge. It would be fatal for the Party leader to be seen promoting confrontation – whether a popular crusade against the Party, or a reformist intra-Party faction. He must avoid the divisive rhetoric that

had been a failing of the Prague Spring. Only by avoiding publicity
and polarisation could he safeguard his own political position,
reassure conservative interests – and achieve anything. By the 1980s
a reformer who was Party-based was inevitably a reformer of
gradualism and continuity; he must try to hold the middle ground
and present himself as a man of compromise and consensus.
Many of Gorbachev's favourite tactics were related to this need to
command the middle ground. He was a master at introducing new,
disturbing content whilst retaining the familiar, comfortable phraseol-
ogy. His programmes often included superfluous items that he would
later 'concede' in return for support. He pushed people into presenting
their case explicitly and in public (something not encouraged in the
CPSU tradition) – and often they ended up discrediting themselves, or
the two extremes were enticed into an exhausting brawl.[7]

There are two subsidiary precepts. The reformist leader needed allies
distinct from the Party functionaries who were themselves part objects
of reform. But these allies should be chosen with greatest care; he must
avoid any appearance of using them to supplement or by-pass his
official servants. And the constraints on his role suggested that he
should buy time and capitalise on quick successes wherever possible.
The Soviet system was internally coherent and its problems not easily
detached from the Gordian knot of centralisation and political
monopoly. But in 1985 there were a few which could. Afghanistan
was an example: a short-sighted adventure, not directly linked to
Soviet strategic interests. Another was the dissidents: not only were
people like Sakharov in exile for advocating what was soon to become
government policy, but the techniques of the dissidents themselves,
and the techniques of suppressing them, were no longer central to
regime control of opinion. A regime which wanted to stop the spread
of wrong ideas in the 1980s should have directed its attention, not to
lone intellectuals, but to ham radio operators, photocopying, imports
of personal computers and video-cassette players. Neither Afghanistan
nor the dissidents were near the core of Soviet problems, and in such
cases a relatively quick and low-cost solution could be offered, and
credit gained.

In all this should one look for a deeper 'hidden agenda'? I am
inclined to doubt it. Considered carefully, Gorbachev's initial position
was a good deal more constrained than his exuberance suggested. In
addition we have seen that he disliked being bound by programmes
and prized his capacity for experimental and improvised response.
And his thinking seems to have taken a quantum leap in maturity and

grasp during 1986, perhaps in consequence of the Chernobyl' disaster. He is unlikely to have seen politics like a chess player, as a tree of alternative strategies branching out from different contingencies on the board.

## FIRST MOVES: *GLASNOST'* AND INFORMAL GROUPS (1986–87)

By the middle of 1986 Gorbachev had begun to outgrow Andropov's legacy and to espouse priorities that were genuinely novel. Political participation began to replace acceleration, modernisation and discipline; the claims of the individual began to ease out those of the state; from invigorated leadership attention shifted to the balance of power between leaders and led.

After Chernobyl' something had to be done to restore public confidence and rally support, and it would be useful and popular to direct the energies released against bureaucratic irresponsibility. This pointed to a prominent role for public relations and the media in the new phase of policy,[8] and this in turn suggested allies – in the form of professional communicators and intellectuals in the creative arts. These groups were influential (in some ways more so than intellectuals in the west); they had been shabbily treated by Brezhnev and were eager to contribute; and in general they were Party members. The choice was not one that would threaten the *apparat*, which in any case would be involved in supervising the calibrated relaxation of controls. The decision to begin with public relations thus became an offer of alliance to professional groups, and fortunately some of the latter's agenda were precisely of that low cost, non-systemic kind that the administration could readily concede. Dissidents could be released, banned authors published, churches brought back into public life, Jewish emigration encouraged, investigations into Stalinism started, and this would not be a challenge to central features of the regime.

This, then, was Gorbachev's initial strategy: begin by allying with professionals and especially professional communicators; with their help and skills muster renewed support and participation; and only on that basis move on to the harder questions of political structures and rights. Specifically the initial moves were the **glasnost'** policy in the media and the toleration of **informal groups** (**neformaly**). The first of these widened the range of subjects and opinions treated in public; the second gave informed and active people chance to share knowledge and experience and to organise the presentation of their case. The result was a dramatic improvement in the availability of information and in public awareness, interest and morale. It began in the big cities of European Russia and among educated people, spread rapidly to the Baltic Union-Republics and then, more gradually, into the provinces, the south and the east.

The moves were very similar to the earliest moves of the Prague Spring, and they went further than any previous Soviet attempt to solicit collaboration from society (rather than act upon it). Yet in one respect they were cautious and easily reversible. Both censorship and the registration of associations had an obscure legal basis dating back to the early 1930s, but the laws' application had gravitated into the hands of the Party. The changes of 1986 seem to have been Party directives to relax the way the rules were applied, going as far, in the case of *neformaly*, as instructions to waive the law itself; (the nickname 'informal' arose because these were tolerated, but not formally registered associations). But to hint that people had new opportunities because the laws were being waived – and not to spell out the exact boundaries of the new freedoms, and to leave the old officials and secret procedures in place: that was hardly conducive to confident public participation.

Indeed it soon became apparent that *glasnost'* and the emancipation of the *neformaly* by themselves were half measures or pilot projects; they aroused people's appetite for substantial change without giving them that substance. And this was to be expected of any reform based on public relations rather than on rights: the predictable consequences were either the dissimulation and orchestrated enthusiasm of an old-fashioned campaign, or undisciplined and irresponsible self-expression. Examples were the Alma-Ata riots or the rapid spread of the Russian chauvinist *Pamyat'* movement. What was needed was institutions in which people might take part on clear and public terms.[9] That such implications were perceived by society is suggested by the spread of the question 'can *perestroika* be made irreversible?' by the end of 1986.

At the same time the Party Central Committee was beginning to oppose Gorbachev, and evidence was accumulating of bureaucratic obstructionism and of the brittle rigidity of existing institutions, of their inadequacy as vehicles for enhanced participation. The answer, it seemed, was **new** institutions that should give social interests legal and public form, and means to affect policy – and should supplement, even by-pass, existing bodies.

## *PERESTROIKA* AND ITS IMPLICATIONS (1987–89)

This meant true *perestroika* (reconstruction) of institutions, and it began to be planned during 1987 after the slogan had lain dormant for a year. Reform measures of this second phase were floated and debated in public in the spring of 1988, accepted in principle by the XIX Party Conference in July, passed into law late that year, and began to be implemented in 1989. Their essential points were, first, representative and responsible government:[10] a parliament chosen by free, competitive elections should approve or reject legislation and appoint and dismiss the executive. Second was limitations on government: officials (state and Party) might serve no more than two five-year terms, and, for the first time in Soviet experience, elements of the separation of powers were to be introduced. Third a start was to be made to the rule of law, implying *inter alia* a new and serious role for the constitution, constitutional review, legal clarification of the Party's position in politics, and the Party's subjection to law. Once this got under way Gorbachev no longer imposed covert measures of reform using the Party network, but had them debated and amended as legislation in the parliaments. The final point: the Party had accepted that *perestroika* entailed changes to itself.

It was the decisive step in the development of reform. To be sure, it was not yet a decision for competitive politics on equal terms. The Party would still be the only Union-wide political organisation, and would retain its administrative privileges and priority of access to policy-making. Nevertheless the programme went further than the Prague Spring or any other attempt at the reform of communist government. It was a watershed decision in two other respects also. It set processes in motion that would lead (and must have been expected to lead) to self-generating competitive politics – and so to a massive challenge to the Party. And it served notice on communists to equip themselves for the new politics or turn against them.

Can this second stage in reform thinking be dated? In the minds of Gorbachev and his personal advisers it must have begun by January 1987 when the proposal for a special Party Conference was made. Gorbachev first used the word 'pluralism' on 10 July 1987; he was careful to qualify it as pluralism of opinions, not of institutions, but the usage suggests that institutional pluralism had at least been considered. In a speech in Leningrad on 13 October 1987 the following was relayed on television but, significantly, omitted from the published text in *Pravda*:[11]

When I put the matter this way, I do not at all want it to be understood as an appeal – as was once the case during the years of the Cultural Revolution in China – to bombard headquarters. No, no, comrades, that would be a mistake.

The prospect of challenges to the Party in some form must surely have already been in his mind. Not for nothing did his talk of a new revolution become routine about this time.

The impact of the XIX Conference, and still more of the elections and new parliaments the following year, was (in Hosking's words) nothing short of a **rediscovery of politics**. Even the use of the word 'politics' changed. In November 1988 V. M. Chebrikov, who two months earlier had been head of the KGB, was urging an Estonian audience against undue haste; they must have been bemused to hear him, of all people, say that 'high politics, as we know, is the art of the possible'.[12] Not only had a Soviet politician taken to quoting Bismarck, but he was acknowledging that bargaining and compromise are essential to politics. Politburo members had never talked like this before; gone was the engineer with his blueprint or the priest with special access to the verities.

From this time phrases like 'high politics' and 'political methods' became clichés in the Gorbachev leadership. What were they trying to convey with the new usage?

First, politics are argument, debate, controversy – and not the giving of orders. And they are argument in public, not fixing things in private. Problems should be identified, and solutions worked out in consultation with those affected, and, without this, solutions – even if theoretically 'correct' – should not be imposed. The army should march as fast as its slowest member, no longer at the pace dictated by generals and general staff. There were no longer to be social interests that were by definition illegitimate and to be suppressed; even repugnant points of view, like secessionist nationalism, should be allowed expression, and other methods than coercion used against them.

Politicians must be seen confronting their opponents in public. They must learn to suffer fools gladly, to put up with public abuse, to lose arguments and votes, and to live with short-sighted decisions that commanded electoral appeal. (One consequence was the need to distinguish between routine issues and issues of confidence, something utterly obscured by democratic centralism.) The vocation of politics is a demanding one and its practitioners should 'shape up or ship out'. Gorbachev was robust about politicians under pressure: 'So what, that's what they're leaders for. If they're worth anything, they'll cope with it all, and still work out policies that meet general needs . . . '.[13]

Political methods were reason and argument, not force, intimidation, trickery or manipulation. One provincial first secretary claimed in 1989 to have set up crash courses for his subordinates in the new political methods, which included maxims like the following: 'Be there where the disputes are!' 'Provoke those disputes – but never let go of the initiative!' 'Straight answers to awkward questions!' Another, less *au courant*, complained that no-one had actually told him what the new 'political methods' were, and, as he understood them, they didn't always work![14] Political methods implied bargaining among groups with independent access to resources, and in competition, in the last analysis, not just over policy, but for power. They included all the familiar techniques of bargaining: bluff and calling others' bluff, finesse, brinkmanship and 'ambit claims'. Outsiders must assume a pluralism of rhetoric in place of the old *agitprop* monopoly; they must remember to ask, '*cui bono?*', as much of the spokesmen for obscure groups as of the Politburo, now that there was real competition for popular attention.

Much of the intellectual background to the new politics is contained in two remarkable articles in *Pravda* 2 and 3 May 1989, written by a Central Committee official, V. M. Legostaev. His title, 'The Intellectual Quality of the Party', was hardly eye-catching, but his message was shocking and pessimistic. The underlying theme is a contrast between **politics** and what he calls **technology**. Politics are concerned with needs, values, interests, priorities; technology with working out technical solutions to problems set by others. There are right answers in technology – but not in politics because every decision is a compromise among competing interests, and a choice of the least among evils. The CPSU leadership has been infatuated with the technological side of the industrial revolution, and has treated social and political development as if it were a set of engineering problems with right answers. Hence the Party is stacked with engineers – who are doubtless competent at solving problems handed to them, but are helpless and dependent when it comes to identifying and posing problems. The Party has stopped selecting people who are good at politics, who (it is suggested) are to be sought among those with arts education.[15] No wonder its best talents are leaving to play a leading role in the *neformaly*; the Party has bred its own opposition.

This reveals another novelty of the new politics: repudiation of the traditional claim to be able to plan and control social development and a recognition therefore of spontaneity and evolutionary change. 'He stopped being a ruler and became a politician',[16] and the concept of a politician is a modest one: merely one among many kinds of social actor, incapable by himself of changing very much, someone who must learn to live with uncertainty, 'muddling through', popular ingratitude and sudden reversals of fortune. And the implications are far more than pragmatic: abandonment of the illusion of social control means abandonment of revolution from above. And what of the 'final goal' of socialism/communism? In *The Socialist Idea and Revolutionary Perestroika* Gorbachev made it clear that he no longer thought in terms of revolution from above or of planned socialist goals; socialism was for him a process: 'the way is the way, and there's an end'. It was part of his claim that the Soviet Union was returning to world civilisation.[17]

## THE PROBLEM OF THE PARTY

Inauguration of competitive politics was indeed a fine achievement. But its public reception was clouded by two gathering problems for which *The Socialist Idea* . . . offered no convincing answer. The first was the role of the CPSU in the new politics.

The Party's traditional role was threatened by *perestroika*. What became generally obvious after the 1989 elections will have been dawning on alert or well-informed Party members since 1988 at the latest: contested voting in elections and parliament was incompatible with *nomenklatura* practices; free parliamentary voting on issues was incompatible with Party steering and discipline, and therefore with democratic centralism; constitutional review must mean (at the very least) publicity for hitherto secret Party operations. Many thought that the Party's *raison d'être* was under challenge – from the Party leader!

Gorbachev had to meet such charges, whether simply to fend off the backlash against himself, or because he hoped to find a different and stable role for the Party in the new politics. He did this in two ways. First he redoubled his urging of internal reform on the CPSU, reform for which he could now claim a mandate. It should in particular renounce direct administration and undertake to represent or argue with people from the whole spectrum of social interests. Implicit in this was the beginning of a demarcation of state from Party, and of a redefinition of the latter's political monopoly.

Linked with this the 1988–9 *perestroika* package contained clear concessions to the CPSU. It remained the only legal, Union-wide political organisation and thus entered political competition with a massive advantage in resources. Gorbachev's treatment of pluralism (and later of the Article six controversy) signalled his readiness to retain 'the shadow of ancient customs':[18] to let the Party evolve and avoid as far as possible formal constitutional revision of its role. Party officials were given an incentive to cooperate in the scheme whereby a Party first secretary should combine this office with chairmanship of the local soviet, which was now designed to assume greater importance; he would need to retain the confidence both of his Party committee and of the soviet – but he was being given an inside track to a new political role.

Nevertheless Gorbachev must have had his doubts about the Party's capacity for self-renewal under pressure, and from 1988 if not earlier we can discern his pursuit of three other objectives. First was the preparation of an alternative political base for himself, independent of the Party: this was the new position of Head of State which included chairmanship of the Supreme Soviet. At the same time his behaviour towards potential leaders of opposition was designed to offer them no excuse to move against him. And he made sure of his own hold on the Party leadership – because, even if he had other resources, a hostile General Secretary in charge of a hostile *apparat* would have been fatal to him.

This was reflected in his tactics towards the CPSU after June 1988. There were no more attempts (like that of March 1986) to stack the Politburo or Secretariat with close adherents, and committed supporters of reform remained only Yakovlev and Shevardnadze. Instead he sought to present himself as occupying the middle ground and as presiding over warring factions; it became useful to have Yeltsin applying pressure from the left to offset Ligachev's conservatism, and he encouraged publication of Central Committee attacks on himself. With the shift in mid-1989 of some powers from the office of General Secretary to that of Head of State, the Supreme Soviet gained a certain capacity to counterbalance the top Party bodies – and to provide a base for Gorbachev, should he lose the position of General Secretary. A repetition of October 1964 might still have been possible, but by mid-1989 it would have been no straightforward matter.

It may seem surprising that Gorbachev's opponents did not make use of this 'window of opportunity' between July 1988 and May 1989.

For all we know the emergency Central Committee Plenum in September 1988 may have been such an attempt. But from their perspectives the opportunity may not have been clear-cut: not just in the trivial sense that there was no apparent candidate who could match Gorbachev's coherence and stature, but, more seriously, because (however much it was begrudged) none of them could challenge the thrust of the reformers' analysis. Published attacks on reform (examples are the speeches of Yu. V. Bondarev at the 1988 Conference, or of V. I. Brovikov at the February 1990 Plenum)[19] tended to be brilliant in style, but primitive, no more than anecdotal, in analysis and policy. Ligachev and his ilk were no such romantic dogmatists: they knew that the Party faced a crisis, with or without Gorbachev, and they suspected he could be the one to salvage something from the wreckage. So they had to stick with him.

Little of such manoeuvres was appreciated outside the Party. As new groups of activists gained in confidence they seized on the weak point of Gorbachev's compromise: competition that was not based on **equal** rights and access to resources did not hold out real chances of a change of political power, and the reforms were therefore little more than paternalistic cooptation. Real politics could after all begin only when the CPSU lost its constitutional monopoly, and competed on equal terms with others. The monopoly was enshrined in Article six of the Constitution and thus began the agitation against that article.

Gorbachev was in a paradoxical position: he was leader of the Party, yet he had started the processes and ideas that were challenging its traditional role – and yet again he could not afford to be seen taking the initiative against it! In the second half of 1989 he fought a rearguard action against change to Article six, arguing that the Head of State should take no initiative on a constitutional issue unless social pressures were overwhelming, and stressing the need for some 'consolidatory' institution which would hold an otherwise centrifugal society together. It was a half-hearted and brittle argument, especially when compared with those of *The Socialist Idea*.

Yet we can surmise that two other processes were going on behind the scenes. Gorbachev must have been preparing another fall-back position for himself. The signs are that he had become disillusioned with the Party's capacities to reform itself and was transferring his interests to the new parliaments. In December 1989 he reminded the Party that 'history never gives anyone a mandate for permanent political leadership'.[20] Further, since he still needed to keep the Party from turning against him, he seems to have been working on an implicit understanding whereby the Party could agree to the amendment of Article six and a dignified withdrawal from the monopoly.

## CRASH THROUGH OR CRASH?

Competitive election campaigns, the grilling of ministerial nominees in parliament, the abolition in 1988 of the Party's economic departments which had intervened in factory management: none of these could have occurred without the withdrawal of direction from above and the unleashing of an indiscipline and confusion shocking by Brezhnevian standards. It is clear that the leadership consciously let this happen. Competition among interests **meant** conflict, and conflict (within rules) was functional to politics; it was part of the 'school of democracy' that people should learn how to conduct disputes. Implicit in this was a belief that society was mature enough to evolve through confusion to a new coherence, rather than break down as it had in 1917–18. The arrangements made in connection with the Presidency after March 1990 seem to confirm Gorbachev's picture of a society that had shaken off the obstacles to normal, civilised politics. At the top the General Secretary and Politburo were replaced by a President and Presidential Council, but in the provinces no attempt was made (despite urgings) to set up any other institution or line of communication in place of the CPSU; the soviets, it seems, were expected to emerge from Party tutelage and assume the role that they had never really exercised after the Revolution.

If this was the thinking it was highly unrealistic: social disorder, the collapse of trade, administrative non-compliance went from bad to worse, and with it Gorbachev's popularity, high until mid-1989, ebbed away. He was accused of half-measures, wasted opportunities, lost control, and general lack of policy or concept; increasingly calls for an 'iron hand' began to be heard. Let us examine this critique, together with something of Gorbachev's case, for the light they throw on his objectives at this time.

First the charge of half-measures and lost opportunities. The *perestroika* of 1988–9, it was alleged, had been flawed because the leadership had been too ready to compromise with the Party and bureaucracy; it could have succeeded if more radical measures had been taken. There is evidence in favour of this: the drafters of the Law *On the Enterprise* seem to have been blithely unaware of the antisocial 'robber-baron' monopolies they were unleashing; the Estonians demanded a revision of Soviet federalism in November 1988, long before Gorbachev was prepared to contemplate it.

Yet Gorbachev's answer makes sense. More radical schemes presupposed that the Party monopoly had already been broken. The main reason, for instance, why federalism was a sham lay not in the Constitution (defective though that was) but in the capacity of the unitary Party to work behind the scenes to stamp out autonomous politics. Far from having been wasted, most of the opportunities had only just arisen. And the CPSU was a dangerous enemy which should not be driven into a corner; by negotiating its peaceful retreat he had let people make the most of these opportunities.[21]

Concerning his political analysis up to 1990, it is a cogent answer. His analysis after the inauguration of the Presidency is much less easy to defend. There is so much that seems to have been wrongly assessed: the capacity of society at large for initiative and self-management, or the speed and smoothness with which people could learn; the conflict between personal, familial and local interests on the one hand, and society-wide interests on the other; attitudes to the Centre among non-Russians and Russians alike; the sheer scale of CPSU involvement in administration. The misjudgements are all ones we can readily associate with the approach of a Russian Marxist and of a middle-class professional. Further, by not setting up a Presidential *apparat* he had left himself vulnerable and disarmed, whilst policy implementation remained largely in the hands of a demoralised, mutinous bureaucracy of Party members. It suggests an optimism bordering on the irresponsible.

One can piece together elements of a reply to this: the device of a Presidential *apparat* is an old instrument from the arsenal of revolution from above. Nothing more is to be achieved by imposed solutions, by 'hounding people into the Good Life'.[22] During the Presidency debates in March 1990 A. N. Yakovlev spoke of making 'a break with the thousand-year-old Russian paradigm of unfreedom, . . . a turn to free development'.[23] People in Gorbachev's circle had evidently been thinking about the cyclical and ultimately self-defeating nature of revolution from above, and had conceived the ambition to break out of the vicious circle.

Whether this was indeed the rationale – rather than a romantic rationalisation – of the administration's objectives after March 1990 remains to be examined in the rest of this book. It was certainly taken seriously by some intellectuals who pleaded with Gorbachev not to embark on something without historical precedent: no society had ever accomplished, at one and the same time, decolonisation, the transition to democracy, and that to a market economy.[24] To pursue all three together was not merely doomed, but the inevitable disaster would undo even the good the reforms of the past five years had brought.

# 6  *Glasnost'* and Interest Groups

| | |
|---|---|
| ROPER: | So now you'd give the Devil benefit of law! |
| MORE: | Yes. What would you do? Cut a great road through the law to get after the Devil? |
| ROPER: | I'd cut down every law in England to do that! |
| MORE: | Oh? And when the last law was down, and the Devil turned round on you – where would you hide, Roper, the laws all being flat? This country's planted thick with laws from coast to coast – Man's laws, not God's – and if you cut them down – and you're just the man to do it – d'you really think you could stand upright in the winds that would blow then? Yes, I'd give the Devil benefit of law, for my own safety's sake. |

(Robert Bolt, *A Man for All Seasons*)[1]

## *GLASNOST'*: MECHANISMS AND OBSTACLES

The earliest reform policies were those that began to affect the media and informal groups in 1986. Concerning these and some others the chapter will ask: What exactly happened? What were the mechanisms, scope and limitations of the policy? Its effects? And what can it tell us about the overall programme of reform?

*Glasnost'* can easily be misunderstood. It was no instant unshackling of press freedom, and the reasons lie in the structure of the Soviet media. This was in principle a centralised state monopoly, and in the case of television and radio, media that lend themselves to centralised organisation, that remained broadly the case until the 1990s.[2] Most printing presses were owned by the CPSU, and this provided the Party's main source of income apart from members' dues. In the case of the print media it is hard to organise local news gathering, publishing and distribution except on a local basis, and here some modification of centralisation was admitted. Newspapers and journals, from the *raion* up to the All-Union echelon, were published by local branches of state or official organisations. Thus the newspapers of Union-Republics, provinces or cities were usually put out jointly by the Party and state organs of their region; institutions devoted to specialised tasks – the Party, Komsomol, Army, many of the ministries – published newspapers for their members, employees and clientele; newspapers for, say, teachers, doctors or railway workers were joint organs of the relevant ministry and trade union. The publishers were in fact the 'proprietors', but, because of central coordination of official institutions, this did not seem important until the late 1980s.

This delegated the practical operations of journalism, editing and publishing, whilst keeping media policy under central control. Within its own region or task sector each media outlet had a position of near monopoly. It was not the case, for instance, that one could choose between two West Siberian papers, one supporting and the other opposing the extension of oil drilling to the shores of the Arctic. One did not find the trade union publication there disagreeing with the Ministry for Oil Extraction, nor would two union papers present the job of unions in different ways. Only perhaps in the field of literature – where journals based in different regions might support different cultural fashions or schools – did there develop any serious competition among media outlets offering contradictory viewpoints.

To this pattern of institutional control was added censorship. This was not the censorship with which we are more familiar, namely the imposition on the media of a list of 'off-limits' topics. The Soviet principle – reminiscent of the same feature in Soviet law – was that editors might publish only that which was explicitly permitted, and according to guidelines handed down by the censors.[3] This is often referred to as 'preparatory censorship'. Journalists in 1990 spoke of information having to go through the censors' office 'before it could reach the newspaper zone'.[4] The outcome was media notorious for their tedious uniformity and clichés, and hence their discouragement of debate.

Most editors and journalists had to be Party members, and Party committees confirmed the appointment of editors under *nomenklatura* procedures. The CPSU Rules provided for discussion in public of issues not so far resolved – but not of settled policy or of political personalities.[5] It would thus have breached Party discipline and put their jobs at risk, if a journalist had submitted, or an editor published, a story, say, of a proposal being defeated in the Politburo or Council of Ministers, or drawing inferences about the balance of power on those bodies. Further, although laws on defamation and contempt were weak, 'anti-Soviet agitation and propaganda' was classified as a crime against the State until 1989. Here were powerful deterrents to independence among media personnel, and good reasons for many of them developing a bureaucratic attitude to their job and employers. The chief editor of *Moscow News*, E. V. Yakovlev, illustrates it well:[6]

> *Moscow News* was the only Soviet newspaper that immediately published the news about the landing of Mathias Rust on Red Square . . . No-one prohibited the publishing of the news in my newspaper. Later I discovered that one distinguished deputy editor-in-chief of a major publication in Moscow used most of the day to find out by telephone whether it would be possible to publish the news story. He found ten agencies and all gave a positive response. Then, the eleventh time, someone said 'no'. And he was very glad that he had such a response.

But professional communicators had to be drawn from among educated people. How to maintain their morale, when the intellectual independence of the nineteenth century had not been forgotten? It seems to have helped that the Bolsheviks were of intelligentsia origin themselves: they seem not to have doubted, for instance, that their public relations should be in the style of systematic philosophy, and **that** meant opportunities for intellectuals, some of whom were seduced into the role of hierarchs for the regime. The authorities kept the media relatively serious and high-brow, avoided a tabloid press, and allowed 'encrypted' political information to be published which only educated insiders could decipher. These became skilful at decoding *podteksty*, 'subtexts' or 'things read between the lines', some of which were evasions of censorship – and others regime signals for people in the know. The prospect of belonging to an elite of *cognoscenti* was attractive, and it became all too easy to confuse decipherment with participation.

This temptation, and the problems it posed, can be illustrated by a curious exchange that took place in the pages of *Pravda* in March 1990. The newspaper was running a debate between supporters of the official CPSU Platform for the XXVIII Party Congress, and supporters of a 'Democratic Platform', drawn up by the first faction to be tolerated since 1921; both debate and publication of the minority platform were milestones in *glasnost'*.[7] A major way in which the two platforms differed, said A, of the Democratic Platform, was that the text of the latter had been scrutinised and amended over weeks by its supporters; the official platform, by contrast, had been prepared in the *apparat* and was first seen by Central Committee members two days before they had to endorse it. Not so, said the more orthodox B: this was to ignore years of theoretical work; and he went on to list important Gorbachev speeches and newspaper editorials since January 1987, as evidence of widespread contribution to the new platform. In vain did a third discussant point out that the Party had frustrated many of the ideas in Gorbachev's speeches. For B, to read or hear ideas was, by some mysterious process, the same as to participate in their debate and clarification. He trusts that what functionaries draft and a Plenum endorses is a synthesis to which all have contributed, and turns a blind eye to evidence of smothered controversy or stage-managed consensus. His stance reminds us that educated people had not merely been made servants of the media monopoly, but many stood to lose authority from a free press.

We have seen that the word *glasnost'* gained an increased currency in early 1986 and that the Chernobyl' disaster elevated it a key status for the new administration – the label for its new media policy. *Glasnost'* means 'openness' or 'frankness', with overtones of 'publicity', perhaps 'public relations', but without the psychological overtones of 'sincerity'. What did the policy change amount to in practice? This has to be reconstructed from its apparent consequences that published treatment became more varied, and a wider range of topics began to be aired. It was reported in the West in mid-1986 that the censorship administration had been wound up; this was not in fact true, but journalists may have picked up echoes of the replacement of Brezhnev's chief censor by someone a generation younger,[8] and of confidential directives which altered censorship practices profoundly. There continued to be officials whose job it was to scrutinise copy prior to publication, but it seems that preparatory censorship began to be replaced by freedom to publish on matters not specifically banned; and the list of these topics was clarified and over the next two years reduced.[9] At the same time liberal editors took over some of the most prestigious journals.[10]

But *glasnost'* did **not** touch patterns of media ownership, nor people's rights to publish independently, nor their access to publishing resources. Neither did the Party Rules or the criminal code change – to say nothing of personal psychology: the pioneers of *glasnost'* never numbered more than a few score – mainly dedicated, experienced journalists or professionally concerned academics from the research institutes, both often with foreign experience.

THE SCOPE AND LIMITS OF *GLASNOST'*

Against this background let us survey the achievements and failures of *glasnost'* up to 1990.

It began in **literature and the fine arts** where there was a backlog of works that had been banned but were otherwise ready for publication From such modest beginnings as poems of the monarchist Gumilev in April 1986, a short story by Nabokov in August and Abuladze's film *Repentance* in January 1987, progression was made to Akhmatova's 'Requiem' in March 1987, Pasternak's *Dr Zhivago* and Grossman's *Life and Fate* (January 1988), Orwell's *Animal Farm* (September 1988) and large parts of Solzhenitsyn's *Gulag Archipelago* in August 1989. At the same time the 'special deposits' in libraries were sorted through and works banned on political grounds shifted to open access. Émigrés of the Brezhnev period, some of whose names had been unmentionable, began to write in Soviet papers and some were invited to resume their old jobs.

The purpose of winning new allies was clear in this, and if such people were to be re-engaged in public affairs they needed information about their own society. Discussion was opened up during 1987 and 1988 of a wide range of **social problems** previously taboo: crime, prisons and corruption; drugs, prostitution and sexually transmitted disease; infant mortality, public health and the abuse of psychiatry; strikes and unemployment; official pay and privileges; pressure on judges and the extortion of confession. Many of these were issues whose existence had simply been denied, something which contributed to the atmosphere of make-believe that benumbed political life. Again the bid to win allies was clear: exposés of the parlous state of hospitals and hospices, for instance, often made it clear that some of their functions would be performed better if they were handed over to the Churches.

**Economic issues**, by comparison, received meagre treatment before 1990. Whatever might happen in detail to the economy, there was general awareness that it must involve retrenchment or retraining for millions of people and that urban food prices must rise steeply. Given the state of public anxiety, the media gave surprisingly little attention to its causes or to options for change.[11] Would there to be unemployment pay, and at what rates and terms? Income supplementation for the poor, the unemployed or pensioners? Devaluation or confiscation of savings? What was fuelling inflation – what **was** inflation! – and why was it so hard to control? Such questions were hardly explored outside the specialist literature. Here the media were taking the soft option – the Soviet Union had few trained economists – but one cannot help suspecting that they were also letting the administration set their agenda.

It is in its relationship to Soviet history that we begin to see the dilemma of *glasnost'*: was it a government campaign or the unleashing of forces that could end up putting the government at risk? The Soviet regime had systematically controlled the historical record and used this control to mount one of its main claims to legitimacy; was it prepared to forego this? In February 1987 Gorbachev announced the objective of filling in the 'blank spots' in history, and in October had a Politburo commission set up 'for further study of the repressions of the thirties, forties and early fifties'.[12] The effect of the former was that by late 1989 public exposés could be read of such notorious 'blank spots' as the Katyń massacre, the Molotov-Ribbentrop Pact, the forced amalgamation in 1946 of Ukrainian Catholics with Russian Orthodoxy, or the nuclear accident in the Urals of September 1957; Khrushchev's Secret Speech was published in Russian in March 1989.[13] The Politburo commission saw to the public rehabilitation of most of the senior politicians executed under Stalin, beginning with Bukharin in February 1988, as well as of some 845,000 other 'repressed' persons (out of a total, according to the KGB, of 3.8 million).[14]

These developments suited Gorbachev's purposes. He was becoming increasingly aware of the affinities between his policies and those of some of Stalin's opponents, especially Bukharin. More important, he was clearly persuaded by the intellectuals who urged that the Soviet experience simply could not make sense, and that accordingly neither *glasnost'* nor invitations to wider participation could be taken seriously, without a coming to terms with Stalinism. Excellent reasons – but this was still to use historiography for government purposes. Episodic revelations about 'blank spots' would not serve to make sense of the Soviet period as a whole. And notice the *terminus post quem* for the commission's activities: victims of the collectivisation period might now seek some sort of public apology (because the commencement of Stalin's crimes had been pushed back from 1934 to 1930), but not those of the 1920s – among whom Academician Likhachev was a distinguished public figure.[15] The Revolution, it seemed, must still be followed by a sacrosanct period, off-limits to free historical inquiry.

This had two consequences. As long as such zones of mystification remained it was impossible in principle for the public to piece together a coherent account of the Soviet period, and this left it at the mercy of 'underground' histories and social philosophies of which the Andreeva letter is an example. Meanwhile radical journalists and historians were encouraged to probe the historiographical frontiers, pushing them back to 1924 and then into the Lenin period itself. How could Gorbachev, the advocate of independent judgement, gainsay them? The years 1930 and 1924 represented turning points in some, but only some, fields of policy: Stalin, appointed in 1922, had merely developed Leninist policies on (for example) law, nationalities and religion; and Gorbachev himself was feeling his way towards reappraisal of some key Leninist policies such as democratic centralism and the ban on faction.

By late 1989 he had to tackle the problem of Leninism explicitly, insisting that the Revolution had not been a mistake, yet posing the question whether 'breaches of socialist legality [and] infringements of democratic rights . . . became possible in the environment of the new social order'.[16] From here he proceeded in two directions. He attempted, first, a major reinterpretation of Lenin, highlighting opinions on, for instance, Party organisation, federalism or the market at variance with canonical Leninism, shifting the focus away from the Party and towards the soviets, even doubting the wisdom of some of Lenin's actions.[17] At the same time he began, I believe, to de-emphasise both Lenin and the justification of government in historical terms and to look for legitimation rather in terms of achievement and civilised values; let there be no more searching of Lenin for authority, thus closing him to historical research. When A. N. Yakovlev spoke of Russia's 'thousand-year-old paradigm of unfreedom' the implicit inclusion of Lenin in this thousand years is hardly likely to have been accidental.[18] In August 1990 a Presidential decree rehabilitated all victims of collectivisation and of political, social, ethnic and religious persecution 'in the 1920s to the 1950s',[19] and sought thereby to close this evil chapter in Soviet policy and to withdraw government from historiography.

Media treatment of **current affairs and politics** likewise shows the stark choices implicit in *glasnost'*. Chernobyl' was the starting point: from a censor's point of view accidents and current affairs present similar problems! Accidents (both natural and man-made), strikes, trials and civil unrest now began to be reported on a routine basis and in 1988–9 this coverage spread to other kinds of current events. In early 1988 restrictions were seemingly withdrawn from coverage of policy and political institutions (with the significant exception of top Party institutions), and published discussion began of such issues as nationalities policy, the role of law, the composition and behaviour of the Supreme Soviet, or the structure and functions of Party committees and the *apparat*.[20] It extended during 1989 to the structure and composition of the armed forces and to the 'federal' structure of the USSR, and even touched such sacrosanct matters as Article six or the powers and accountability of the KGB.[21] *Verbatim* proceedings of the Congress of People's Deputies – though not of the Supreme Soviet, nor of most Central Committee Plenums – were published.

Yet such reporting still differed significantly from its equivalent in western democracies. There was reasonably wide and unbiased coverage of events and they were discussed in public, but the investigative and interpretative tasks of journalism remained underdeveloped. Much political reporting took its cue from the administration.[22] Often it lacked context and retained an anecdotal quality. After the spring 1990 elections to Union-Republican Supreme Soviets, Lithuania (already well on the road to secession) was the only republic in which full election results – votes for both victorious and defeated candidates, by constituency – were published; their omission elsewhere suggests a continuing wish to restrict politics to insiders.[23] The careers, records, interests and personalities of top politicians, or their interrelationships at the top did not begin to be explored until 1990; there was still no equivalent of the lobby correspondent speculating on the background to policy decisions, on the probable course of a Cabinet debate or the balance of power there.

The affair of the Andreeva letter in March 1988 provides an illustration of these weaknesses. Nina Andreeva was a chemistry teacher at an Institute of Technology in Leningrad. Her blend of sentimental conservatism with neo-Stalinism is fairly widespread, and her presentation of it was confused and emotional. Why should a national newspaper see fit to give her a whole page, one-sixth of an issue? It was generally agreed that the contents did not warrant such prominence, and, since the letter contained snippets of what looked like inside information, it was assumed that the letter was a 'signal', placed by someone very senior and hinting at a retreat in media policy. The finger was pointed at Ligachev. The interpretation was strengthened by a drying up of media debate over the next three weeks and by *Pravda*'s apparent need to rebut Andreeva in a sophisticated and magisterial policy statement on 5 April (rumoured to have been written by A. N. Yakovlev).[24]

Andreeva's letter did read like a plant, though in whose interests is obscure; and both letter and sequel left a taste of the old-fashioned surrogate politics in which unseen hands manipulated media puppets for inscrutable ends. The press seemed to play a passive role, simply printing what was placed with them; there was little attempt to analyse the background or interests of people like Andreeva or to investigate who really wrote the letter, how *Sovetskaya Rossiya* got its copy, who sanctioned publication or who stood to benefit from it.[25] And the explanation would seem to lie not in censorship, but in Party discipline and the sanctions Party politicians could use against editors under prevailing patterns of media ownership. It was a frightening episode, showing the fragility of *glasnost'* so long as it was not anchored in a bedrock of rights.

## THE ADVENT OF PRESS FREEDOM

*Glasnost'* was thus a programme, initiated from above, and one that retained a strong element of management throughout. It was aimed both in content and technique at the more aware and informed middle class public, those who read and wrote newspapers. Its programmatic nature accounts for many of the inadequacies of the Soviet media up to 1990. Their fare was often piecemeal, incoherent and superficial: it would have been difficult for a citizen to develop informed judgements (let alone a critique of the system) from internal sources alone. Few journalists or editors made the breakthrough to investigative, political journalism at the national level, and the best journalism still took some courage, because few of the new freedoms had been formalised or made justiciable. Above all, changed media content was not matched by changes in the pattern of media ownership or control; on important issues the media could still be manipulated by their bureaucratic owners, whilst many interest groups and some institutions lacked media access.

There were two achievements of *glasnost'*. First it made an abundance of new information and ideas accessible, and promoted a corps of editors and journalists more enterprising, courageous and experienced than in 1985, and better equipped to defend freedom of expression. These galvanised the *neformaly* into action and won a public following of people who appreciated being told unvarnished facts, trusted the media more than ever before, and would be less easily fobbed off in future with public relations. The elections of 1989–90, the new parliaments, the end of the CPSU monopoly, the popular defeat of the August coup would all have been unthinkable without *glasnost'*. The second was to start a social process, which was soon straining at the bounds of *glasnost'* as a programme: by 1988 (at the latest) Gorbachev had the choice either of halting it – as so many previous experiments with liberalisation from above had been halted – or strengthening it with institutional and legal guarantees, which would be to loose it from control.

The legal changes that were to bring real press freedom began in July 1989 when the Supreme Soviet struck 'anti-Soviet agitation and propaganda' out of the Criminal Code and replaced it with 'incitement to violent overthrow or change of the Soviet state and social order'.[26] In early December the draft of a law *On the Press and Other Media of Mass Information* was published. Its authors – two Standing Committees of the Supreme Soviet – clearly intended to challenge Party powers over the media. But the Party monopoly collapsed before the bill could be debated, and this meant that the CPSU from March 1990 had rights only over the media organs that it 'owned'; and media independence here too was improved when the July 1990 version of the CPSU Rules allowed its members to criticise politicians and institutions in public. These were of course changes to rights only: most media staff were still communists, and the Party still owned most publishing facilities (85 per cent in the RSFSR).[27] Even in those it did not own, editorial policy might not change unless someone was prepared to demand the new rights, and there were still plenty of Party officials eager to interfere in policy or appointments. Nevertheless the changes combined to have a marked effect on the reporting of high level politics. From mid-1990 speculative or hostile writing about named politicians can be taken for granted in such papers as *Izvestiya*, *Literaturnaya gazeta* or *Moscow News*; non-communist social theory began to be explored; and openly anti-communist or anti-Leninist material to be printed.[28] *Izvestiya* even managed to farewell E. K. Ligachev without especial vindictiveness.[29]

The law *On the Press* . . ., passed in June and effective from 1 August 1990, consolidated these gains and sought to tackle more deep-seated problems.[30] Censorship was declared abolished and the numbered censors' stamps duly disappeared from the back of printed material on 1 August. Instead media were liable to be prosecuted for publishing libel, pornography, incitement to violence etc – together with 'secrets specifically protected by law'.[31] Far more important were its provisions regarding media structure and ownership. The law sanctioned what amounted to private enterprise in information: any group of citizens might found a media organ and register it with the local authorities, and the courts were to adjudicate disputes over registration or media content. Employees of existing organs were given a certain freedom to choose their 'founder' (i.e. sponsor and proprietor) and the staff of many newspapers seized the opportunity to break with their founding institution (most commonly the CPSU) and either seek another founder, or set up as independent cooperatives;[32] the latter course was taken by such powerful papers as *Literaturnaya gazeta, Argumenty i fakty, Ogonek* and *Moscow News. Sovetskaya Rossiya* (publishers of the Andreeva letter) soon came into conflict with the RSFSR Supreme Soviet under Yeltsin and contrived to get itself transferred to the CPSU Central Committee, leaving the RSFSR Supreme Soviet without a mouthpiece, until the foundation in November of *Rossiiskaya gazeta.*[33] Several other independent newspapers were founded about this time – *Kommersant, Megapolis-ekspress, Stolitsa* and the excellent *Nezavisimaya gazeta*; in the capital they soon began to supplant the traditional names. By the spring of 1991 one found oneself asking a question inconceivable five years earlier: in what way are these different from the best papers of the democracies?

Two problems the law did not touch. Until the August coup the CPSU continued to own perhaps half the media and most of the printing equipment; the fighting around media buildings in Latvia and Lithuania in early 1991 suggests the tension this provoked.[34] Second it made virtually no difference to television and radio: it was technically very difficult to compete with these state-run operations and, with the appointment in November 1990 of L. P. Kravchenko to head Central Television, its journalism became a byword for conservatism. But in its effects on the print media the Law *On the Press* . . . was one of the most effective pieces of legislation of the *perestroika* period. A year later the free press made a vital contribution to breaking the August coup.


## THE NEW INTEREST GROUPS

The initial objective of *glasnost'* had been increased participation in public life especially among middle-class professional groups. But a communications policy by itself could only be part of such a programme: it had to be coupled with a reappraisal of the restrictive Soviet attitude to interest groups.

## Informal Groups

Since the early 1930s all spontaneously formed societies or associations were supposed to be registered with the local soviet, which could refuse registration and close a group down.[35] It is clear that it was *ad hoc* Party policy, rather than codified rules, that determined which groups might be registered, and that the CPSU sought to prevent the formation of groups it could not control. There were elaborate measures against evasion of this supervision: the Party Rules provided that wherever three or more Party members found themselves together in an organised gathering, they should coordinate a Party role in it;[36] the Komsomol was supposed to coordinate all youth activities in Party interests; behind both, the KGB tracked down serious evaders. During the Brezhnev period pressure against this tutelage grew, in part out of Khrushchev's thaw and the rise of dissidence, but also as a general consequence of improved education and material comfort. The regime's reaction was to modify some aspects of the registration policy – the societies concerned with the cultural heritage (see p. 34) are an example – and it is likely that a blind eye was often turned to unregistered but innocuous group activities. These were the first *neformaly*.[37] But arrests for illegal group activity – often hard to distinguish from illegal publishing – continued into the 1980s.

The experience of Boris Kagarlitsky illustrates what happened next, and may help clarify the underlying policy.[38] Kagarlitsky was imprisoned from April 1982 to some time in 1983 for his connection with neo-Marxist discussion groups and *samizdat* publications. After his release he paints a picture of rising intellectual pressure, meeting (at any rate in Moscow) with increasing sympathy on the part of officials; he says the 'first informal clubs began to form in 1985' and mentions several factors that helped the emergence of the 'club movement', of which only one[39] predates 1986. In 1986 he helped found a 'Club of Social Initiatives', apparently after winning approval of [Yeltsin's Moscow Party] authorities. By August 1987 the movement had become so widespread that this club could organise a conference of some fifty left-wing *neformaly*! To my mind the proliferation of *neformaly* in most major cities by the end of 1987 – especially after the recent repressions – suggests not just rising social pressure but also the dissemination of a central decision. Such a decision would most probably have been taken, like that on *glasnost'*, in the second quarter of 1986 – when the relevant new officials were in place and after the Chernobyl' shock.

As a result thousands of groups, involving millions of people, emerged; by the end of 1987, according to *Pravda*, there were some 30,000 of them, and by early 1989 more than 60,000. Most involved were young people and most *neformaly* were concerned with popular music, sport, hobby and leisure activities, but up to a quarter had moved into such quasi-political concerns as protection of the environment and cultural heritage.[40] From early 1988 many of the latter began to form regional federations with titles like 'Popular Front for the Support of Perestroika', and from 1989 such Popular Fronts existed in most big cities and in most of the Union-Republics. The earliest were in the Baltic republics, and it was there that the Popular Fronts scored their most spectacular successes.[41] As elsewhere their leaders were professionals, either locally respected non-communists, like the musicology professor V. V. Landsbergis, or disillusioned Party members, like the professor of journalism Marju Lauristin, daughter of Estonia's first communist Prime Minister. By late 1988 they had clearly seized the political initiative from the local CPSU branches, and they came to dominate their republics' politics during 1989. They won most of the local seats in the elections to the Congress of People's Deputies, and a year later, after the republican elections of early 1990, were able to form the first non-communist or coalition governments since 1918.

All this while their status was 'informal', i.e. illegal but tolerated. One official attempt to draft a legal basis for citizens' associations was leaked to Moscow activists in February 1988:[42] it proposed they should all be attached to some existing institution (trade-union or factory, for example), which would have been in a position to close them down without recourse to law! It illustrates the widening gulf between officialdom and the *neformaly*. Yet how was it possible to draw up consistent and credible rules about the access of public organisations to state officials, the press or resources, or of their members to office or employment, when the largest 'informal' of them all enjoyed privilege in these matters? Effective legislation was dependent on some resolution of the Party's legal status.

It was thus not until June 1990 that an acceptable draft law *On Public Associations* appeared, and not until October that it was passed by the Supreme Soviet.[43] This provided for groups to register their charters (and subsequent changes of rules) with local authorities, or the Ministry of Justice in the case of Union-wide formations. Registration might be refused where a group proposed such purposes or methods as the overthrow or violent change of the Constitution; violent breach of Soviet territorial integrity; propaganda of war or violence; organisation under arms; or incitement to class, racial or religious dissension. Disputes about these and other matters must be settled in court. The law stated that attempting to gain power was a basic function of a political party. The activities of public organisations might not be conducted in working hours or at another's expense (as a great many CPSU activities had been). State officials and those of public organisations might not give directives to or receive them from each other; membership or non-membership of a public organisation might not be grounds for discrimination, *inter alia* in state employment. It was excellent no-nonsense legislation – and the CPSU had to amend its Rules before it could be registered.[44]

## Producer Cooperatives

The administration must have been encouraged by the early results of its experiment with the *neformaly*. In May 1988 concessions began to be extended to interest groups in the economic sphere. The first was the removal of restrictions on economic cooperatives, small-scale business enterprises in sectors such as repairs, retailing and services that state enterprises had always handled incompetently. Under the Law *On Cooperation* people might now combine into profit-sharing cooperatives to produce or deliver services outside the state plan and at their own prices.[45] The members who combined must work in their cooperative, at least part-time, and their incomes were subject to a progressive income tax. Cooperatives might hire non-members as employees and raise capital by issuing bonds to other institutions or to their own employees. They must register with their local soviet, but the latter might not prevent their formation or operation provided they kept within the rules. If the experiment worked, cooperatives stood to improve consumer satisfaction and morale, to soak up personal savings rather than state investment funds, and to redeploy labour from heavy to light industry.

Cooperatives had a rapid impact on the economy. After two years operation under the new terms there were more than 150,000 of them, employing five million people (3.7 per cent of the workforce) and producing perhaps seven percent of national income.[46] In 1990 they were said to be attracting skilled staff from factories and ministries.[47] Yet from the outset cooperatives were beset with difficulties. The administration seems not to have foreseen the strength of Russian feeling against 'tall poppies' and the way that this would play into the hands of the bureaucracy. Complaints soon began to mount about cooperative prices (many cooperatives were in a position of virtual monopoly) and it was implied that the criminal underworld was making millions by exploiting decent citizens. Local authorities seized on this and began refusing registration, closing down or otherwise harassing cooperatives. Nor was it hard to find pretexts. Cooperatives had to get their materials and equipment ultimately from the state sector, in theory by contracting to buy uncommitted supplies from factories. In conditions of chronic shortage there were few such spare supplies, and the hazy borderline between legal enterprise and corruption was easily crossed – strengthening the image of criminal connections.

### Tenant Farming

It was a similar story with Gorbachev's plan for agricultural leaseholds unveiled in May 1988, and pursued (again) as a Party measure through *apparat* channels.[48] Would-be tenants (employees of a farm or out-siders) might now approach a collective or state farm and contract to lease a piece of land or a service such as transport, repairs or marketing; leases, it was later agreed, might run for up to fifty years. How leaseholders fulfilled their contracts was their own business, and after payment of the agreed rent they could do what they liked with their earnings. In practice the terms of the relationship between tenants and the 'landlord' farm might range from temporary delegation, through subcontracting to virtual independence – but the more radical contracts did away with control of a farmer's operations from above, and **that** meant that those who wanted to opt out of collective farming could do so. In symbolic terms it was an important break with the past.

In practice the symbolism went largely unnoticed. Sixty years after collectivisation the farming workforce had become disproportionately old, unskilled and female; few had any idea of the management or trade aspects of farming, and some may no longer have understood the full cycle of farming operations. Furthermore processes of self-help and self-improvement meant social stratification. The land or farming tasks that might attract tenancies were the most profitable. So it was in farm managers' interests to discourage tenancies, for otherwise the land and labour remaining to the farm would be its least productive portions. There were reports of farm managers telling 'their' peasants to take out leases – naturally of the least disruptive kind. In some agricultural provinces managers forged an alliance with local officials and representatives of the agricultural ministries, making it clear that to seek a lease here was to challenge the establishment. Except in the Baltic (where collectivisation went back only to the late 1940s, and it was still just possible for a farmer to regain land he had lost forty years earlier!) few farmers seem to have been able and willing to take up leases. In mid-1991 in the RSFSR private farmers occupied less than 0.4 per cent of agricultural land.[49]

Affairs in the Black Earth province of Ryazan' illustrate the problem, as well as much else about provincial politics.[50] The free elections of spring 1990 brought a popular Afghanistan veteran, Lt. Col. V. V. Ryumin, to the chair of the Ryazan' city soviet. By this time the Party had lost its monopoly, but the *obkom* first secretary, L. I. Khitrun, a former head of two agricultural ministries, was still directing officials and farmers and nominating appointments as if nothing had happened. Khitrun had mobilised a clientele of obedient peasants to oppose Ryumin's election, and afterwards got him vilified in the local press and banned from local television. No one in the province was granted an agricultural lease. In mid-1990 the coalition of bureaucratic and *kolkhoz* interests demanded the services of 2000 skilled urban workers, or it would withhold food supplies to Ryazan' city. Ryumin's riposte was to commandeer all official chauffeurs!

Under legislation of February 1990, those prepared to make use of land were permitted to hold it for life and will it to their heirs, but not to buy, sell or exchange it.[51] A comparison with the legislation on the media and on public organisations is instructive. In all three cases a 'private' reform initiative of the Party leader was converted into law, and the latter, like all legislation, defined the limits within which self-interested activity was to be permitted. But rights are not incentives, nor do they abolish disincentives; legislation cannot in itself deliver social change unless people want to change. The laws on the media and on public organisations met pressing and articulate social demands and this was one reason for their success. But the balance of forces on the farm was more confused, and legislation alone could do little to alter matters. In the words of V. A. Tikhonov, one of the leaders of the cooperative movement:[52]

The *Law on Land* provides for the right to own land, to inherit it. Still 98 per cent of all land is owned by collective and state farms and there is no mechanism to hand it over to private farmers. Peasants can see that those of them who dared to take land on lease were crudely put out of business ... 'Peasants aren't taking the land!'. . . 'Did you let them have it?'

## GORBACHEV'S SOCIAL POLICIES

Examination of these four cases – *glasnost'*, the *neformaly*, cooperatives and agricultural leases – suggests a great deal both about
Gorbachev's social policies and about him as a politician.

Note first that, although Gorbachev initiated the changes from
above, he did not – unlike all other communist leaders but Dubček –
try to stop the processes from becoming self-sustaining. Nor indeed, in
the case of cooperatives and tenancies, did he seek to impose his
policies by bureaucratic *fiat* when they encountered resistance;
Khrushchev would not have been so cautious. The two latter policies
were publicised at a time (May 1988) when it was abundantly clear
where the policies of *glasnost'* and free organisation were leading. We
must conclude, I think, that self-sustaining social processes were part
of his objective, and with them evolutionary development and some
kind of competitive pluralism; (the precise role envisaged for the Party
is immaterial). We can go further: his policies were successful where
frustrated 'entrepreneurs' – pioneering journalists, leaders of Popular
Fronts – were pressing for rights and where incentives did not have to
be applied from above. They failed where people were apathetic or
manipulated, but Gorbachev did not turn on the conservative institutions (eg the collective and state farm structures) that kept them from
'realising their true interests'. It suggests not merely encouragement of
social evolution but a refusal to get involved in social engineering.

What he created or tried to create was a political alliance of an
unusual kind for Russia. Social interest groups were encouraged to
organise and express themselves, but without their affairs being
directed from above. Where such groups supported *perestroika* they
did it out of their own self-interested stake in reform, not from
clientelist allegiance; indeed by 1990 much of this support was
accruing, not to the leader who had let it emerge, but to B. N.
Yeltsin. This did not of course mean that no-one in the future would
seek to manipulate ideology, nationalism or charismatic leadership to
muster a political following; but another sort of politics was at least
strengthened, one in which citizens united freely to further rational
interests. There is perhaps one other figure in Russian history who
espoused such policies. Under the programme of Russia's third Prime
Minister, P. A. Stolypin (1906–11), peasants could apply to withdraw
from the commune and set up consolidated small-holdings. Stolypin
hoped that the independent yeomen farmers who resulted would both
stabilise and develop society; it was called a 'Wager on the Strong'.

Gorbachev's and Stolypin's policies were similar in two ways: each sought to promote individualism and each took a gamble in initiating social processes that promised little advantage to himself.[53] The policies were designed to strengthen the new middle classes, the educated and professional products of Soviet industrialisation. The stress on self-motivated initiative and avoidance of social engineering focused attention on these groups. But in interests and temperament Gorbachev was in any case one of them; they represented for him what yeomen farmers had for Stolypin, the group most interested in, and best equipped for stable social development.[54] They were eager to shoulder responsibility, to break the 'alliance of despotism and parasitism' and to gain what they saw as their rightful place in politics. The Union of Scientific and Engineering Societies, its president told *Pravda* in May 1988, was ready to 'come out as a real partner, or, if necessary, as an opponent of the state system of administration'.[55] Such people came to the fore over the next two years in the new legislatures and the movements pressing to supplant the Party. Deputies with jobs in 'middle management' – examples are factory and farm directors, headmasters, heads of hospitals or laboratories – were seven per cent in the 1984 Supreme Soviet, but 35 per cent in the 1989 one. Deputies with tertiary qualifications rose from 52 per cent in the 1984 Supreme Soviet to 76 per cent in the Congress of People's Deputies – and to more than 90 per cent in the parliaments of the RSFSR and Ukraine in 1990! The most common of these qualifications was engineering: trained engineers were 37 per cent of RSFSR deputies and 30 per cent of the delegates to the First Congress of the Popular Movement for the Reconstruction of Ukraine (*Rukh*) held in September 1989.[56]

Not only did his policy work to middle-class advantage but 'organised labour' played a strikingly unobtrusive role in politics under Gorbachev. So much – from the curbs on alcohol and quality control measures of 1985–7 to the economic collapse of 1990–91 – could have presaged trouble from this quarter: but the official trade unions did not make it;[57] independent trade unions were set up but did not capture a large following; neither showed the initiative or assertiveness of the *neformaly*. There was little sign of the rapprochement between professionals and blue-collar workers that had made Polish Solidarity so powerful. Instead (as the figures above suggest) there seems to have been widespread acceptance of local leadership by professionals,[58] and where this failed the alternative was often disorganised rioting.

The serious coalminers' strike of July 1989 might seem a different matter. This did involve an alliance between workers and specialists, indeed of virtually all the population in the two regions where it was most effective, the Kuzbass (Kemerovo) coalfield, and the Ukrainian Donbass. And it resembled Solidarity in other respects: it blended industrial with political demands, in particular for a regional say in coal sales; and its strike committees were not dissolved and became a kind of 'shadow' local government.[59] Yet it was surely features of coalmining (a highly organised monoculture) rather than of working class activism that produced effective coalitions in the Kuzbass and Donbass. The evidence, both general and particular, points to two things: a demoralisation in which people trusted only close and familiar social bonds; and, second, where coalitions did manage to impinge on politics, it was because some rallying force – regional patriotism, professional morale – had survived.

Here we begin to see what was wrong with Gorbachev's social analysis. Yes, the new middle classes were the leaders of the future and showed that society was readier than it had ever been for democracy and pluralism. But he misjudged the strength and precise interests of the middle classes and overestimated their social authority. Whatever Marxist and liberal models may have indicated, they were not greatly interested in the financial independence of the entrepreneur but rather in unimpeded pursuit of their professions. Hence the experiments with leases and cooperatives were a flop. What they needed was support in finding an independent voice. And the middle classes were no model for society as a whole: professional values of economy and cooperative organisation had not permeated deeply; indeed many professionals were attracted by the uneconomic and disruptive ideas of regional autarky and nationalism. This mistake had political consequences that were important.

# 7 *Perestroika* and Political Institutions

'The rules . . . are a human invention which makes the job of ruling considerably harder. They favour the ruled, but when a government falls they also save its ministers from being shot.'

(Ludvík Vaculík, 1967)[1]

## THE NINETEENTH PARTY CONFERENCE (June–July 1988)

We have seen that the focus of Gorbachev's planning shifted towards institutions and legislation during 1987, but that little of significance occurred in this field before late 1988. Measures of 'reconstruction' before that time were cautious and ambiguous, suggesting political struggle and compromise. The obvious point of leverage, the Party, had to be approached with utmost care.

He had proposed a special Party conference on reform policy in January 1987, and had met with resistance; but he got his way in June and the conference was convened a year later, in June 1988. It was preceded in the first half of 1988 by what seemed to be the first public debate in the media about Soviet political institutions – how they worked and how they ought to work. Only the top Party institutions were exempt.[2]

The XIX Party Conference,[3] much of which was televised, was for most of the public (as well as of its delegates) an introduction to open political debate. For the first time since the 1920s delegates voiced opposition to leadership policies and voted against the final resolutions – but in each case not many of them. It was the kind of operation that Gorbachev managed with skill. He made full use of the contrast between his own assertiveness, clarity and fluency and others' inexperience and fear of unpopularity. He knew when to polarise issues, when not to pursue divisive clarity and when to bid boldly – giving himself room for public compromise. In comparison with the surprises of debate, the Conference resolutions seemed bland and vague; but precisely this feature gave the General Secretary discretion to pursue **his** interpretation of them for the next two years. The core of the resolutions lay in the fields of institutions and law.

Public accountability was the focus of two new procedures: competition was to become the norm in the selection of representatives and office bearers, Party and state; and office bearers were to be limited to a maximum of two successive terms, with five years becoming the standard term of elective office at the provincial echelon or higher.

Little here to alarm the Party seriously: limited terms had been a pet project of Khrushchev, and the impact of contested elections could be blunted through democratic centralism, or, outside the Party, through an enhanced role for 'pre-election assemblies', designed to whittle down the number of candidates, and a gift for any well-organised lobby. The key to elections, *nomenklatura* was handled with kid gloves. True, 'the formal *nomenklatura* approach to the selection and placement of cadres [was] out of date', but Party committees should still concentrate on personnel training 'with a view to its possible recommendation to leading posts in accordance with democratic procedures. The final decision on staff questions should be determined by the results of elections.'[4] The most obvious way of reading this was that several recommendations, rather than one, would become the norm, but that the principle of Party recommendation remained. Left ambiguous was whether **all** nominations **must** be backed by the Party.

Other measures were designed to raise the confidence of those elected. Hitherto the infrequent and unpaid sessions of a soviet had been dominated by its standing executive (or *ispolkom*), a committee of paid officials who took their orders in practice from the local Party. Employees of a soviet were now to be ineligible for election to it, that is, to join the assembly that could vote them their job. Ministers therefore might no longer be in the Supreme Soviet, and members of *ispolkomy* might not belong to their soviet[5] – and deputies should learn to make policy without them. The principle of payment for elected representatives was introduced, giving them a measure of independence and immunity to pressure; with this the emergence, for the first time in the Soviet period, of professional, experienced legislators became a possibility. From May 1989 such payment was available to members of the Supreme Soviet and of its standing committees.[6]

The aim was to make soviets more effective and independent and less easily manipulated. But the changes did not touch the informal, extra-legal influence of the Party. The device chosen to regulate this was an unexpected and subtle one, one whose real implications emerged only gradually. It was proposed that the chairman ('speaker') of a soviet (not to be confused with the chairman of its *ispolkom*) should 'as a rule' be the local Party first secretary, but that the latter should be elected separately to each of these positions. The obvious consequence would be to push the chairman of the *ispolkom*, who had ranked next to the first secretary, into the background; by introducing the senior Party figure as speaker of a soviet, Party status and authority would be lent to that body and it would be strengthened in relation to the executive. The measure was presented as a return to the revolutionary slogan of 'power to the soviets'.

There was more to this than was spelled out at the time. The change would serve to bring Party first secretaries out into the public limelight, where previously they had been able to pull strings from the background. They became doubly accountable; they must get and keep the confidence both of the Party committee that chose them and of the local soviet. It was made clear during 1989 that first secretaries who lost the confidence of either of these bodies were expected to resign from both, or face dismissal. Putting Party first secretaries in charge of soviets thus served to put the Party on notice that it must earn its claim to leadership by winning public confidence. At the same time (can this implication have been thought out in advance?) Party secretaries gained first refusal of a new and possibly powerful non-Party office; this could prove a useful insurance for them, should the Party come under real pressure.

Applying the same principle at the All-Union echelon it was resolved to merge the largely ceremonial duties of Head of State (Chairman of the Presidium of the Supreme Soviet) with those, hitherto light, of presiding over the Supreme Soviet; this strengthened post of Head of State was to be held by the General Secretary. (A clear implication was that Gorbachev would replace A. A. Gromyko who had been Chairman of the Presidium of the Supreme Soviet since July 1985.) The old Supreme Soviet was to be replaced by two bodies: a large Congress of People's Deputies which would meet twice a year; and a new much smaller Supreme Soviet which would be in session for the greater part of the year, like western legislatures. The large size (1500) and infrequent, short sessions of the old Supreme Soviet had been major reasons for its ineffectiveness.

A further Conference resolution declared the Party's intention to work towards a 'socialist legal state'.[7] In February 1988 it had been announced that the authorities would no longer entertain anonymous communications (often denunciations).[8] In the next few months a series of major articles by senior lawyers explained such concepts as the presumption of innocence, the irremovability of judges and that 'anything is permitted except what is specifically forbidden by law'. They also documented what people had taken for granted for years – that judges and prosecutors had often no more than a primitive understanding of law and legal concepts, and that the Party interfered systematically in legal processes. More than half of judges (elected at the same time as local soviets) thought they had been subjected to improper influence, typically by Party officials who could determine whether they would be nominated for reelection. Yet 56 per cent of the legal profession were happy to see convictions even when the prosecution evidence was not compelling![9] The Conference therefore called for an overhaul of the legal codes in the light of the newly recognised principles; the retraining of most legal personnel (this was clearly running into trouble two years later[10]); and the definition in law of much that hitherto had been a matter of unwritten (and implicitly Party) policy. Specific recommendations were that judges be elected not in their own locality but by soviets at a higher echelon, and that a Committee of Constitutional Supervision rule on the validity of government acts; this was set up in December 1989.[11]

Implicit in these proposals, and especially the last, was something momentous: acknowledgment of the principle that no person, institution or procedure should be outside or above the law, and hence that the role of the Party (and of the KGB) should be defined in public. Yet these were **Party** proposals, and the Conference had accepted in principle that they meant internal change for the CPSU. How much did the Conference delegates understand of what they were approving? The high-level Party disputes of the next eighteen months suggest many did not. But many others were exposed to their first rational, rather than mystical, treatment of Party power.[12]

## THE CONSTITUTIONAL AMENDMENTS OF DECEMBER 1988

At the All-Union echelon the political structures recommended by the Conference were set up by a series of constitutional amendments passed at the beginning of December 1988.[13] In formal terms the amendments created three new institutions. A **Congress of People's Deputies** should meet twice a year, with the principal duties of electing the Supreme Soviet and the Head of State and of amending the Constitution; its 2250 deputies were to be elected, 1500 directly by territorial constituencies, and 750 by the various 'public organisations' (of which the CPSU and the Trade Unions had a hundred seats each). A **Supreme Soviet** of 542 paid deputies was to be elected by and from the Congress and function as a full-time legislature. And an office of 'Chairman of the Supreme Soviet' replaced that of Chairman of the Presidium of the Supreme Soviet as the Head of State; to avoid confusion this post will be referred to as '**Speaker of the Supreme Soviet**'.

Gromyko had retired in October and Gorbachev replaced him as Chairman of the Presidium of the Supreme Soviet; the latter's acquisition of the new post of Speaker thus seemed automatic. But the new relationship **between** his two posts, that of General Secretary (which was not mentioned in the Constitution) and that of Speaker, was a most significant part of the constitutional amendments. The true implications of the change took time to emerge, but it represented a subtle shift of power away from the General Secretary and towards the Speaker/Head of State. Among the latter's duties were to chair sessions of the Supreme Soviet and Congress of People's Deputies; to nominate the Prime Minister and a number of other senior posts for the Supreme Soviet to vote on; and to head the Defence Council, an executive body which had run the country during the Second World War and still served (apparently) as the ultimate political control of armed operations. It was the Supreme Soviet, chaired by the Speaker, which was to accept treaties, appoint the Defence Council and High Command, and vote to commit troops abroad in peacetime. Under the old Constitution none of these powers had lain with the full Supreme Soviet or with the Chairman of its Presidium; a good many of them had simply not been specified in the old Constitution – and the General Secretary normally exercised these. Stalin had headed the Defence Council, and it seems to have been in this capacity that Khrushchev managed the Cuban missile crisis and that Brezhnev sent troops into Czechoslovakia and Afghanistan. But from December 1988 in law, or from May 1989 in fact, this power lay with the Speaker. Overall the clarification of powers shifted certain duties in the fields of defence, internal security and foreign affairs from the General Secretary to the Speaker/Head of State.

Did this matter? Since October 1988 Gorbachev had been both General Secretary and Head of State; his own position would have been unaffected. But it still mattered to distinguish between the posts of General Secretary and Head of State and to attach certain powers to one rather than the other. Imagine the situation if the Central Committee had tried to depose the General Secretary as they had deposed Khrushchev. After May 1989 they could have stripped him of his Party posts, but he would still have been Head of State and of the Defence Council. They might then have tried to recall him as a deputy (he was elected from the reserved Party seats), with legal consequences that were unclear, or Gorbachev might have resigned, as on his own admission he had an obligation to do. But he might have tried to tough it out, using his legitimate control of the armed forces and calling on support from the elected parliaments. In other words there would have been a constitutional crisis of a kind unprecedented and undreamt of in the Soviet Union hitherto – and it would have been because Gorbachev had started to build himself a political base independent of the Party.

Particularly revealing in the constitutional amendments was a clause stipulating that the full Supreme Soviet should vote before a body of troops could be dispatched beyond Soviet borders in peacetime. The word used for 'body of troops' was 'contingent' (*kontingent*) and that word could not fail, with Russians of the 1980s, to conjure up the euphemism 'limited contingent of Soviet troops in Afghanistan'; this was the only way the media had described these forces. It was shortly after this that statements were issued to the effect that Gorbachev had not been involved in the decision to invade Afghanistan (though he was a Politburo candidate at the time), and had been disgusted both at the decision and at the way it was taken. The new clause in the Constitution signalled that such decisions should be taken out of the hands of the General Secretary and entrusted to a more representative and accountable body.[14]

December 1988 was the first time that anyone had tried to introduce into Soviet politics the notion of checks and balances, or of the separation of powers. Indeed it was only from this time that the Soviet Constitution (and those of the Union-Republics) began to be treated seriously as a set of rules for the regulation of political conflict. But this could not mean very much until people saw the Constitution being worked to serious purpose – which they did in May–June 1989 – and until the contradiction between constitutionalism and Party absolutism had been resolved.

## THE GENERAL ELECTIONS OF MARCH–MAY 1989

A new electoral law was passed along with the constitutional amendments.[15] It is often thought that this law made possible the dramatic elections of March 1989 and subsequently, but this is incorrect. Instructions on Soviet ballot papers since 1936 (thus even during the Great Purge!) read 'Cross out the names of the candidates you are voting against', and to win such an election a candidate, even a single candidate, had to receive at least half of the votes. These formal rules were not changed by the 1988 legislation, though procedures were added that served to make multiple candidacies and secret voting look less like conspicuous defiance. What happened at the general elections of March-May 1989 (particularly in the territorial constituencies, but to some extent also among the public organisations) was not so much that people had new opportunities, but rather that they gained the confidence to use **old** opportunities. They **used** their right to cross names out in a way never seen before, and particularly where a single candidate was standing. The consequence in hundreds of constituencies was that, where there were one or two candidates and these were defeated (ie half the voters crossed out their names), a new election had to be declared; and where there were three or more candidates, run-off ballots between the top two had to be held. The elections ran to four distinct polling days (and in one constituency to a fifth) and so lasted more than two months.[16]

What happened to elicit this surge in confidence? It seems clear that Party committees were instructed not to apply pressure to have the number of candidates reduced to one; and other public organisations and *neformaly* were given to understand that they could lodge complaints with electoral commissions if they thought nominations or campaigns were being obstructed.[17] This did not always work: officials often tried to 'manage' things in the traditional way, and on polling day voters had no choice in some 27 per cent of constituencies. But on the whole electors were able to exercise their choice.[18] This seems to have been the final occasion on which the General Secretary used the Party machine to push through change from above – and many in the Party never forgave him for it.

It was high-profile Party and state officials, in big cities and the Baltic Union-Republics, who were the particular target of voters' anger. The defeats should be seen in perspective. I identified the defeat of some 70 senior officials, the sort who before 1989 would have taken their place in a Supreme Soviet for granted; there could be more – no consolidated lists of candidates were ever issued, but the defeats would still be no more than a small fraction of the 2250 places in the Congress of People's Deputies.[19] (Most of the Politburo, including Gorbachev, were elected from the CPSU.) Nevertheless here was a symbolic humiliation that cut deep: it included almost a clean sweep of the top officials in cities like

Moscow, Leningrad, Kiev, Minsk, Kemerovo or Alma-Ata. Meanwhile B. N. Yeltsin, who had been sacked as Party first secretary in Moscow, won more than 90 per cent of its votes!

It was a revolt against officials but not against the CPSU as a whole. Indeed the proportion of deputies who were Party members rose from about 72 per cent in the 1984 Supreme Soviet to 87 per cent, and this trend was to be repeated in the Union-Republican elections of 1990. How to resolve this paradox? In April 1988 Yurii Burtin, one of the pioneers of *glasnost'*, had published something unprecedented in its time: an occupational analysis of the 1984 Supreme Soviet, together with inferences about its probable capacities for political independence. Burtin found that 39 per cent of Supreme Soviet deputies were selected literally *ex officio*, whilst 46 per cent were token workers and peasants, two thirds female; calling the two groups 'bosses' and 'silent partners' he suggested that legislative confidence would be improved by the introduction of authentic **public figures**, 'economists, historians, . . . journalists, writers, stage and screen directors and actors'.[20] It was a remarkable forecast of subsequent election results, if it did somewhat overestimate the role of the creative arts. Officials did not forget their humiliation in 1989 and became increasingly reluctant to stand, and both then and later far fewer 'dairymaids and loom operators' were nominated as candidates. The people who took their place were typically from the middle classes and especially from jobs that the public valued more than did the Party: hospital doctors, teachers, lawyers, technicians, research assistants, 'middle management'.[21] They were professionals but not decision makers: that was a responsibility they were anxious to shoulder. They were not radicals and not overly sympathetic, say, to the poor or to intellectuals; as state employees (most of them) they favoured gradual change and were suspicious of private enterprise. The Muscovite intellectual, Yu. N. Afanas'ev, was to sneer at the 'Stalinist-Brezhnevite Supreme Soviet',[22] and in this discerned correctly that deputies' interests were not those of the intelligentsia. And they were Party members because such membership was a precondition of responsible white-collar employment; but they were a long way from toeing the Party line.

## THE NEW LEGISLATURES

The new Congress of People's Deputies – the first freely elected legislature since the short-lived Constituent Assembly of 1917 – met on 25 May 1989 and was in session for about a fortnight; it met again for similar periods in December 1989, March and December 1990 and September 1991. The new Supreme Soviet was in session for about two out of every three months over the same period.[23] The new legislators made an enthusiastic start to their tasks. Under Khrushchev and Brezhnev laws were usually given preliminary approval by the Presidium of the Supreme Soviet, put into immediate effect and enacted by a sleepily unanimous Supreme Soviet as much as six months later. In the new parliaments debate was vigorous, sometimes stormy, from the start. Deputies voted against each other (even Politburo members were observed doing this). They rejected or amended government bills and motions.[24] They subjected Ryzhkov's nominees for ministerial appointment to searching interrogation and rejected about a sixth of them; in one case (the environment portfolio) the job finally went to a non-communist, for the first time since the Civil War.[25] Numerous parliamentary inquiries were set up, into current scandals like the Tbilisi killings of April 1989, or the case of the popular detectives Gdlyan and Ivanov (suspended for allegedly exceeding their powers in investigating corruption in Uzbekistan), and into such 'blank spots' in history as the Hitler-Stalin Pact, or the nuclear accident in the Urals in September 1957.

Two things helped this confidence. Gorbachev sought to convince deputies that the Party's electoral defeats had been no fluke and that the new legislatures were seriously meant. Few senior Party politicians were nominated for the Supreme Soviet (and, as we have seen, ministers were excluded); from the Politburo and Secretariat there were no more than three, Gorbachev, Luk'yanov (the Deputy Speaker) and Vorotnikov.[26] Deputies were thus given the opportunity to work out distinct viewpoints, undaunted by baleful figures from high politics. In addition the initiative was seized by the deputies of professional background, so long frustrated in political access, and now flushed with their recent victories.

The primary business of the new assemblies was legislation. Formal, publicly-accessible, uniformly-applicable laws were needed to replace informal, private regulation by Party officials in almost every walk of life – publishing, taxation, property, land, religion, association, state security . . . Some of this legislation addressed problems never tackled before in the Russian or Soviet periods. It was a prodigious task, and it was to be the Supreme Soviet's main business for the next two years. Deputies had no experience or precedents and had to develop parliamentary skills from scratch. They were criticised for the time they spent on standing orders and other procedural wrangling; but in this they showed their determination to be independent and take law-making seriously. And laws gained rapidly in quality. Soviet laws in the past had suffered from a confusion of legislation in the strict sense – delineation of the boundaries of the permissible – with policy-making and policing. When one compares, say, the 1987 Law *On the State Enterprise*, or the leaked 1988 draft of that on *neformaly* (see p. 102) with the 1990 Laws *On the Press* . . ., *On Public Associations* or *On Freedom of Conscience and Religious Organisations*, one notes the improvement in clarity, foresight and succinctness, and the impact of the doctrine that 'everything is permitted except what is expressly forbidden'.

Leaders of authority and parliamentary skill arose: S. S. Alekseev, future chairman of the Committee of Constitutional Supervision; the reactionary Colonel V. I. Alksnis; the Leningrad lawyer and future mayor A. A. Sobchak; the ethnic relations specialist G. V. Starovoito-va (a Russian elected from an Armenian constituency); N. I. Travkin, future leader of the Democratic Party of Russia.[27] In late July 1989 a group of deputies mainly from Moscow and the Baltic and including communists and non-communists set up the first organised parlia-mentary fraction, the Inter-regional Group of Deputies – in effect the parliamentary wing of a yet-to-be-formed opposition party. Led by Academician Sakharov and B. N. Yeltsin, it commanded about 400 votes in the Congress of People's Deputies and about 90 in the Supreme Soviet.[28] This was followed in February 1990 by Colonel Alksnis's *Soyuz* ('Union') group of about 100 deputies.[29]

But the problems and defects of the new parliaments also began to emerge. The queue of urgent business grew ever longer: the Supreme Soviet session of September-November 1989 started with 34 items on its agenda,[30] of which it finalised perhaps a third. Complaints began to mount of dilatoriness, of hasty, capricious decisions or of decisions railroaded through by the Speaker. Competent legislative work was also impeded by rules or habits of mind that had, until recently, been central principles of Soviet politics. To reject a nominated minister and substitute someone of the deputies' own choosing was an infringement of the *nomenklatura* system; to reject a bill meant that the Party was no longer in everything 'the leading and guiding force'. Criticism of other communists and voting against them could be construed as a breach of several CPSU rules, and to mobilise like-minded communist deputies to win a vote was a serious breach of the ban on faction. On this score Gorbachev was clear that CPSU members who were also elected representatives had a primary duty to their electorate; they had to be able to speak and vote against each other, and he proposed disregarding the relevant Party Rules in respect of deputies; Party unity should be maintained only on matters of basic principle and strategy (which he did not define).[31] It followed from this that the Party group in the Supreme Soviet – or indeed in any soviet – should modify its former activities; it should no longer try to coordinate debate and voting in advance, nor to narrow down candidacies to a particular person. These 'rights' had been at the heart of Party power: the implications for the role of the CPSU in public life – for its future – were revolutionary.

Many deputies must have been itching to be free of Party discipline but they chafed also at the lower levels of discipline without which parliamentary business is hard to conduct. Important sittings often lacked a quorum. Despite Colonel Alksnis's success in beating the Inter-regional Group into second place by December 1990, policy-based parliamentary parties never really consolidated themselves, nor indeed any clear and stable alignment of forces. Deputies could belong to more than one parliamentary group;[32] would-be 'whips' or 'numbers men' must have had a nightmare. The real beneficiaries of the end of CPSU discipline were the republican and regional leaders, especially when in autumn 1990 some began to organise boycotts of parliament. The procedures for electing the Supreme Soviet and even the seating arrangements favoured regionalism.[33]

And deputies and their constituents had inflated expectations of the new legislatures. They looked to the Supreme Soviet, not just for law-making and the formation of governments, but for considered long-term policy, versatile response to emergencies, day-to-day control over the executive, even the revival of local government – and in all these for it to replace Party functions. These expectations were quite unrealistic: many would have been inappropriate for experienced parliaments; in the Supreme Soviet deputies still knew little of places and issues other than those they represented, and they faced a well organised and experienced bureaucracy. The inevitable consequence was disappointment with a Supreme Soviet that 'did nothing but talk', and a rise in calls for a 'firm hand'.[34] When the Supreme Soviet was tempted to try executive action the results could be disastrous. At the end of November 1989 it voted to abandon central rule in Nagorno-Karabakh;[35] this turned a guerilla war into a civil war and sparked off racial violence which required intervention by the regular army.

The new parliaments, in short, could tackle only a fraction of the problems emerging as the Party retreated, and these problems could not themselves be grasped in full until the question of the Party monopoly was settled. This was the background to the decisions of early 1990 to amend Article six of the Constitution (which will be discussed in Chapter 8) and to establish an executive Presidency.

## THE PRESIDENCY

It was a straightforward decision for supporters of the new parliaments to challenge the Party monopoly: it stood in the way of crucial pieces of legislation, like those on the media or public organisations; it frustrated the working of other laws as well as effective parliamentary business; and these were merely the outward signs of the basic incompatibility of constitutional with mono-organisational government. But should anything be put in the place of the CPSU, and if so what?

Merely to pose such a question was to reveal things about Soviet policy-making and the nature of the Party that had been little understood before this time. Suppose the CPSU became in law one among many organisations that might participate in politics. There would then be no **legal** obligation on media editors or army officers – or any 'public' servant – to be Party members, to follow Party instructions in their work, or indeed anyone's instructions except those of their legal administrative superiors. There would no longer be any legal reason for the latter to give prior consultation to communists, indeed to consult them at all; no reason for the government to listen to, or consist of, communists. But most policy was **made** by bodies that were legally Party not state bodies. To confine them to their legal tasks would be to open up a gaping hole at the apex of Soviet politics. It was a stark illustration of the fusion of Party and state into a state-party.

Two functions of government would suffer in particular: political analysis and the drafting of policy initiatives; and the response to day-to-day events (especially foreign events and local emergencies) that required not just execution but the interpretation of policy. These are the responsibilities in all democracies not of legislatures but of smaller bodies like cabinets or national security councils. In the Soviet Union too they had been the business of a small body, the Politburo, serviced by the Central Committee Secretariat, and they had robbed the Council of Ministers (the 'government') of experience and facilities in these functions of government. New institutions must now be set up to perform them and they must be true **state** institutions, neutral in respect of parties, accessible to policy input from all quarters and – it was to be hoped – respected by all, communists and non-communists. Gorbachev made a show of reluctance to contemplate new institutions and (according to A. N. Yakovlev) this may have been more than a show.[36] Article six was debated briefly in the Congress of People's Deputies on 12 December 1989, and within the next month there was violent revolution in Romania (a brutal illustration of an intransigent monopoly going down); anti-Party riots occurred in important cities of the RSFSR and Ukraine; insurgents took over Party buildings and frontier posts and then unleashed pogroms against Armenians in Azerbaidzhan; and on a visit to Lithuania he found widespread, firmly argued support for secession. The Party was not trusted, yet these were simply not issues which could be dealt with by the Supreme Soviet or the Council of Ministers alone. The need was clear and urgent for an executive institution able to give day-to-day orders and capable of rapid response to events. Its creation could also be used to strengthen the separation of powers and the impartiality of the Head of State.[37] The issue seems to have been given priority consideration during the first fortnight of January 1990,[38] and the decision was probably finalised in his mind after his return from Lithuania on the 13th, the day pogroms broke out in Baku. The Central Committee agreed to move the amendment of Article six on 7 February and the Constitutional amendments were passed by the Congress of People's Deputies on 14 March.[39]

The institution of **President of the Soviet Union**[40] that replaced the CPSU monopoly combined the functions of a Head of State with those of a Chief Executive very much after the pattern of the United States (and indeed no secret was made of the debt to the constitution and experience of the United States). The President took over from the old Speaker/Head of State its formal and ceremonial duties (signing legislation, representing the Soviet Union abroad, awarding decorations, granting clemency etc) and the more important right to nominate to the Supreme Soviet the Chairman of the Council of Ministers, the Chairman of the Supreme Court and the Procurator-General. (The office of Speaker of the Supreme Soviet remained, but it was now exactly what the title suggests; it was taken by A. I. Luk'yanov.) To these were added the right to move the dismissal of ministers or the government; to suspend the working of acts of government; to issue Presidential decrees within the framework of his powers and in furtherance of the laws; and to delay legislation by sending it back to the Supreme Soviet – in which case the Soviet might overrule the delay by a two-thirds majority. The President could also move, in the Congress of People's Deputies, the dissolution of the Supreme Soviet and the election of a new one – but only in the event of irreconcilable deadlock between the two houses of the Supreme Soviet. Note in all the above the precision which must now be attached to words like 'nominate', 'move' or 'suspend'. Such language had not been used previously to demarcate the powers of one institution from another. The President was **not** empowered to nominate members of the Committee of Constitutional Supervision (that rested with the Speaker), since this body might be asked to rule on the constitutionality of the President's actions; nor might he move the dismissal of the Chairman of the Supreme Court.

From the General Secretary (in so far as that role had been clear cut before 1989!) the President inherited general duties of policy initiation, and specific 'national security' duties in the fields of foreign policy, defence and maintenance of order: he was to conduct international negotiations and appoint diplomats; act as Commander-in-Chief, appoint generals, impose martial law, order mobilisation and declare war, in the last case with immediate submission of the issue to the Supreme Soviet; and declare civil emergencies, including direct Presidential rule, with **either** the consent of the Supreme Soviet of the Union-Republic concerned, **or** support of two-thirds of the All-Union Supreme Soviet. It seems probable that the heads of the KGB and MVD were subordinated to the President rather than to the Chairman of the Council of Ministers. The 1988 stipulation (of which Gorbachev was clearly proud) that only the Supreme Soviet could commit troops abroad in peacetime was left untouched.[41]

The President was to be elected for a five-year term and might serve no more than two terms; he or she must be at least 35 and no more than 65 years old and might receive no other salary than the Presidential one. If a President died or became incapable of performing his duties, new elections must be held within three months; in the interim the duties should descend to the Speaker of the Supreme Soviet, and then to the Chairman of the Council of Ministers. The President might be dismissed for breach of laws or Constitution by a two-thirds majority of the Congress of People's Deputies – but no other grounds for impeachment were cited, nor any procedure for determining a President's incapacity. The form of election was one borrowed from Swiss and United States practice: in a general, direct election the successful candidate must receive a majority of all votes, and a majority in a majority of Union-Republics. This is an interesting constitutional device[42] – but Gorbachev did not follow it when he was selected as President on 15 March 1990. Instead under special legislation he was elected by a simple majority of the full membership of the Congress of People's Deputies; he received 1329 votes, 206 more than he needed.

General Secretaries had acted in theory on the advice of the Politburo which had played the role of state cabinet. Two new advisory councils replaced the Politburo in this function: the Council of the Federation and the Presidential Council. The former was to be concerned with the Soviet **Union** as a multinational federation, and its members were the 15 Presidents or Speakers of the 15 Union-Republics; these were now elevated above first secretaries as the chief office-bearers in the republics (unless, of course, the same person held both posts). The Presidential Council was made up of the Chairman of the Council of Ministers (N. I. Ryzhkov, *ex officio*) and 15 (later 16) other members; in keeping with the Presidency's national security emphasis, these included the Ministers of Defence, Foreign and Internal Affairs and the Chairman of the KGB. All except Ryzhkov were appointed at the President's pleasure; one cannot help recalling that General Secretaries rarely had complete control over the member-ship of the Politburo! In his appointments Gorbachev went out of his way to include representatives of the main opinion and interest groups, in a way that had never been true of the Politburo; outspoken radicals and conservatives were there, writers, a natural scientist, a metal-worker, a farm manager who had issued shares to its employees, five non-Russians and one non-communist Orthodox Christian; women were the group most obviously overlooked.[43]

ASSESSMENT

For more than seventy years up to May 1989 the power of the CPSU had been unlimited and unaccountable; when this was enshrined in the Constitution of 1977 it merely underlined the fatuity of that document. Then, for the ten months May 1989 to March 1990, the Party accepted some minor limitations to its powers: ministers appointed by and accountable to parliament, parliamentary legislation that it had not itself approved, the concession of some rights to the Speaker. But the turning point that marked the end of the mono-organisational state came in March 1990: after this the CPSU was still the strongest political organisation and still the dominant influence on policy, but it was subject to law and obliged to compete openly, legally and on equal terms over policy and for power.

The Soviet government was still in western terms a 'communist' government but after March 1990 the Politburo was no longer the engine of state policy. The latter continued, of course, to meet (under Gorbachev's chairmanship!) and was reported as discussing Party matters only; E. K. Ligachev was to complain in June that government policy on marketisation had never been brought before it.[44] The displacement of the Politburo was merely the most conspicuous way in which state institutions now began to be quietly disengaged from the CPSU: Party committees were no longer the exclusive source of policy advice; directives were no longer sought from them; holders of high office need no longer be communists. V. G. Rasputin in the Presidential Council and V. V. Landsbergis in the Council of the Federation had never been members of the CPSU; the latter was joined by several other ex-communists before the end of 1990. All over the country holders of state office began to resign, first from simultaneous CPSU office, and then, like Yeltsin, Sobchak and G. Kh. Popov (by mid year respectively Speaker of the RSFSR Supreme Soviet and mayors of Leningrad and Moscow), from the party itself. The Trade Unions announced that people of differing party allegiances were welcome in their leadership.[45] When the Committee of Constitutional Supervision met for the first time it announced that no CPSU organisation would be formed there 'since [it was] an organ of the State'.[46] Other judicial and police organs began to follow suit, especially in the Baltic and Transcaucasia. Everywhere these processes accelerated after the CPSU Congress in July, which also saw the decision to separate 'Party' from 'political' organs in the armed forces.

The institution of the Presidency meant change for the Council of Ministers also. Since the 1930s it had handled two kinds of business: management of the state economy, to which more than half of its ministries were devoted; and traditional 'political' tasks such as foreign affairs, defence and law and order. The two domains clearly drew on different skills and it was commonly thought that the political had suffered from the predominance of economic management. When the national security ministries got representation in the Presidential Council they were not removed from formal membership of the Council of Ministers, but it was clearly a move towards something F. M. Burlatskii had proposed, the separation of political and economic government, with a diminution in the powers of the Council of Ministers.[47] And economic ministries would be abolished as a market economy spread; in 1990 it was possible to forecast the demise of the Council of Ministers, leaving the executive wholly subordinate to the President.

Political life was further affected by the Committee of Constitutional Supervision which began work in early 1990. The Committee was composed of twenty jurists elected by the Congress of People's Deputies on the nomination of the Speaker of the Supreme Soviet; its chairman was the academic lawyer S. S. Alekseev. It had powers to suspend or to move the repeal of formal legal acts of soviets or their executives where they were found to contravene existing laws or the Constitution. Public bodies (but not individuals) could initiate complaints through the Congress of People's Deputies, or Committee members could initiate cases themselves.[48] It could proceed however only in matters that arose from 'juridical norms', and thus (to the consternation of many) had no powers in relation to the army killings in Vilnius in January 1991.[49] A further defect, about which Alekseev protested repeatedly, was that, pending the signing of a new Union Treaty, acts of Union-Republican authorities were outside the Committee's purview. But during one year of work the Committee tackled some of the most notorious complaints of Soviet citizens. Official registration of residents was declared legal, but not the long-standing MVD practice of making residence conditional on a permit (*propiska*). All legal acts affecting citizens' rights or obligations must be published, and those that still remained secret by March 1991 (claimed at the hearing to be 70 per cent!!) would lose their validity. The Committee made legal history when it declared unconstitutional a Presidential decree seeking to regulate demonstrations in central Moscow. In February 1991, while investigating another Presidential decree on joint police and army patrols, the Committee uncovered serious illegalities in army and police regulations: these, it emerged, had not been updated since CPSU disestablishment and commanders were still supposed to obey CPSU organs![50]

The March 1990 Constitution was superior in two ways to previous Russian or Soviet constitutions. It allowed a clear boundary to be drawn between the legal and the illegal; Stalin and the CPSU (in different ways) had benefited from obscuring this distinction. And it made a start at dividing state power among institutions and at clearly demarcating their spheres of competence. The Presidency was clearly the most powerful of these institutions but it would have been difficult for the President legally to assume complete control. He had wide powers to initiate and carry out policy, but he could not dismiss and replace the legislature or the chief judicial officers, and if he were wise he would remember the limits on his term of office and the possibility of impeachment. He could block legislation or rule by decree over large parts of the country, but only after convincing two-thirds of the Supreme Soviet. He was required to act in pursuance of, and within a framework of law, and the Committee of Constitutional Supervision and the Congress of People's Deputies had means of enforcing this. Here were institutional checks that a willing society could use to prevent a relapse into absolutism.

How easily could the Constitution have been subverted? It was certainly not foolproof, and the conspirators of August 1991 exploited one loophole – the lack of an agreed procedure for determining a President's incapacity. Like previous Soviet Constitutions it was far too easy to amend, requiring no more than a two-thirds majority in the Congress of People's Deputies.[51] It soon became apparent that combinations of two or more institutions could do it considerable damage: a Supreme Soviet unwilling to displease a President, a President unwilling to cross the armed forces (as in January 1991), an executive in collusion with the armed forces and officers of the Supreme Soviet (August 1991).[52] But this is no more than to say that, for constitutions to work, people must be willing to work them.

The weakest feature of the March 1990 Constitution lay not in its design but in this dependence on people; it was a constitution for the legitimate government of a stable and cohesive society. But after seventy years of CPSU monopoly (not to mention economic collapse and ethnic conflict) it needed more than a decent constitution and laws to bring people to cooperate politically and to stick to legal and public methods. Gorbachev compounded this by a serious mistake at the outset: to let himself be elected by an extraordinary procedure was not only to forfeit the chance of a popular mandate, but to treat the Constitution with disrespect and to set the strongest of precedents for it to be rewritten as soon as might be.

# 8 Gorbachev and the CPSU

'He who desires or proposes to change the form of government in a state and wishes it to be acceptable, and to be able to maintain it to everyone's satisfaction, must needs retain at least the **shadow of its ancient customs**, so that institutions may not appear to its people to have been changed, though in point of fact the new institutions may be radically different from the old ones. This he must do because men in general are as much affected by what a thing appears to be as by what it is, indeed they are frequently influenced more by appearances than by reality.'

(Machiavelli, *The Discourses*)[1]

## THE PROBLEM

Was Gorbachev a cuckoo in the nest? Could he have been aiming all along to bring the Communist Party down? One can be forgiven for entertaining this question: Gorbachev's relations with the CPSU require a chapter to themselves.

Gorbachev was made by the Party, and rose to head it. Without the CPSU he would have had no means of realising his political vision; to embark on *perestroika* he made full use of the wide discretionary powers vested in a General Secretary. And yet the *prima facie* evidence is compelling that he deliberately made trouble for the Party: that he criticised it, encouraged outside opposition to it, weakened it, and then cast it aside.

In 1987 he began saying that *perestroika* was a social movement, and that the Party either risked lagging behind, or **was** lagging behind a more dynamic society. Few people hearing this will have missed the suggestion that the Party, far from being the vehicle of political reform, stood in its way. Nor will the departure from Leninism have been missed: Lenin had always stressed the dangers of social spontaneity, and the need for the working class to be led from outside.

From August 1988 he began cutting down the size, scope and activity of Party institutions. The number of Central Committee departments was reduced from twenty to nine, principally by pulling officials out of intervention in economic management, and the same cuts were extended to provincial committees.[2] The latter no longer received a steady stream of central directives but were told to appraise and resolve their problems for themselves. For years the Politburo had met at least once a week; but during 1989 – to judge by press announcements – its sessions were held more like once every **three** weeks, and occasionally five weeks elapsed between meetings. It is hard not to connect these changes with the departure of nine politicians from the Politburo in September 1988 and September 1989, and with the 'resignations' in April 1989 of 110 Central Committee figures. Some of these may have been ordinary retirements, but for the outsider the central message was one of struggle at the top and hence of divided councils, wasted energy and weakness.

Still more damage (Party officials thought) was caused by the external pressure Gorbachev unleashed against them. By tolerating or encouraging the *neformaly* he had an instrument for mobilising society that bypassed the Party. Give them *glasnost'* and they were able to create a climate in which every Party worker became 'a bureaucrat who stops people living well'.[3] Officials could scarcely oppose free choice in public, so they blamed this climate for their defeat in the 1989 elections.

Consider the following sequence of events over a three month period in 1989:

**25 April**: Over a hundred people announce their resignation at a Central Committee Plenum. We read their speeches in the hope of learning whether they jumped or were pushed, but they follow Party discipline and are circumspect. But we do encounter a tide of resentment, some of it muffled and incoherent, some caustic. Its main theme is that the Party has lost authority and effectiveness; no wonder that its membership is beginning to fall, and its officials refuse to stand for election! In particular, speaker after speaker blames the *neformaly* and the elections – and the unspoken charge is that Gorbachev has loosed these calamities on the Party. At the end, and with an air almost of challenge, Gorbachev gains the meeting's permission for the speeches to be published *verbatim* in *Pravda* of 27 April;[4] publication of such debate has been rare in the past and it is almost unprecedented for the publication to be immediate. The Soviet public is thus able to read the full proceedings; and they must have caught the note of bewilderment in the speeches of those frustrated old men. Some of them, it is plain, had not taken Gorbachev seriously until this occasion – and they wanted to know what had hit them.

**2 and 3 May**: The articles of V. M. Legostaev are published in *Pravda*. They make a point of suggesting that many Party members are unfitted for politics because they have been chosen as technicians. Legostaev is a Central Committee official, and such opinions, printed when they are, sound very like an officially sponsored comment on the speeches of the previous week.

**25 May**: With the last run-off elections concluded, Gorbachev opens the Congress of People's Deputies – and calls on Academician A. D. Sakharov to make the first speech. He has no need to recognise Sakharov, and must be aware of the symbolic importance of the gesture: it is an invitation to another free politician – for Sakharov has made it clear that he owes him no political allegiance. Gorbachev spends the best part of the next month presiding, exhorting, cajoling, adjudicating – exercising his histrionic and debating skills to the full (and surely enjoying himself!).

**18 July**: Another meeting is held of leading Party officials.[5] There is more moaning and groaning, and this time it might be more serious. N. I. Ryzhkov says ' . . . we should all help the General Secretary to devote more of his attention to his Party obligations. We should free him from the trivial questions that overwhelm him'.[6] No-one could have missed the point that Gorbachev had spent most of the previous two months in major foreign visits, or presiding over sessions of the new legislatures. Trivial questions? In reply Gorbachev seems to mock the meeting: 'Revolution isn't comfortable . . . We summoned [it] up by our own policy. Do you mean to say we didn't understand that when we considered it?'[7] 'Some comrades are treating the transfer of power to soviets as amounting to the collapse of the universe. Even if one concedes it's a collapse, then it's the collapse of a warped universe!'.[8] His implied contrast between the two legislatures, the new and vigorous state parliaments and the tired and querulous Central Committee is not far beneath the surface.

To my mind, then, there can be little doubt that Gorbachev deliberately exposed the CPSU to challenge, and that he was disappointed with the results.

## GORBACHEV'S POINT OF VIEW

Let us look at it from Gorbachev's point of view. Other Communist Party leaders had become impatient with their own single ruling parties, and turned against them. But Gorbachev was different from Stalin or Mao Zedong in two ways.[9] He lacked their megalomania and urge to bend people to obedience. And from July 1988 he could claim a mandate to reform the Party. This was an important factor in his survival; so long as a sizeable number of Party members agreed that reconstruction could not proceed without intra-Party reform, then Gorbachev was not an aggressor or tyrant. One should think rather of a team at the bottom of the league recalling a former player as coach. Team members know they will be put through the wringer – but they trust a coach who is one of their own to do things for their own good.

Gorbachev had thought about Party reform since at least early 1987 but his developed ideas about it belong to 1988–9. The CPSU had to change its practices and structures along two related lines.

First, earned authority should take the place of administrative rights and privileges: the Party should withdraw from economic administration and from directing the affairs of non-Party bodies. This amounted to an attempt to separate Party from state and to set limits on the Party's sphere of competence.[10] It was with this aim that the Central Committee staff was completely reorganised and its economic departments closed down during the last quarter of 1988.[11] Only when the Party ceased to be a '**state-party**', not merely duplicating but fused with the state's powers, could it begin to develop, in A. N. Yakovlev's later words, as a **party**.[12] By October 1989 the Central Committee Personnel Commission, chaired by Gorbachev's supporter G. P. Razumovskii, was recommending 'abolition of the so-called registration *nomenklatura*' of posts in non-Party organisations.[13] The publication of the bill *On the Press . . .* in December 1989 (i.e. before the repeal of Article six) shows the intention to pull out of control of non-Party publishing.[14] Gorbachev and his advisers sought to conceptualise these changes by a distinction between the 'leading' and the 'vanguard' or 'avant-garde' roles of the Party; the former was linked with administrative privilege and the latter with earned authority.[15] Understandably perhaps it was not a distinction that gained currency.

Demarcation of Party from state led to the second item in the prescription: in practice and substance, if not in form, competition must replace monopolistic means of determining policy. Only in a competitive environment could the Party generate sensible, relevant policy and become accountable and legitimate in the public eye. It should recognise the whole cross-section of social interests; adopt the 'new political methods' of debate, negotiation, consensus and free electoral choice; acknowledge the rights of *neformaly* and Popular Fronts, and allow elected assemblies to work unsupervised; and subordinate itself to the rule of law. This would entail changes to the Party Rules that would leach most of the content from democratic centralism and the ban on faction; by mid-1989 Gorbachev was already applying these changes to parliamentary activity.

These were immense sacrifices to demand. In return Gorbachev seems to have offered concessions on his own part. An effort would be made to work a form of competition whose participants were **not** equal in law or in access to resources, to retain a special status for the Party and to avoid a pluralism of **parties**. Its role could evolve, he seems to have hoped (or persuaded it), without any necessary change to the formal trappings, just as it had before 1977. The institutions of monopoly could be transformed, whilst the shadow of ancient customs was retained. With the scheme for first secretaries to preside over soviets, Party officials were offered a respected place in the new order, even an escape route to a new career. But if the Party failed to set its house in order, 'history never issues a mandate for permanent leadership'.[16]

## OPTIONS FOR THE CPSU

*Perestroika* in general and Gorbachev's demands of 1988 brought to the surface a dilemma that had been latent since the 1920s. The Party could **either** have a political **monopoly**, in which case its interests and behaviour merged with those of the Soviet state and nations (in particular the Russian one) and lost their **parti**san content; **or** it could be a political party in the original sense, one that **competed** over policy and for power – and risked losing it. The Party's saturation of the public service, the introduction of Article six into the Constitution, the increasing tendency after Stalin to govern through joint decrees of Party and state organs, or, under Brezhnev, to throw Party meetings open to the general public are all illustrations of the way that as a state-party it had lost its connection with specific policies. We can even detect a whiff of the same thinking in Ryzhkov's appeal to Gorbachev not to waste his time on trivialities! On the other hand its neglect of law or its treatment of peasant farming, religion and other outgroups show how tenaciously it clung to its partisan origins, and refused to face the logic of the state-party. Now it had to choose between a depoliticised monopoly or demonopolised politics.

Further pursuit of monopoly meant to clarify the Party's state role, stripping it of the partisan and making it in truth 'impartial'. It must take over one or more of the functions necessary to any state, regardless of policy – and then allow other organisations to compete over policy. If it kept the name of 'party', that too would have to be depoliticised, and competitive politics conducted by bodies of some other name, 'movements', 'fronts', 'formations' or what you will. It is the kind of evolution that has happened before. When William III accepted the throne as a constitutional monarch in 1688 he was accepting a resolution of a similar problem: in return for renouncing control of policy and politics, he got a new role for the monarchy and one which raised it above contention. Pursuit of such a **depoliticised monopoly** was not a wholly unrealistic option for the CPSU, as emerges if we survey some of the forms it might have taken.

It might first have withdrawn to a position of special ideological authority and sought to turn itself into a **state church**. There were always Party figures – M. A. Suslov is an example – who sensed that political practice sat ill with commitment and who hankered after some means of maintaining revolutionary fervour and doctrinal purity. It is a role reminiscent of that of the Church in Europe before the Reformation, both in fact and as idealised by Thomas Aquinas. The Medieval Church claimed to confine itself to spiritual matters and to stay out of practical politics; when it imposed punishment it handed people over to the 'secular arm' to carry out sentence; yet it reserved the right to excommunicate secular rulers and to call on subjects to overthrow a tyrant. Aquinas's position with regard to pluralism (as we would now call it) was that it was possible for secular rulers – even non-Christian secular rulers – to make advances in human law and in the elucidation of natural law; but the Church kept a position of special authority, because only the Church could sanction these advances in the light of divine law. Implicit in one brand of communist revivalism was the vision of turning the CPSU into something like the Medieval Church, the spiritual arm that might impart Leninist purpose to the neutral, technological State.

A second option for the CPSU could have been to build on its experience of *nomenklatura* and turn itself into a state agency for the selection, training, accreditation and deployment of the **public service**. Many states have found a need for some such system – think of the examination system of Classical China or the French École Supérieure d'Administration – and Soviet and Russian governments had always faced a particular problem in maintaining standards and reliability in their bureaucracy; Solzhenitsyn quotes Stolypin approvingly on the need for an Academy of Administration.[17] One could imagine a 'Ministry of Personnel' evolving from the CPSU *apparat*, whilst the membership became a professional association of administrative personnel!

Still a third prospect might have been its transformation into a generally acknowledged **sovereign** in conditions of ethnic diversity. It was a weakness of the Soviet system, as we have seen, not to have developed institutions that stood above ideological and ethnic differences, respected by communists and non-communists, Russians and non-Russians alike. All too belatedly some Party leaders seemed to realise this and began to preach a 'consolidatory' or 'integrative' role for the CPSU.[18] The argument was used particularly during the debate on Article six; Ligachev put the case succinctly when he said that 'a multiparty system in a multinational state cannot strengthen . . . federation'.[19]

Why did these opportunities come to nothing? First, the time when they were real opportunities was long past: the Party had exhausted its credit with society. There were many who recognised the need for a sovereign, or a skilled public service, or spiritual authority, but they had no intention of entrusting these services to the communists. They might just have been prepared to let the CPSU fade out with dignity – but not to subsidise new experiments.

The second reason formed a central theme of the Legostaev articles: the CPSU simply did not possess the requisite intellectual or moral resources to embark on such enterprises. Too many members had been selected for disciplined obedience, too many had joined not for the sake of ideas or ideals, but of career or power – or simply of belonging to something big. Indeed (to go beyond Legostaev) the problem can be traced back to Lenin, who let Party membership become a bureaucratic perquisite and who showed so much more interest in organisation and power than in ideas or authority.[20] Communist ideas about their own future were marred by nostalgia, wishful thinking and plain confusion.[21] State churches had been authoritative in the days when few people could read and these were all churchmen or allied with the Church; such authority could not be resurrected in a literate population exposed to twentieth century communications without resort to 'secular' censors and policemen. It was hypocrisy to lay claim to a consolidatory role before the Party's links with the state and with Russian interests had been convincingly severed.

If saving some form of monopoly was unrealistic, the alternative of demonopolised **competitive politics** meant profound dislocation and travail for Party institutions and psychology. It would have to learn to live and work with other political parties, with impartial rules of competition and with electoral defeat. It would lose its hold on policy making, from questions of national security at the top down to the humblest newspaper office or village school. Under fair rules of competition it must lose its state-party privileges in respect of appointments, in the armed forces and police, and in the workplace.

And to survive in competition it would need to transform itself internally. It would no longer be able to afford a large *apparat*, and such as was retained must be controlled by the membership. Members' opinions were close to being a cross-section of public opinion, as the diversity among elected deputies – more than 80 per cent communists – illustrates; in conditions of competition many merely formal members must be expected to drop out, and many energetic members to work for the realisation of their true ideas and interests. Implicit factions would become explicit and might split the Party, on ideological or regional lines. Leaders would have to choose whether to rally the old mainstream (with its organisation and assets!) around a vague and catch-all programme, or to lead a smaller party with clear policy objectives; if so, representing what social interests? Worker, professional or bureaucratic? Liberal, conservative or social democratic? There was no avoiding demystification of the Revolution, of Lenin and of most of CPSU history.

## DISESTABLISHMENT

By late 1989 Gorbachev was clearly disappointed in the Party's response to his calls for internal reform.[22] The circumstantial evidence pointed to two more things. His approach to the election results, the attempted distinction between 'leading' and 'avant-garde' roles, the waiving of Party Rules in respect of deputies, the preparations to withdraw from Party control of non-Party editors and appointments all suggested that he meant to undermine the practical effects of Article six. Second, the contrast between his behaviour in Party and in legislative fora, or his failure to convene Politburo meetings suggest that he was distancing himself from the Party, preparing a public image of himself as above party politics.

Article six stated: 'The leading and guiding force of Soviet society and the nucleus of its political system, of all state organisations and public organisations is the Communist Party of the Soviet Union.' It had been introduced in 1977 (from the Party Rules) and had had no equivalent in earlier constitutions. Gorbachev's position was a complex one. He was determined to inaugurate competitive politics and must have foreseen that they would lead to a challenge to the Party monopoly. He had to safeguard his own position and dare not appear hostile to the Party, nor let the leadership get into hostile hands. Yet the Party's inflexibility put a serious fight[23] on behalf of Article six out of the question. His public tactics were to resist formal constitutional change, which, he argued, should properly be made only on the basis of substantial popular demand; the implication was that he should not give a lead and should leave it to others to work out what they wanted and to make the running. He continued to defend Article six until the end of the year, though his defence was often unconvincing and cost him popularity, especially when he clashed with Academician Sakharov over it.[24]

By mid-January 1990 he was ready to move in formal terms against the CPSU monopoly. Yet every effort was made over the ensuing months to save the Party's face and let its exit be smooth and dignified. Suggestions of a defeat for the CPSU and of a triumph for democracy were played down. The measure was presented as a free and considered decision for which the Party thought the time was ripe. Party disestablishment turned out to be exactly that and no more: political appointees were not sacked, legally elected authorities were not dislodged, property was not confiscated, there was no new governing party nor positive discrimination; voices urging reprisals were met with studied unresponsiveness.[25] Especially controversial issues – like the political organs in the armed forces or CPSU media ownership – were smothered. Everything was done to minimise disruption, confrontation and humiliation, and at the same time to counter any impression that he was the Party's hostage.

Why did the CPSU fall in with disestablishment? We have seen how difficult it would have been to retreat to a politically neutral monopoly, and the competitive option had its supporters, especially among professionals and the assertive, 'trouble-shooting' type of official. Nevertheless it seems that the Party as a whole drifted, or let itself be pressured, into the decision. Gorbachev had made up his mind, and the logic of *perestroika* pointed to competitive politics. These were already a reality in the legislatures and in the Baltic, and all over the country anything smacking of centralisation or monopoly had become the object of strong hostility. Against this tide of events the docile, unimaginative and exhausted Party workers described by Legostaev could offer little resistance; it was characteristic that, after much resentful invective, their Central Committee representatives voted overwhelmingly for the change on 7 February 1990; only Yeltsin voted against!

After the February Plenum A. N. Yakovlev communicated the news to the press with the bland statement that the CPSU 'would fight for an avant-garde role in society in equal competition with any socio-political movement'.[26] The understatement could not hide the end of an epoch. After seventy-two years the CPSU had lost its direction of policy and had to face the loss of its administrative privileges and the probable collapse of its morale, prestige, membership and resources.

So drastic was the change that many of its details had not been worked out a year later. Millions, inside and outside the CPSU, did not immediately absorb its full impact, and, as the Ryazan' case (p. 105) illustrates, it never filtered through to remote provinces. Nothing perhaps illustrates the traumatic quality of the February 1990 decision better than the confusion that reigned about the Party's actual and ideal role and the practical implications of demonopolisation, 'depo-liticisation' and competitive politics. The role of the Party as a watchdog against bureaucracy was widely canvassed, apparently without admission that the Party had made the bureaucracy what it was. It was thought that the Party could conjure up its own opposition (the press and the Committee of People's Control were mentioned in this role) or even be its own opposition![27] The separation of Party organisations from political organs in the armed forces (and the transfer of the political organs from Party to state) was widely confused with the abolition of political activity, by any party, among soldiers. After the decision for competitive politics, some CPSU organs were still trying to play the role of non-partisan state-party: in May 1990 the Ideological Commission invited to one of its sessions Academician Likhachev and V. G. Rasputin, both practising Christians and one a former political prisoner![28] Decades too late.

Single ruling parties, as we have seen, divert ever more of their energies into staying in power, and to most outside observers it was hard to imagine such a Party losing power except as a result of armed defeat. For Gorbachev it was a magnificent achievement to have effected an orderly transfer of power from a single ruling party to new institutions, without substantial violence and with the reluctant consent of that Party. A few historical cases present similarities, but Gorbachev's success overshadows them: Atatürk, Sadat and Franco's successors did not have to tackle so entrenched a political monopoly; it is open to doubt whether Nagy or Dubček, supposing they had not been overthrown by a foreign army, could have completed the transfer of power without civil strife.

It was Gorbachev's achievement above all. His vision and sense of responsibility made Party disestablishment a practical option in Soviet politics, and his patience, determination and political skills steered it to completion. The pressure he put on the CPSU was nicely calculated to compel its withdrawal whilst preserving its dignity. It was not achieved without cost. The same deal that allowed the Party to withdraw with dignity and to remain in some sense Gorbachev's party and the party of government, left him the duty after March 1990, not only of working with, but to some extent of shielding the old bureaucracy, police and officer corps. This lent credibility to the suspicion that he had become a hostage of the *ancien régime* and this was to dog him as President.

Two comments must be made about the role of the CPSU. Beneath its facade of a formidable organisation it was shown to have lost a great deal of its **political** capacities; when asked to appraise and respond to problems, as a whole it did not know how to do this. But let us remember the clarity and courage of many Party members – from Yakovlev to thousands like Legostaev, Allik, Latsis or Shatalin – who did not blink this fact. These members of the ruling class accepted rational argument that their time had come. The end of the communist monopoly could so easily have unleashed a dreary cycle of coup and counter-coup; that it was a constitutional transfer of power owed much to them.

## RE-EQUIPPING THE PARTY

How well did the CPSU equip itself for its new incarnation in competitive politics? The question directs attention to two processes: democratisation, and disengagement from the functions and privileges of a state-party. Neither process was ever fully completed, but their main thrust and scope was determined at the XXVIII CPSU Congress in July 1990, a Congress which rewrote the Party Rules.[29]

If Party members were to stay in the CPSU rather than resign or join the opposition, the Party needed to be able to show them that they could make an effective contribution through membership. This meant a new balance of power between centre and local branches, and between members and *apparat*, and the new Rules sought to enshrine this. Entry into the Party now became the business of primary organisations alone; the requirement of references, probation and confirmation by higher organs served little purpose now that the Party had no perquisites to offer, and was dropped. The principle of secret competitive election was established for the selection of all delegates, committees and officials, and as if to underline the point it was specified that candidates might nominate themselves. After July appointments of provincial Party officials were no longer submitted to the Central Committee for 'confirmation'.[30] Office-bearers might not serve more than two terms at the same office, nor sit on more than two committees simultaneously. And communists standing in public elections or serving as deputies got new rights. Party organisations were permitted to enter into electoral pacts with other 'socio-political organisations and formations' (though not with other parties!) and to support their non-communist candidates. It was taken for granted that many communist deputies would prefer to work or organise independently of the CPSU, and the old 'whip system', whereby they were required to join disciplined Party groups in soviets, was abandoned; the only stipulation was that those outside CPSU groups might not call their organisations 'communist'.[31]

The main measure against appointed and paid *apparatchiki* was to deprive them of automatic tenure: elected bodies must now appoint an *apparat* for the same term of office as their own, and have access to the meetings and the documents of their paid staff.[32] Coupled with the fact that there was now less business for paid functionaries these provisions might have been successful in making appointed staff the servants rather than the masters of elected bodies. But it would have taken time to bring this about, and the problem of an experienced, angry and underemployed *apparat* was an immediate one. It was pressure from such elements that led to the foundation in June 1990 of a distinct Communist Party of the RSFSR and the election of the conservative I. K. Polozkov as its first secretary.[33] Many reform-minded Russian communists were furious at being transferred automatically to Polozkov's organisation; part of the intention must surely have been to subject Party members in the central institutions to another discipline than Gorbachev's.

The new Rules kept the phrase 'democratic centralism' and the formal ban on faction, but their substance was reduced to a rudiment of what it had been. Majority decisions must still be carried out by people who disagreed with them, but minorities might now 'defend their positions at meetings', 'have them entered into the record', 'demand that questions be reopened'[34] and insist that controversial items be subjected to a two-thirds majority. They were also permitted to communicate with like-minded minorities elsewhere, by setting up '**platforms**' on the basis of common views, problems or interests; two such platforms, the Democratic and the Marxist, had been formed early in 1990 and their spokesmen were identified as such at the Congress. The creation however of '**factions** with their own internal organisation and discipline' remained forbidden. How a 'platform' differs from a 'faction' was not clarified but is plainly central here. The text envisaged that platforms would generate documents, and they would therefore have needed secretarial assistance, mailing lists and funds, but it would probably have been deemed factious for a platform to raise funds by a distinct membership subscription. If so, platforms would have had little option but to approach the Party, or particular like-minded Party organisations for financial support.

All this may sound like casuistry but the dilemma was very real. The Democratic Platform had flourished because of support from the Moscow Higher Party School; in July many of its members resigned from the CPSU and in November founded the Republican Party of the RSFSR.[35] The following year Gorbachev was to speak of the 'two, three or four parties' struggling within the CPSU framework.[36] Hundreds of thousands of members must have been tempted to leave, or work for a split, so as to organise effective common action with like-minded people; they held back in part because new parties would lose any claim to the CPSU's assets and infrastructure.[37] But this was no dilemma for the *apparat*: their interest in preserving existing structures, and hence in preventing members finding their natural alignments was unambiguous.[38]

Intra-Party democracy evidently included decentralisation, but marrying Party unity with the new recognition of diversity was especially difficult in the ethnic field. In the three Baltic republics communists prepared to work with local nationalists had broken with the CPSU in the first half of 1990[39] and in Lithuania and Latvia these factions were more popular than those that maintained the central connection. Congress's response was to move the fifteen first secretaries of the republican Party organisations into the Politburo *ex officio* and to introduce quasi-federal elements into the Central Committee also.[40] Republican CPSU organisations were now to work out 'their own programmes and normative documents' and decide for themselves 'political, organisational, staffing, publishing [and] financial' questions on the basis of the All-Union Rules and Programme. But this was not legal language and it did not, as federal arrangements should, demarcate the spheres of competence of the republican parties in relation to the CPSU. Failure to solve this issue made the CPSU increasingly irrelevant in the Baltic and Transcaucasia.

Democratisation might succeed in holding the membership together, but what counted for a major part of the electorate was to see CPSU influence expunged from state institutions – whose senior staff, it will be remembered, were almost entirely Party members. This process could take two forms, each labelled, rather confusingly, 'depoliticisation'. There was no doubt that policy-making, for example, had to be 'departisanised' – freed from the influence of one Party so that others might have access – and for Gorbachev such 'departisanisation' was a sufficient remedy for the problem of CPSU influence in the army and bureaucracy. For others, notably Yeltsin, nothing short of the removal of all party-political influence – 'depoliticisation' in a strict sense – would produce a trustworthy public service. It will be apparent that the former was a cautious and conciliatory line which required no more than administrative action, whilst 'depoliticisation' was a political issue affecting the employment of several million persons.

At the highest level of policy-making the President and Presidential Council effectively replaced the Politburo, which after July 1990 contained no ministers or members of the Presidential Council apart from Gorbachev. But below the All-Union echelon the President made no attempt to impose non-communist government on the Union-Republics or provinces; the interplay of local political forces was left to take its course, and where lower-tier authorities, especially Yeltsin's in the RSFSR, sought to force the pace of Party disestablishment, they were met with legal obstacles that looked vexatious.[41] This was doubtless the constitutional, democratic and prudent course of action, but it left Party bosses like Khitrun in Ryazan' with a control that was little altered, and such examples may have encouraged other Party officials to interfere in administration, or bureaucrats to seek Party 'instructions'. A confidential Party document of August 1990 showed a Central Committee Secretary apparently issuing instructions on the exercise of their duties to Party members in the police and judiciary of Lithuania.[42]

The Party had enjoyed a number of 'administrative privileges' the more easily to dominate political life, privileges which in principle had been ended by the amendment of Article six. But legal curtailment left significant problems in practice. Take the example of *nomenklatura*. After March 1990 the CPSU had no right to approve any appointments other than its own; but it was still in possession of personnel files on millions of people, and tens of thousands of communist employers will have had little idea how to conduct a fair and competitive job search (and probably less inclination). Congress did not resolve matters by deciding that Party committees should continue to 'recommend communists and non-party people to particular positions of state, economic and public activity. Using political methods they are to assist their election or appointment to the said responsibilities . . . '.[43] All this was within its democratic rights, and such recommendations could always be challenged; but a CPSU that still kept files on non-communists was unlikely to win trust, and it is clear that some Party organs continued to demand staff changes of their choice and that some employers obeyed them.[44]

Party organisations had always been set up at the workplace rather than at places of residence, and CPSU business had been conducted on factory (office etc) premises, in factory time and in other respects at cost to factories – privileges that cost-conscious managers would scarcely want to extend to a variety of political parties. Even before the Law *On Public Associations* prohibited political activities in working time, there were signs of management (sometimes with workers' support) seeking to depoliticise the workplace.[45] But to ban party activity in working time was not the same as to ban work-based party organisation, and in government offices, for example, one can well imagine that the continued existence of a Party organisation of senior staff made a difference to the way people did their jobs. The issue was fought hard until Yeltsin's decree of July 1991 prohibited political organisation at workplaces under RSFSR jurisdiction; that was still before the Committee of Constitutional Supervision when the August coup settled the question.[46]

The workplace controversy was linked to that of CPSU property. The Party had assets that it valued (perhaps conservatively) between 4.9 and 7.7 billion roubles, much of it administrative buildings in city centres, or hotels and sanatoria. It was also a substantial entrepreneur: of its annual income of 2.7 billion (more than the budget of the smaller Union-Republics) forty per cent derived from economic activity, principally publishing.[47] Party leaders insisted that its assets were protected by law and Constitution, but many were none too scrupulous about clinging to material perquisites; members of *obkomy* and Central Committees, it emerged in November 1990, were still exempt from customs inspection.[48] Pressure mounted for it to divest itself of property, with or without compensation. A case could be made that it had acquired much of its property not by purchase but by simple transfer from the state. And Party media holdings, and still more its ownership of printing presses, came so close to monopoly, it was argued, as to constitute a threat to democracy.[49] This is the background to the fighting around communications premises in Lithuania and Latvia in early 1991; the Riga Press Building was the only publishing facility in Latvia.

For the CPSU the 'jewel in the crown' had always been its organisations in the armed forces, KGB and MVD. These 'political organs' were not set up and run by their members (as was formally the case with civilian Party organisations) but by a distinct corps of political officers, who were in turn appointed by a Main Political Administration (MPA) of the Central Committee. It was characteristic of the state-party amalgam that political officers were paid by the state but answerable to the Party. However managed, the severance of this nexus was bound to threaten Party power and at the same time abolish a discipline that had kept the Army out of public politics. Gorbachev's solution, decided in March 1990 but not completed until a year later, was the compromise one of 'departisanisation': command of the political officers was transferred from Party to state so that they became a body of morale, education and welfare officers with duties not unlike those of padres and the education corps in a western army. At the same time party activity (any party!) was not forbidden in the armed forces, and CPSU members were told to form their own organisations with elected committees and without any special relationship with the political officers or the Central Committee.[50]

This was a compromise characteristic of Gorbachev but a risky and unstable one – as is seen if one asks whether Islamic fundamentalists had the right to organise in the armed forces! Granted, that might not happen quickly, but in the meantime the membership (and activities?) of most CPSU cells stayed unchanged and off-duty political officers must have continued to run many of them. The arrangement had three other consequences. It allowed the officer corps to treat depoliticisation as not serious: we have noted the failure to amend military regulations and CPSU secretaries still had *ex officio* membership of regional Defence Councils in November 1990.[51] It freed political officers to enter public politics: best known among them were Colonels V. I. Alksnis and N. S. Petrushenko of the *Soyuz* group. And most serious: there was no longer anyone with the formal duty of reporting to the President on the mood of Party members in the armed forces.[52]

Together these were the Party reforms that Gorbachev engineered at the XXVIII Congress. It was probably his most brilliant campaign and characteristically it was conducted in the Party's familiar ordered environment. More than forty per cent of the delegates were paid Party workers and many were determined to get him overthrown; many too had had the chance to coordinate their tactics at the Congress of the RSFSR Communist Party a fortnight earlier. In the event Gorbachev managed to stay General Secretary, to avoid a major split and to turn the CPSU into a party which for most of its members was still a tolerable framework for the pursuit of their political interests. What he failed to achieve was a party equipped to pursue electoral and constitutional politics in the Soviet Union of the 1990s. In that sense it was a hollow victory and his energies would have been better spent elsewhere.

The problem he failed to solve was that of the *apparat*. The paid Party functionaries continued to immobilise the energies of ordinary members whilst deterring non-communists from trusting the Party. They had major financial and organisational resources, and powerful allies especially in the armed forces. And they knew their future was at stake. Dislodging or neutralising them could not have been done by rules or legislation; they were a social and political problem. This was the key to Gorbachev's relations with the CPSU in 1990–1, and in particular to his decision to combine the posts of General Secretary and President. Attempts to confront the *apparat* (he seems to have thought) would succeed only in driving them underground into a subversive and armed subculture; but enough of them might still be won round to the service of a reformed Party and this process would serve to blunt the efforts of the rest; and he was the only senior Party figure with the commitment, experience and authority to bring it off. The approach entailed trying to hold the Party together – something that was in any case dear to his heart. But in the event he failed to avert reaction and the costs of the failed policy were enormous: energies were diverted, options foreclosed, urgent agenda postponed and precious support dissipated.

## TWO, THREE OR FOUR PARTIES?

At disestablishment the CPSU had 19.2 million members. Some 6.8 million were blue-collar workers in industry and agriculture, while 6.4 million were white-collar employees in production and services apart from administration; the latter absorbed 1.4 million – including somewhat less than 200,000 Party *apparatchiki* – and 1.2 million were in the armed or security forces, mainly as officers; the remaining 3.4 million was made up of pensioners, housewives, students and others outside employment.[53] Between January 1990 and July 1991 the Party lost 4.2 million or about a fifth of these members. Losses were slightly higher in the non-Russian Union-Republics than in the RSFSR – the Party had virtually collapsed in the Baltic and Transcaucasia – but even in Russia losses approached two out of 10.4 million.[54] Falling membership meant loss of income from Party dues, and many members stopped paying their dues without resigning; in 1990 Party income from its members fell by almost half. This was not all. The Law *On the Press* had crippled the Party's publishing income: prestigious journals rejected Party ownership, more orthodox ones like *Pravda* suffered a massive fall in sales and the Party was under pressure to hand over its publishing facilities. Long before the August coup it was clear that the CPSU was running a deficit and drawing on its assets.[55]

Those leaving the Party came disproportionately from the blue-collar or non-employed groups,[56] and it is easy to see why they were the first to go. They had come under great pressure during *perestroika*. As living standards declined and social confidence rose they were pushed more and more into isolation and odium, whilst rewards for their role in the shape of preferment or community respect had dried up. Once the state-party, and with it sanctions against resignation, were gone, it was a simple choice to rejoin their communities. The departures threw into relief the contention between two remaining groups for the Party's future: the *apparat* with its allies; and the group that was probably now most numerous, professionals outside the bureaucracy, people for whom membership had traditionally been a condition but not the source of their employment.

Professionals had done well under *perestroika*. Most deputies belonged to this group and it had produced most of the new breed of politicians – people like Sobchak, Alekseev, Nazarbaev, Popov or Khasbulatov. Such people were confident and had more room for manoeuvre than the *apparat*, though they had not made serious inroads into its power. Their general interests were in a modern and efficient system with a mixed economy, and *perestroika* had clarified for most of them the connection of these objectives with democracy and the rule of law. It was noted in earlier chapters that they were not entrepreneurs; their experience was in big state-run establishments and they tended to take large-scale organisation for granted. They were the type Gorbachev seemed to have in mind when he wrote *The Socialist Idea and Revolutionary Perestroika* or when he strove to reform the Party.

Two things weakened their political effectiveness however. The Party had performed for them many of the functions we would expect of professional associations, so that despite their ambitions they did not produce many able organisers. This is a further reason why they did not readily abandon the Party. And they were not clear-minded or united in their attitude to nationalism. From the vantage point of a Gorbachev or a Yakovlev, of course, professionalism was plainly incompatible with such romantic irrationality, and in a Union-Republic like Kazakhstan it offered an attractive secular alternative to the clash between Russian irredentism and Islamic fundamentalism; but away from Moscow many professionals had come to give highest priority to decentralisation and they often found their firmest allies in the nationalists.

If the Party was to have any chances of electoral success it needed to retain the loyalties of this middle class. Although a certain number left the Party over particular issues like the Vilnius killings (see Chapter 10), it seems likely that the majority sought in it, not specific policies, but political effectiveness combined with democratic organisation. Hence the importance to them of the XXVIII Congress and the dilemmas over the *apparat* and Party unity. Gorbachev was calling on moderates to rally;[57] the largest and most experienced body of such centrists was in his own Party, struggling to find a distinct voice.

As for the *apparatchiki*, CPSU disestablishment, the winding down of the state-run economy, the prospect of new relationships between the Centre and the Union-Republics had all served to consolidate a political alliance around them. Their cause was clearly shared by other Party members who faced redundancy because their jobs depended on the state-party: political and many security officers, teachers of ideology, government media officials. Readily drawn into coalition was a much larger number of those whose jobs – or conventional understanding of their jobs – had been threatened by *perestroika*: military, security and police officers; bureaucrats from the economic ministries, especially from planning and defence industry; judges, prosecutors and leaders of the official trade unions. Simply to list their occupations suggests what policies, beyond simple conservatism, this alliance would espouse: defence of the external and internal empires that had served to justify a large army and armaments industry; Russian nationalism – since state-party, empire and army had been run mainly by Russians. Increasingly this nostalgia took on the mystical overtones of nineteenth century Slavophilism.

What was emerging was an 'Imperial Superstructure'[58] of those whose power, status and values had been threatened by *perestroika*. There were about a million army officers, and if we add officers of the KGB and MVD (another half million), the CPSU *apparat* (200,000), the All-Union echelon of the state bureaucracies (perhaps a further 200,000) and an unknown number of enterprise managers linked with the Union, we reach a total of almost two million persons (without dependants) with interests in maintaining the old order; well over half of them were armed and organised. Add two social groups that looked to the 'Imperial Superstructure' for protection (the only hope it ever had of electoral success): Russian minorities from outside the RSFSR; and peasants from remote and backward provinces like Ryazan'. It was an ironic denouement for the Communist Party – to be rallying a nationalist administrative and military elite, plus peasant clients,[59] against an inexperienced but vigorous majority that wanted twentieth century progress.

It was an alliance that controlled massive resources. It had reason to think that most of the country's armed force was at its disposal. Even if Party membership and income collapsed, its 'machine' linking over a million primary organisations and Party groups would still be largely intact. The *nomenklatura* system had left it with personnel files on millions of people (and the KGB would doubtless be glad to supplement them). Here was a communications network that deserved to be envied by any political activist, together with a vast, informal web of allies, colleagues, patrons and clients, linked to each other, to management and the media, to armed forces and security, and to non-communist outsiders. Let old obligations, contacts and habits of obedience be put to use! Beneath the surface the Party could continue to manipulate the bureaucracy, police, courts, media and above all the armed forces. It must have been a tempting fantasy. But it was not of the contemporary world. The more the *apparat* armed itself in the way it knew best – symbolically a return to the pre-revolutionary underground – the more it threatened the CPSU as a political party and indeed the prospects of centrist or constitutional politics.

Gorbachev's dealings with the *apparat* stand out as central to the Party's fate. He had compelling reasons to avoid armed reaction, but also to promote centrist politics; his compromise course achieved neither. Had he any alternatives to this course? Possibly two. He could have resigned as General Secretary in order to become a non-aligned President like Yeltsin or General Jaruzelski. Such a response to the pressure to oust him could have been presented as a move of constitutional principle and would have kept him some of the non-communist support that he lost in 1990–1. But the arguments against it were the same as in autumn 1989 and still decisive: whether or not resignation led to a Party split it would leave an *apparat* more desperate and unrestrained and probably under hostile control.[60]

A better prospect would have been to work to divide the *apparat* from Party members of democratic inclination and precipitate a major realignment of politics: the *apparat* would be pushed into public alliance with the reactionaries whilst Gorbachev could be prominent in an alliance of communist and non-communist democrats.[61] This would have provided a much-needed political base for himself and a rallying-point for millions of moderate communists whose energies had been frustrated in the *apparat*-centred Party. The same appeal to secular professional ideals and rational problem-solving could also have been addressed to the officer corps; Yeltsin was to show that many would respond. With skilful manoeuvring the reformists could have taken over what they wanted of the CPSU's organisational network and assets. The move would have required careful preparation of a kind Gorbachev was good at; he need not of course have figured personally in its public presentation.

That this was a realistic option is suggested by two things: the evident alarm and rapid retreat of Party conservatives when Gorbachev was moved to offer his resignation in April 1991;[62] and the success of Colonel A. V. Rutskoi (NB an officer) in founding Communists for Democracy as a counter to the *apparat*-inspired Communist Party of the RSFSR.[63] There were perhaps two favourable opportunities for initiating such a move: after Gorbachev's victory against strong odds at the July 1990 Congress; and at the April 1991 Plenum when the Novo-Ogarevo Agreement (pp. 174–5) had temporarily freed him from *apparat* pressure. Why was no such move made until July 1991, when Yakovlev, Shevardnadze and others founded the Movement for Democratic Reforms, and why was

Gorbachev's attitude even then ambiguous?[64] The loyalties of a lifetime were apparently too strong; he could not be the one to go down in history as the 'splitter' or 'grave-digger', and this fear seems to have strengthened a vision of Party unity that was ultimately unrealistic. It is a loyalty that emerged from his sadly inappropriate but revealing words when he was released from captivity: 'I shall do everything in my power to banish reactionary forces from the CPSU. . . . I think it is possible to unite in the Party everything that is good, progressive and thoughtful'.[65]

## THE END OF THE CPSU

Whether or not because of missed opportunities the Party's democrats never threw off the hold of the *apparat*. But the struggle seems to have weakened the latter also, and over the Party's last eighteen months of political life the *apparat*'s intellectual and moral exhaustion is striking. Its energies went into politicking against its own democrats, into illegal or legally dubious machinations to protect its privileges or keep its clients pliable, into salting away hard currency – all of it reactive and defensive.[66] But it had nothing to say about current problems, its opinions were at best blinkered and banal, it 'could not even promote a leader capable of rousing simple human . . . respect, let alone agreement'.[67] Perhaps its only flicker of initiative was the attempts to retrain functionaries as commercial entrepreneurs, and even this could not escape suspicion of money-laundering and worse. Its world of hollow make-believe is revealed in the November 1990 decree of the Secretariat 'On Urgent Measures in Connection with Gathering Anti-Military Manifestations in Many Regions'.[68] This recommends various Party bodies **together with the MPA** to devise strategies in support of the army. It is on the fringe of illegality as the MPA is no longer a Party institution – but these are only recommendations, to do nothing more radical than mount a press campaign, and the MPA was not definitively subordinated to the state until January 1991. The Secretariat is acting on a submission of the Party's military-political commission, which it quotes: this turns out to rest mainly on information from the Minister of Defence and the Head of the MPA. A breach of law here perhaps? But Marshal Yazov and Colonel-General Shlyaga reveal nothing that has not already been in the press. On the surface the 'decree' is a taunt to the Constitution; on closer examination, pompous blether.

The initiative in Soviet conservatism shifted markedly during 1990 and 1991 away from the CPSU. Military figures like General Makashov or Colonel Alksnis (the latter openly contemptuous of the Party), neo-Stalinists like Nina Andreeva, populists like V. V. Zhirinovskii dominated the verbal stage. The *Appeal to the Soviet People* of the August coup leaders never mentioned the Party, nor hinted at Marxism-Leninism and the eight-man Committee for the State of Emergency contained no representative of the *apparat*. The July *Word to the People* – seen as a forerunner of the coup and signed by some of its plotters – managed to mention the Party – in ninth place after workers, peasants, engineers, scientists, the Army, the intelligentsia, the Church and other believers. Public relations are not the whole story, of course; but at Vilnius we note that the 'Committee of National Salvation' did not move without army and KGB support. The CPSU Secretariat cooperated willingly with the August coup, its launch was known beforehand in the *apparat*, and one Politburo member, O. S. Shenin, seems to have helped plot it.[69] Nevertheless it is probable that the coup leaders not only kept the Party out of their public relations, but kept all but chosen *apparatchiki* out of their planning.

But neither did the Party go to any trouble to defend its General Secretary, and it was not until 21 August – when the coup had clearly failed – that the Secretariat issued the limpest of calls for his release.[70] It cannot have been surprised when on 24 August Gorbachev resigned as General Secretary and recommended that the Central Committee dissolve itself; as President he froze CPSU assets and suspended Party activities in the bureaucracy and armed forces. Five days later the Supreme Soviet voted to suspend all CPSU activities, pending judicial investigation.[71] The Central Committee never met again. On 6 November – so as to announce it on the anniversary of the Revolution – Yeltsin used the excuse of parliamentary findings on the Party's role in the coup to decree the end to its activities, dissolution of its organisations and nationalisation of its property in the RSFSR.[72] There were legal questions to ask about its treatment and nationalisation set a bad precedent; but few stood in the way or mourned its passing.[73]

Why did the CPSU fail? Not because of the stupidity of the coup: we have seen that it was already in serious decline before then, and the coup saved everyone the effort of controlling its final agonies. The cause of its downfall went back to Lenin's decision to try to blend the functions of Party and state. Two things stemmed from this. Sections of the Party absorbed the traditions of the Russian state and empire and became a traditional ruling class with the vanity and short-sightedness characteristic of such a class. By itself this could have been predicted and a distinct Party organisation was retained as a means of injecting new vision and flexibility into the ruling class. It did not work out like that, principally because the state-party's leaders would not give the Party side of their leviathan even this degree of independence. The consequence was a membership policy aimed at conformity and obedience rather than at ability or understanding. When the CPSU had to shed its state functions in 1990 it had neither the ideas nor the capacity to act as a political party.

# 9 Society and Politics under the Presidency

'I don't like extremists and fanatics. Politics is the art of balance. It is much harder to stay in the centre. Russia has always had a tradition of professional revolutionaries and it has played a negative role. In this sense I'm in complete agreement with Solzhenitsyn.'

(G. Kh. Shakhnazarov, January 1991)[1]

## POLITICS UNBOUND

Party disestablishment in March 1990 did not leave *tabula rasa*. The CPSU had been dislodged from the apex of politics but, except at the very top, nothing was put in its place, in the form either of institutions or of leadership. Party organisations had now to refrain from some of their former activities or at any rate pursue them with circumspection, but they and their personnel were not otherwise tampered with. They were left to take their chances in the new environment and, since most people in responsible jobs were Party members, this meant that administration had little need to change even if there was a non-communist majority on the local soviet – unless and until someone was prepared to challenge them, as Ryumin did in Ryazan' (see p. 105). In some parts of the Union, notably the big cities, the Baltic, West Ukraine and Transcaucasia, communists were displaced rapidly and CPSU membership collapsed. Elsewhere, especially in remote rural provinces, policy and personnel might change very little. Many situations fluctuated wildly and the pattern of developments was piecemeal.

Revolutionaries or founders of new dynasties in Russia had traditionally brought in their own personal staff of agents and executives, and the bureaucracy often kept a sense of being the ruler's personal retainers; the obligatory CPSU membership of senior officials was an updated form of this. On this model it was widely expected that Gorbachev would introduce a Presidential *apparat* or network of plenipotentiaries to expedite compliance with legislation and his own decrees.[2] Yeltsin and other non-central leaders were to do this subsequently,[3] but Gorbachev did not and it is a striking omission. When pressed hard in November 1990 he was willing to concede a 'state inspectorate'[4] but his failure to develop an executive network, even when the evidence of bureaucratic disobedience was overwhelming, amounts, we must conclude, to deliberate refusal.

He was not, as we have seen, likely to get loyal service from the CPSU *apparat* which stood between him and his supporters in the Party, nor did he take any steps to build up any other base of political support.[5] The consequence was that he was more isolated than he had ever been. A dominant theme of the politics of 1990–1 was attempts by the major institutions and interest groups to 'capture' Presidential policy and advisers for themselves. On different occasions we can see radical intellectuals, the Supreme Soviet, the leaders of the Union-Republics and the Party *apparat* all doing this. In November 1990, for example, Yeltsin – by then Speaker of the RSFSR Supreme Soviet – proposed that the Union's Prime Minister and Ministers of Defence and Finance should be nominated by his parliament.[6] Above all the two strongest institutions that had outlived the CPSU, the ministerial bureaucracy and the armed forces, could not fail to move into the power vacuum. Gorbachev's preference for playing a lone hand made him a particularly vulnerable target; on top of his policies of continuity and social conciliation, these pressures made central policy markedly conservative.

At the same time changes in Gorbachev's public manner and style became evident. Three examples from May 1990 illustrate the basic features. On May Day he had to beat a not-very-dignified retreat from the Lenin Mausoleum in the face of hostile crowds. On 23 May he made the mistake of criticising Yeltsin to the RSFSR Congress of People's Deputies in an attempt to ward off Yeltsin's election to Speaker; his argument that Yeltsin was abandoning socialism suggested a serious lack of awareness of what was on deputies' minds. Four days later he spoke on television in defence of his Prime Minister's marketisation plan: his style was awkward and nervous, he seemed ignorant of economics and of specialist and public reactions to the plan, and his intervention spread unnecessary public confusion.[7] Yet there were times when he could regain all his old confidence and mastery: the XXVIII Congress, for example, or the 1990 November 7 Parade, when he combined a fine speech about the meaning of revolution with a walkabout among (carefully managed) crowds.[8] He seems to have found it a difficult transition from institutional to mass politics and from the mobilisatory duties of a General Secretary to the impartiality of a sovereign.

The seemingly powerful institution of the Presidency was in fact extraordinarily weak, and its introduction was the signal for a social and political free-for-all. This may have been due to Gorbachev's exhaustion and his work in a state of political siege, but some at least of the evidence points to the deliberate choice of a *laissez-faire* policy: to let society grope towards its own way of doing things and to dissociate his administration from revolution from above. A Soviet newspaper caught the mood of withdrawal in April 1991 with the headline, 'Will Gorbachev become Queen of England?'.[9]


## THE DESCENT INTO AUTARKY

Neither the supersession of the Party nor the inauguration of the Presidency had anything like the impact on ordinary people that would have been the case five years earlier. The increasing difficulties of day-to-day life were drowning out politics. Crime and street disorder were rising, less and less could be achieved through the bureaucracy, and shortages (always endemic) began to affect staples such as bread, milk, cheese, macaroni, soap and tobacco. People dreaded anarchy and spoke of a return to the Time of Troubles (see p. 5). Society was dissolving into its ancient natural communities, each fending for itself.[10]

The 1987 law *On the Enterprise*, a principal purpose of which had been to clamp down on loss-making – and hence subsidised – enterprises, had also made it easier for an enterprise to raise pay in accordance with productivity and, in consultation with its ministry, to raise the price on its products (especially if they were, or could be presented as 'new' products). Workers feared for their jobs, managers and ministerial planners wanted to avoid liquidations. What more natural than that the parties should come to 'sweetheart deals' whereby wage and price rises were based less on productivity or innovation than on mutual protection. Workers got more in their pockets, failing firms could show a paper profit, and the ministry could show an upturn in its sector of the economy; only the consumer lost out, and as inflation gathered pace, so did the consumer's distrust of manufacturers and suppliers. The vast Gosplan monopoly which was the Soviet economy was breaking down into competing ministerial monopolies, each seeking to advance its own interests first.

This was an economy in which everyone – shoppers, enterprises, ministries, regions – bought whatever was available and hoarded it, because one never knew when the next consignment might arrive. It was only a matter of time before ministries began to instruct their enterprises to fulfil 'in house' contracts before dispatching supplies outside their sector, and shortages of extra-sectoral supplies soon built up. Where there was substantial overlap between sector and region (clearly the case, for example, with coal, cotton or oil), shortages soon generated pressure to satisfy regional interests before trading 'across state lines'. Such trade barriers were supported by the local population: in July 1989 coal miners in the West Siberian Kuzbass (see p. 108) demanded local control of the price and distribution of coal and of the proceeds from its export; it was a claim for the economic autonomy of the Kuzbass. Moscow wanted to deal with the hundreds of thousands of commuters from the hinterland who stripped its shops bare, so it resolved to sell only against a Moscow residence permit; the surrounding provinces responded by cutting off supplies of foodstuffs.

Shortages and empty shelves were puzzling because the decline in output, though evident, was not severe. It was trade and formal distribution that was collapsing, not production. Increasingly goods were being distributed before they reached retail outlets – at the workplace by enterprising management,[11] 'under the counter' to favoured customers or those who could pay more, or simply hijacked by criminals. Increasingly barter was coming to replace monetary transactions, and the currency (the equivalent of a year's wages was in savings banks alone!) coming to be treated as near-worthless 'lottery tickets'. By late 1990 many regions or republics were paying wages partly in ration coupons. It is worth noting who stood to lose and who to gain by these processes. Pensioners, invalids and others outside employment, or those without established contacts (immigrants, commuters, foreign correspondents) had to depend on the public economy. Regions with specialised economies suffered, and cities like Moscow (or, on a smaller scale, Ryazan') that could be portrayed as administrative parasites, came under siege. But peasants, regions of all-round development, people attached to major institutions or with resources or contacts were relatively immune; things were not so bad for the old elite and the new middle class.

This dissolution of the Soviet Union into scores of self-sufficient, isolationist mini-economies had its natural political consequences. Where remote and meaningless orders conflicted with local ones that were popular and made sense, a bureaucrat had little real choice. Laws and Presidential decrees began to be flouted openly.[12] Where there was a climate of nationalist, separatist or anti-Central sentiment, it was easier still to sever contact with other administrations. It was a process extraordinarily like that after 1917, as if seventy years of state organisation and transformism had left no mark – except to keep real aspirations in cold storage. In Nagorno-Karabakh a quarrel was revived in the form in which it had been suppressed in the early 1920s. Decades of economic privation had made people selfish and decades of authoritarianism had focused them on symbolic issues and robbed them of political skills. Their natural preferences were for small-scale community politics.

## THE ETHNIC REVIVAL

Upon this resurgence of autarkic communities was superimposed an ethnic revival.[13] We saw (pp. 34–5) that Soviet policies had generated a non-Russian white-collar elite, involved in public affairs as executors but not as policy-makers. The fifteen Union-Republics were in theory a federation but the distinguishing feature of federalism, demarcation between 'federal' and 'state' spheres of competence, was absent from the Constitution; local personnel could not alter the Central policies they had to implement, and had no access as of right to Central policy making.

Two factors embittered this experience further for non-Russians. The first was the priority given to Russian and Russians. Russian was the language of administration in the non-Russian Union-Republics (until autumn 1988 apparently)[14] and crucial Party and state posts were held by Russians seconded from the Central Committee *apparat*. In some areas Russian encroached on schooling in the native language; in others Moscow disposed of the profits whilst swamping the local economy with unskilled Russian settlers. What in Russian local government was no more than burdensome centralism, outside Russia could readily be seen as rule by foreigners, while 'communism' looked like a flimsy disguise for the ancient Slavophile sense of mission, that is, for imperialism. The second factor was the harshness, often brutality, of Soviet rule, particularly under Stalin. Nations were subjected to deliberate famine, deported *en masse*, or their elites singled out for transportation. Small but ancient cultures were threatened with extinction. Few non-Russians thought that their grandfathers had consented to joining the USSR, and some could look back with nostalgia to home rule. The consequence was powerful resentment of the Soviet order. It was largely suppressed resentment; to express such grievances or explore the politics of ethnicity in public had been forbidden for almost three generations. This had had the effect of driving ethnic perceptions inward and underground; they were dissociated from rational argument and negotiable interest and gained in emotionality and abstractness.[15]

Thus when controls began to be relaxed under Gorbachev it is not surprising that non-Russians saw their opportunity. The first to overcome their suspicions were Estonians, Latvians and Lithuanians, and, next after Moscow and Leningrad, it was in the Baltic Union-Republics where the *neformaly*, the Popular Fronts and competitive politics in general developed fastest. By late 1988 the Popular Fronts there and in Armenia had become articulate critics of the Soviet system and record (despite the presence of many communists in their leadership), and this had won them the political initiative and over-whelming support in the non-Russian communities. The demoralised CPSU organisations had either lost all authority, or were trying to cling to shreds of effectiveness by a show of patriotism and independence of Moscow. The Estonian Supreme Soviet, in November 1988, was the first to declare the sovereignty of its republic, and at the same time called for a rewriting of the Union Treaty (of 1922) on which Soviet 'federalism' was based;[16] it was told not to be impatient and to stick to the General Secretary's reform agenda.

The episode seems to have concentrated minds in Moscow and in September 1989 a Central Committee Plenum was devoted to nation-alities policy. Gorbachev praised federalism, saying that Soviet citizens had 'not yet lived in a real federation',[17] and an elaborate programme, *The Nationalities Policy of the Party in Contemporary Conditions*, was adopted.[18] For the CPSU it was enlightened – the trouble was it been drafted in the Central *apparat*; it was still unthinkable to consult the republics formally about the sort of Union **they** wanted, and mean-while republican public opinion had long overhauled that in Moscow.

Events were moving fast in the Union-Republics. By the end of 1989 three more (Lithuania, Latvia and Azerbaidzhan) had declared their sovereignty, and the rest followed suit by October 1990; by the end of the year most Autonomous Republics, some autonomous provinces and even some Russian *oblasti* had joined them.[19] 'Sovereignty' itself had little legal significance: the participants of many federations consider themselves sovereign, meaning that they claim the ultimate power to determine their form of government, including the transfer of elements of it to someone else. But in some Soviet republics sovereignty was clearly a euphemism for independence, and in many others it was interpreted as the shedding of external obligations, with the insistence that republican legislation could override Union legislation on any matter. In vain did the best legal scholars remind that no country, even the strongest, was sovereign in this sense (adherence to international treaties, for instance, represented a constraint on domestic legislation).[20]

Belatedly and reactively the Union authorities tried to grapple with these issues. Three major pieces of Union legislation were passed in April 1990. The status of Russian and non-Russian languages was codified (the Law *On the Languages* . . . ); a provisional attempt at demarcating the Union's from the Union-Republican sphere of competence was made (*On the Delimitation* . . . ); and a *Law on Secession from the Union* was adopted.[21] The demarcation was not thoroughly clear and prohibitive conditions were imposed on secession; nevertheless this was pioneering legislation that addressed some of the most notorious flaws in the Constitution.

In the Union-Republics the first free elections (analogous to the Union elections of 1989) were held in 1990, mostly in the spring. Their results prompted Lithuania in March to declare independence and attempt to secede;[22] it was subjected to three months economic blockade by the Union. After affairs in the new parliaments had settled down, three Union-Republics – Lithuania, Moldavia and Georgia – emerged with anti-communist and anti-Unionist governments; those of Latvia and Armenia were similar in ideals but more constrained in their policies by local circumstances. In the Ukraine, Belorussia and Azerbaidzhan communist governments faced anti-communist oppositions. The RSFSR and Estonia were headed by coalitions of reformist communists with non-communists.[23] It was with these administrations that the President dealt in seeking to negotiate a new Union Treaty (see Chapter 11).[24]

## DEVELOPMENTS IN THE RSFSR

Russians in 1989 were 50.8 per cent of the total Union population; the Russian Republic (or RSFSR) included about half the Soviet population, more than half its natural resources and industrial stock, and three-quarters of Soviet territory. The tough administrators, officers and policemen who had 'built communism' had been mainly Russians, and their communism was hard to distinguish from Russian nationalism and Slavophile imperialism. One can understand why the word 'Russian' came to be confused with 'Soviet' inside and outside the USSR. Yet the mood of the Union's largest ethnic group was often hard to gauge and too readily taken for granted.

Russians, especially Russians from the poor lands of rural Muscovy, had had an inside track to Union employment and had dominated the Union's politics and its bureaucracy, security, officer and diplomatic corps. With the aim, possibly, of holding them to this tradition the RSFSR had been kept with relatively few of its own institutions and for many purposes its provinces were subordinated directly to Union authorities; there were, for instance, before 1990 no Central Committee, Komsomol, KGB, MVD, Trade-Union Council or Academy of Sciences of the RSFSR. Russians came to be identified with everything that was liked or disliked in Soviet policies, but Russia as a country had even less means than the other republics of expressing its specific interests. Outsiders easily forgot that millions of Russians had fallen victims to Soviet policy, most of them under Stalin who – Russians remembered – was not one of them.

By the 1980s many Russians were not at all sure about the special relationship between Russia and the Union; the automatic equation of 'Russian' with things Soviet, Central or communist was coming under increasing scrutiny. One trend in this thinking inclined to an insular Russian nationalism, rid only of its imperialism (and sometimes hostile to intellectuals and Jews). Russian and Soviet interests, it began to be said, did not always coincide and some Soviet policies worked to the detriment of Russia: centrally-fixed raw materials prices held back Russian development and subsidised that of the other Union-Republics;[25] Russian minorities outside the RSFSR felt inadequately protected and migration patterns were beginning to prove it. A second group, inspired by authorities like Solzhenitsyn or Academician Likhachev, sought to restore moral and spiritual focus to the Russian identity; they stressed the connection of abstract evangelism and foreign ambition with rapacious growth, destruction of heritage and environment, persecution of dissent and contempt for the weak – and they sought to dissociate Russia from all this. The war in Afghanistan and the Chernobyl' disaster must have won many into sympathy with them. Common to both trends of thought was the idea that Russia too had been a colony of the 'administrative-command' system, and that it shared with the other Union-Republics a common enemy in the Centre.

Such anti-Centralist motives became widespread in Russia at the end of the 1980s. The change of mood formed the background to RSFSR politics in 1990–1 and especially to Yeltsin's challenge of the Union authorities, first as Speaker of the RSFSR Supreme Soviet (from May 1990) and then as RSFSR President (from June 1991). As a politician Yeltsin is very much the reverse of Gorbachev: impulsive where Gorbachev is measured and diplomatic, charismatic where the latter is aloof outside structured environments. He inspires great loyalty, knows how to delegate, and is capable of symbolic gestures that are brilliant. His initiative in recognising republican Declarations of Sovereignty (where Gorbachev showed a legalistic ungraciousness) did a great deal to convince nationalists that some Russians at least were sincere about more equal relations with non-Russians.[26] He showed himself in tune with the popular mood by adopting Solzhenitsyn's idea of a Slavic Union. But such gestures may also be disastrous: in August 1990 he told a Tatar audience to 'take all the power you want', appalling his own advisers, giving disintegrative and autarkic forces a boost, but without securing the Tatar Autonomous Republic for the RSFSR;[27] after the 1991 coup a brief statement about Russia's borders from his press office dissipated non-Russian good will towards him. His intervention during the XXVIII CPSU Congress, when he threatened implicitly to loose the mob on conservative officials, may have turned the Congress in Gorbachev's favour.[28] Nine months later he was urging the mob against Gorbachev.[29]

His populist methods first came to public notice in 1986–7 when he was Party first secretary in Moscow. He was hounded from that office in November 1987 but made an unprecedented return to politics by standing in the Moscow electorate in the 1989 elections. Here was a victim of the system and a battler for the ordinary Russian; he could be trusted to fight the Centre and to put Russian domestic interests first. In the Russian Supreme Soviet in May 1990 he was backed by an alliance of urban radicals and anti-Centralist conservatives against the supporters of Polozkov's Communist Party of the RSFSR – which represented the maintenance of Russia's special relationship with the Centre.[30] He was elected Speaker by a margin of four votes only, and since then he has not been assured of a majority except on issues that assert Russia's interests against the Centre. Russian defiance of the Centre explains why the repeated attempts at cooperation between Yeltsin and Gorbachev always broke down, and why Yeltsin showed such scant enthusiasm for the Union Treaty.

He was clearly driven by strong personal motives: his humiliation in November 1987 (see p. 43) and wish to get even with those he held responsible; the knowledge that his political talents had been undervalued, including by Gorbachev. Yet the personal element in his feud with Gorbachev has been exaggerated. Seventy years of communist monopoly had obscured an elementary fact: in free politics a Russia that was larger than all the other Union-Republics together was virtually bound to be at loggerheads with the Union authorities. Perhaps this is why earlier Party leaders had kept Russian institutions weak. It is significant that Bismarck in a similar situation to that of Gorbachev made sure that the Federal Chancellor should usually also be Prime Minister of Prussia.[31]

THE ARMY IN POLITICS

Party disestablishment set the armed forces free as an independent factor in Soviet politics. Russian and Soviet history had been remarkably free of military intervention: the failed *coups d'état* of the Decembrists in 1825 and of General Kornilov in 1917 are the only examples that come readily to mind. Civilian government had drawn so much on military models and priorities that there was little to be gained from militarising it. But Gorbachev civilianised government and the military had to take thought for its own interests.

The armed forces numbered over five million when Gorbachev came to power. Their formations were subordinate to three different ministries: the 'Soviet Army and Navy' of the Ministry of Defence (about ninety per cent of the total); the Frontier Forces of the KGB; and the Internal Forces of the Ministry of Internal Affairs. The distinction between officers and NCOs (together over a million) and ordinary soldiers was more salient than in most western armies: officers were almost all career soldiers, whilst the men were conscripts, called up for two or three years service from the age of eighteen and rarely rising to the rank of sergeant. Conscription was one of the chief means of assimilating non-Russians to Russian and Soviet ways. Officers tended to be well-trained professionals and were almost all in the CPSU; they were also quite disproportionately of Slavic nationality, the great majority Russians. Up to 30,000 of them were political officers; these organised the 1.2 million communists in the armed forces[32] and (another aspect of *nomenklatura*) were decisive in promotions. Until 1990 political officers were responsible not to the High Command but to the CPSU Central Committee.

Officers were accorded high social status and earned considerable benefits – for example in preferential access to housing – upon demobilisation. This, combined with the easy access of the High Command to policy-making, had fostered an assumption of authority by the officer corps in a range of matters that were not strictly within their professional competence: matters of foreign policy, of social order and imperial cohesion. The KGB obscured their supra-legal status with a ghastly romanticism about being the 'sword of the Revolution'. Under Gorbachev such pretensions came under attack. The officer corps had to live with the humiliation of Afghanistan, the withdrawal from Eastern Europe, and the reunification of Germany. It was told to accept reductions in its numbers and procurements, the release of hundreds of thousands of officers into a precarious civilian economy, the repatriation of many more to garrisons that had no housing for them. At home the army was deployed increasingly in riot-control and counter-insurgency operations, and a good many units were transferred from the regular army to the KGB or MVD for the purpose;[33] such operations had to stand media and legal scrutiny. In the Baltic, West Ukraine and Transcaucasia local populations obstructed conscription and harassed garrisons, often with local authority connivance. To cap it all the change to an all-professional army was proposed;[34] the threat to conscription was a threat to much of an officer's authority. One can appreciate the unrest that was building up in the officer corps.

Yet although many officers saw their status or livelihood threatened, it would be wrong to think that this made reactionaries of them all. Those who were proud of the army's role in defending the Soviet system and maintaining its empire, and those for whom obligatory Party membership meant something important, will have inclined to the thinking of the 'Imperial Superstructure'. But there must have been many, especially junior officers, who could see both skill and honour in the defence of a constitution and civil order, and for whom the indoctrination of conscripts or CPSU-controlled promotions stood in the way of straightforward professional soldiering.[35] Many must also have been affected by the new mood in Russia and the Ukraine and seen their loyalties lying with their communities in times of hardship and ethnic strife. Officers must have asked themselves what they would do if ordered to turn their guns on Russian strikers or Ukrainian nationalists.[36]

It is clear that in its last two years the Soviet Army was deeply divided. It was divided geographically, with the Ministry of Defence exercising only slack control and some regional commanders looking very like warlords: in January 1991 the commander in Vilnius tried to topple the local government; by the end of the year an army of the Odessa Military District was working as the defence force of the self-proclaimed 'Dniester SSR', ie for Slavs who opposed Moldavian independence.[37] There was widespread theft or private sale of military fuel and weapons – and in a country where military experience is general among males it was not difficult to equip irregular fighting units. On 15 November 1990 the Ministry of Defence moved to redeploy officers of indigenous nationality from charge of munitions in some republics.[38] The republican leaders knew perfectly well that officer loyalty was crucial to their future; Yeltsin was more open than most in suggesting (in January 1991) consideration of a Russian army and in inviting soldiers to consider the validity of their orders.[39] It is clear that around this time he won some high officers over to supporting him.[40]

## THE COALITIONS FORM

Before 1989 there had been little public opposition to *perestroika*. Even the reactionary *Pamyat'* group had tried to turn the new opportunities to its advantage.[41] Hardly anyone suggested that *perestroika* did not go far enough – until Yeltsin in October 1987, and that was not meant initially for the public. The Popular Fronts were 'Fronts for the **Defence** of *Perestroika*'. It was from the Popular Fronts in the Baltic that the first open opposition from a radical standpoint developed – the Estonian Declaration of Sovereignty in November 1988 is an example – and this theme was taken up by the Inter-regional Group of Deputies in July of the following year. At this stage conservative opposition to *perestroika* was confined almost entirely to the CPSU.

CPSU disestablishment changed the situation. The way in which he handled the Article six controversy made Gorbachev's centrism clear and showed that there was room for opposition to it from both ends of the political spectrum. It also made it possible to found new parties. These tended to be small and poor (certainly by comparison with the CPSU), quarrelsome and prone to splits, to differ one from another only in minutiae and to be centred around some particular personality or region.[42] Few operated beyond the confines of a single republic, and unificatory movements like the Movement for Democratic Reforms were slow to emerge. But by late 1990 the various new foundations and parliamentary fractions[43] had coalesced into two broad coalitions, one more radical and one more conservative than the President. They were loose and heterogeneous coalitions and neither their policies nor their internal dynamics were easy to pin down.

Three groups can be discerned in the radical coalition whose *de facto* leader was Yeltsin: democrats, mainly urban, who had grown impatient with Gorbachev; patriotic Russian anti-Centralists; and the newly empowered elites of the Union-Republics. It was a tactical alliance of democrats and liberals who had graduated from the politics of *perestroika*, and products of the ethnic revival for whom the achievement of national self-government was more important than the political complexion of that government. Further, the strength of the urban democrats within the coalition declined during 1990. There were a number of reasons for this: the democrats were 'all chiefs and few Indians'; they had lost many of their best figures to office in republican or city governments; Yeltsin's charismatic populism had an inhibitory effect; and the deepening social and economic crisis was making people more conservative. It must also be added that many of them showed a poor sense of political realities – about the effects on morale of unemployment, shortages and ethnic violence, about the future of the CPSU and about army interests.[44] By December 1990 registered membership of the Inter-regional Group in the Congress of People's Deputies had sunk from about 400 to 229, less than half that of its conservative opponent *Soyuz*, and Shevardnadze was to complain that democrats had 'slunk into the bushes' rather than defend each other.[45]

This faltering among democrats was all the more striking because they faced hardly any organised or public conservative opposition until late 1990. A conservative backlash against *perestroika* had been predicted since at least 1987 and people had naturally expected it to come from the CPSU *apparat*; but the latter's leaders, people like Ligachev or Polozkov, never struck any kind of public profile.[46] When the backlash came its source was not at all what had been expected: it was pioneered by military politicians who played the political game with an aggressiveness and skill that made the communists look restrained and unimaginative and who quickly supplanted their leadership of conservative opposition. They turned the somewhat passive *Soyuz* (Union) group in parliament into a well-organised force which began to put up the kind of resistance to *perestroika* that many had expected of the Central Committee in 1988–9. In the Congress of People's Deputies in December, with 561 registered supporters, *Soyuz* was revealed as its largest parliamentary fraction; by May 1991 it claimed 740.[47]

Prominent in the leadership of *Soyuz* were two forty-year-old colonels and political officers, V. I. Alksnis and N. S. Petrushenko. Neither was Russian (Alksnis was Latvian and Petrushenko Belorussian) and its support and most of its other public figures were drawn from assimilated non-Russians or Russians from outside the RSFSR. Alksnis showed considerable grasp of legal and debating procedures and combined this with vehement rhetoric and aggressive public relations including numerous articles in the western press;[48] no-one on the conservative side of Soviet politics had behaved like this before. Unlike traditional CPSU speakers he singled out scapegoats for personal attack, and played quite deliberately on mass emotion; but it nevertheless took skill to appeal simultaneously (as he did in his attacks on Shevardnadze's policy towards Iraq) both to Soviet patriots **and** to opponents of foreign involvement. It was a style reminiscent of National Socialists, whilst his stress on leadership and personal responsibility had an almost Prussian ring to it. Alksnis's call was for an authoritarian and centralised Union in which national separatism would be put down and local government and political parties (including the CPSU) suspended. He had no objections to a market economy, and was impatient with the 'demoralised party-state apparatus that [had] half-surrendered power and influence'.[49] He compared his programme to the post-war US administration of Japan – but it is also reminiscent of Pestel' in the 1820s![50]

Why was such resistance so late in emerging? Conservatives had evidently left it to the CPSU until March 1990, and it may have needed the legislation on the media and on public organisations and the activities of the Committee of Constitutional Supervision to convince some of them that its disestablishment was no aberration or tactical retreat. It was Party disestablishment that released political officers like Alksnis from CPSU discipline and into public politics, and the failure of the *apparat* push at the July Congress told them they must shift for themselves. What galvanised them further was the Lithuanian Declaration of Independence, Yeltsin's success in Russia and that of nationalist governments in other republics, and, above all, the Union Treaty negotiations of August 1990.

Yet in the end *Soyuz* failed to become the political mouthpiece of the 'Imperial Superstructure' and of Soviet conservatism in general, and it is odd that it did not. Conservatism was as diverse and disunited as radicalism, and Soyuz represented only one strand in it, '*les pieds-noirs russes*',[51] *parvenus* who in origins, style and ideas had made no mark on the CPSU before 1990. There must have been far more conservatives who wanted to retain the command economy, and far more who rejected parliamentarism; both the latter approaches are likely to have appealed particularly to soldiers. Behind the scenes, apparently, the Party was promoting the more manipulable among the new political parties – and perhaps it thought of *Soyuz* in those terms?[52] Yet *Soyuz* politics were **effective** and the presence of a few generals or career Party officials on its platform would have made them more so. Their absence points up, not just an incapacity for public politics among most conservatives, but a real disinclination to embrace them.

# 10 The August Coup

Mine eyes are full of tears, I cannot see;
And yet salt water blinds them not so much
But they can see a sort of traitors here.
Nay, if I turn mine eyes upon myself,
I find myself a traitor with the rest;
For I have given here my soul's consent
To undeck the pompous body of a King;
(Shakespeare, *King Richard II*, Act IV, Scene I)

## UNDER SIEGE

The assertive 'new conservatism' thrust itself suddenly on public consciousness in mid-November 1990. On 13 November Gorbachev attended a meeting of soldiers who were also elected deputies. The meeting as reported was emotionally charged, and there were claims that its atmosphere was more hostile towards the President than the media suggested. Gorbachev's remarks were a cautious defence of his policies – though he indicated a retreat from the plans for a professional army – and Colonel Alksnis then declared that the President 'had left himself without armed forces'.[1] Three days later in the Supreme Soviet Gorbachev made a Presidential statement which (even as printed text) seemed remarkably calm and bland. The deputies, who had just returned from hearing their constituents' complaints, were angrier than they had ever been in the Soviet period – about the economy, about non-compliance with law, about ethnic violence and secessionism – and they demanded action and a 'firm hand' from the President.[2] More radical again than others, it was Alksnis who gave Gorbachev a month's grace before *Soyuz* would move no confidence in him.[3] *Soyuz* had already singled out the Foreign Minister, E. A. Shevardnadze, for attack, and it now widened the campaign to include V. V. Bakatin (the Minister of Internal Affairs) and A. N. Yakovlev.[4]

One day later, 17 November, Gorbachev returned to the Supreme Soviet with concrete plans for the restructuring of central institutions: the abolition of the Presidential Council, the upgrading of the Council of the Federation to decision-making status, the replacement of the

Council of Ministers by a Cabinet of Ministers subordinate to the President, and even, for the first time, a scheme for a system of Presidential plenipotentiaries, to be called a State Inspectorate. He had produced these finished proposals for a major change of course overnight, it was noted, and they involved the retirement of the Prime Minister, N. I. Ryzhkov, whom he had been defending for months against criticism.

It **was** a major change of course, and, as its implications for policy, institutions and personnel unfolded over the next two months, it became evident that it was not a tactical retreat from *perestroika* but more like its end. Few credited the reverse wholly to the public pressure of *Soyuz*, and the suspicion grew that Gorbachev had capitulated in private to unseen forces and was now their puppet. It was a suspicion that damaged him and the new politics far more than any open defeat could have done. Observers were later to identify the night of 16–17 November as the specific occasion when pressure was brought to bear on Gorbachev. What is likely to have happened?

It was during this night, according to S. S. Shatalin and N. Ya. Petrakov,[5] that members of the Politburo and of the RSFSR communist leadership 'played a reactionary role' in influencing the new plans, and members of the Presidential Council were not consulted about them. Ryzhkov's wife confirmed that the announcement of 17 November took her husband by surprise.[6] There is no reason to doubt that Gorbachev met with lobbyists on this occasion, but it is unlikely that they dictated the new form of state institutions because this was drawn from the draft of the Union Treaty, as yet unpublished.[7] What Gorbachev may have decided between 16 and 17 November, and without consultation, was to bring forward the presentation of the institutional part of the Treaty. It also seems possible (Gorbachev had done this before) that his performance in the Supreme Soviet on the 16th was designed to provoke deputies into specifying their grievances – and so to give him an opening for a substantial initiative.

But there was more to the 'turn to the right' than new institutions. After the *Soyuz* threats against Shevardnadze, Bakatin and Yakovlev, people could not but draw conclusions when precisely these three had left politics by the year's end. The military and the KGB increased in importance whilst that of law and Constitution declined. In late December the KGB chairman, V. A. Kryuchkov, blamed foreign subversion for Soviet problems in terms ominously reminiscent of the old days; in February 1991 the new Premier-minister claimed that foreigners were planning to unleash hyperinflation by dumping roubles from outside.[8] These were not merely voices from the past, but the kind of official paranoia that Gorbachev had discouraged. His role in these changes seemed out of character and he did not try to explain it. It suggested someone whose hands were bound.

Could he have been responding to an undoubtedly conservative popular mood? Colonel Alksnis said he was 'capable of assessing a situation and . . . drawing reliable conclusions' from the protests of soldiers and the Supreme Soviet. In January Yeltsin reported him as saying he was 'moving to the right, because the country is moving to the right'. (To which Yeltsin claims he replied, 'You are wrong, Mikhail Sergeevich. The country is moving to the left'.)[9] But what began to be done after November was more than just conservative, and a simple acknowledgment of popular exhaustion could have been explained in public for what it was; it might even have won him credit. Gorbachev's meeting on 28 November with representatives of the arts hints at something different. For the first time his reminiscences about his background and the origins of *perestroika* had an obtrusive ring of nostalgia to them. He referred repeatedly to 'the last bulwark' which must be defended. He concluded, almost as if asking forgiveness:[10]

> I don't wish to thrust it upon you, but I ask you to think about our conversation. Whoever has a conscience or whose heart is heavy will come, I'm sure, to the same conclusion as I . . . I hope we part company understanding one another better, and understanding the times in which we live. And what they force upon us.

The evidence is circumstantial but telling: some specific and covert pressure was brought to bear, on top of evidence of general dissatisfaction, and probably in mid-November. Gorbachev's meeting with soldiers, the sudden assertiveness of *Soyuz*, the Army order on supervision of munitions, the CPSU instruction to military communists (see pp. 148, 162 – both are dated 15 November!): these all coincide uncomfortably with the date his supporters name for his change of behaviour, and the coincidence suggests – though it does not prove – a concerted operation. On whose part? The military and the KGB above all. They quickly gained a new prominence and influence in politics, and only after that did the confidence of the CPSU *apparat* revive.[11]

How was the pressure brought to bear? Not primarily, we can be sure, through *Soyuz* or the Politburo. Besides the Defence Minister, Gorbachev had other senior generals who reported directly to him, in particular his Presidential adviser, Marshal S. F. Akhromeev, and the Director of the Army's Main Political Administration, General N. I. Shlyaga; it would be inconceivable that such figures were not heard.[12] If the President doubted their opinion there were other sources to which he could turn, but, to judge from what happened, they would have told the same story: there were policies that must change, or Gorbachev must risk mutiny or army intervention.

What policies? Relevant witnesses single out two: coalition between Gorbachev and Yeltsin; and a liberalism towards the Union-Republics that amounted (in its opponents' eyes) to the break-up of the Union. Of these, the former would be likely to interest observers like Shatalin, but it is the latter that would have concerned the army. G. Kh. Shakhnazarov, one of the few liberals to stay in Gorbachev's team at this time, emphasised the pressure from the army.[13]

Had Gorbachev any alternative but to give in? Perhaps not: he could not count on the *apparat*; radical democrats and nationalists had deserted him and the political centre had not been mobilised; it all played into the army's hands. Yet even so he seems to have tried to bargain with the military. His principal concession (and a far more costly one than was perceived at first) was that he would make imperial unity, as he said, 'the last bulwark'. Others were an increased role and status for the army, a 'centre-right' administration that kept Yeltsin out, and the abandonment of economic reform. What he gained was avoidance of emergency or martial rule; the new course should be run by civilian politicians in the Supreme Soviet and in formal accordance with law and Constitution. And Gorbachev lived to fight another day.

## THE TURN TO THE RIGHT

When the Congress of People's Deputies met in December 1990 to pass the new institutions,[14] reactionary pressures on the President were strengthened by the replacement of the Presidential Council with a Council of Security, most of whose members were drawn *ex officio* from the national security sector.[15] In place of the old Council of Ministers there was now to be a Cabinet of Ministers formed by and directly subordinate to the President; its chairman was renamed Premier-minister.[16] The heads of the twenty Autonomous Republics were introduced into the Council of the Federation, more than doubling its size; many of these were conservative and their presence was resented by the larger Union-Republics.[17] Finally the Congress renewed part of the membership of the Supreme Soviet, and mainly with conservative deputies.

But not everything went according to plan. What was less in the interest of the 'Imperial Superstructure' was the increased power of the Council of the Federation. This became a decision-making rather than advisory body; it had to be consulted over nominations to the Cabinet and Council of Security, and with a two-thirds majority could bind the President to issue its decisions as decrees.[18] And the plan to create a State Inspectorate, the most significant of Gorbachev's concessions of 17 November, was defeated by the Congress. Both these decisions worked to the advantage of the autarkic republican leaderships that were competing with the military for a hold on Central power.[19] It was quite incorrect to portray this Congress as strengthening the President's powers;[20] it revealed instead something close to stalemate.

The plan had been to put a newly-created Vice-President in charge of the Inspectorate. When the latter was rejected Gorbachev seems to have given up the idea of nominating a prominent non-Russian – Shevardnadze or Nazarbaev, perhaps – as Vice-President. Instead he chose or accepted a colourless bureaucrat from the (official) trade-union movement, G. I. Yanaev, as his deputy and the man who would become Acting-President in an emergency.[21] This mistake was to have serious consequences.

In policy terms the 'turn to the right' meant the shelving of economic reform and the reimposition of controls on the state-owned media, particularly television. More important, it raised the profile and influence of army and KGB in politics. These interests refused to contemplate the independence of any of the republics or inroads into the powers of the Central government.[22] A scheme was begun of joint patrolling of urban areas by police and army personnel – in apparent contradiction of recent legislation that restricted the civilian use of the army to declared states of emergency.[23] Most mysterious, but perhaps central to the August coup, was the development of combined military, KGB and police structures for internal security purposes; their chains of command are unclear, but it is possible that Army General V. I. Varennikov was a key figure in them.[24]

This new course was particularly marked in personnel terms. Television programmes became noticeably more subservient to the regime after the appointment of a new chairman of the State Committee on Radio and Television, L. P. Kravchenko.[25] The popular and liberal Bakatin was dismissed from the Ministry of Internal

Affairs, and replaced by B. K. Pugo, a former KGB chief in Latvia; as Pugo's first deputy, the commander in Afghanistan during the withdrawal, General B. V. Gromov, was appointed.[26] The new Premier, V. S. Pavlov, was a disastrous choice: touted as an economist, he was really a financier, and he thought he could take the non-economist President for granted.[27] In disgust at what was happening the Foreign Minister, E. A. Shevardnadze, resigned at the end of December, warning that unknown hands were preparing dictatorship;[28] this was followed by the withdrawal from Gorbachev's advisers of other experienced liberals such as A. N. Yakovlev and S. S. Shatalin.

Yanaev was placed in charge of ministerial nominations[29] and may have had Pavlov's name put forward. He may also have had links with the KGB,[30] and the KGB influence on government was further reinforced by Pugo at Internal Affairs. Appointments like these may well have been part of a coordinated plan to isolate the President, suborn policy-making and prepare the ground for a more overt power seizure if necessary. They may already have been working through the head of Gorbachev's Secretariat, V. I. Boldin; Boldin was later said to have exercised systematic control over all the information and persons that reached the President – to have tried, in fact, to construct a counter-reality around him.[31]

## VILNIUS

Affairs in the Baltic Military District (headquarters Riga) had been especially important in alienating the officer corps and prompting the November intervention. At the heart of their anger was, of course, secession, which all three Baltic republics were pursuing with deliberation, and its implication of an army withdrawal or of its dismemberment. But officers were able to point to grievances with more direct bearing on army work.

First were actions of the new freely elected governments that seemed to discriminate against those not of Baltic nationality. The Lithuanian Law *On Political Parties* outlawed the political parties of 'other states' and allowed only registered voters to be active in parties.[32] This put communists at a disadvantage (which they could overcome by severing their ties with the CPSU) and hampered political activity among immigrants, most of whom were army officers and hence mainly Russian communists. A Latvian ordinance suspended the right of officers to get an automatic residence permit (*propiska*) when they were posted to Latvia, which made it difficult for them to get housing and sometimes impeded access to education, child and medical care; Colonel Alksnis (himself a Latvian) complained that he was charged 1500 roubles for his children's education.[33] The target of such policies seems to have been not so much local Russians – many of whom had come to support independence[34] – as immigrants and the Soviet Army.

Second was the campaign of public hostility to and interference with army personnel and installations in the Baltic. On 18 November several local residents were injured when soldiers broke up a demonstration outside a base in Vilnius, and Marshal Yazov followed this up with instructions to the commanders of military districts authorising the use of firearms if soldiers were attacked, the take-over of public utilities if it was necessary to safeguard normal work, and the protection of Soviet monuments and graves.[35] The last clause in particular seemed to give an excuse for the emergence of vigilantes. On 7 January paratroopers (why paratroopers?) were ordered into the Baltic, Transcaucasia, Moldavia and West Ukraine to enforce conscription.[36]

The officer corps seems to have had a particular preoccupation with the Baltic and to have persuaded Gorbachev to share it. Why the Baltic, rather than Georgia, Azerbaidzhan or Moldavia? Georgia (to take that example) was also bent on independence. In December the Gamsakhurdia administration there abolished the South Ossetian Autonomous *Oblast'* whose inhabitants mainly supported Union; and many more lives were lost in the ensuing fighting than in Vilnius and Riga.[37] There was talk of restricting Georgian citizenship to those who could prove that their ancestors had lived there in 1921 – or even in 1801![38] The declaration of a state of emergency or Presidential rule in South Ossetia would have been legally justified and locally welcomed. In Georgia, to be sure (where the blood feud lasted into our own times), guerillas would have made a fight of it. One has to surmise that in officers' perceptions the Balts, with their reasonable and orderly pursuit of independence, constituted a greater threat to military interests, whilst offering readier targets for intimidation.

With such purposes the army had gone beyond the strictly military or strategic and was involved in civilian politics. November 1990 was a signal to officers in the Baltic to pursue their purposes more openly. It created a climate in which they would have found it easy to embellish instructions in transmitting them and in which hotheads and opportunists were encouraged to try what they could get away with. On 10 January Gorbachev warned the Lithuanian Supreme Soviet that he was considering the introduction of Presidential rule.[39] It would have been preferable if he had imposed it. His message included the charge that Lithuania was aiming at the 'restoration of the bourgeois order'. It was an unpardonable thing to say. The word 'bourgeois' has no legal meaning (and in historical terms was not Gorbachev himself a 'bourgeois' restorationist?); in political terms it suggested his abandonment of pluralism and constitutionality, and was surely read as an invitation by the army.

Early on 13 January the commander of the Vilnius garrison, Major General Uskhopchik, responded to an appeal by a 'Committee of National Salvation' and sent troops to take over the Vilnius television centre; at least fourteen people were killed and scores wounded.[40] It is possible that Uskhopchik consulted the deputy commander of the Military District in Riga before moving.[41] The Salvation Committee's aim of assuming power in Lithuania had been aired by Moscow Central Television shortly before the operation began; its membership was never revealed, but spokesmen for it were officials of the (pro-CPSU) Lithuanian Communist Party. Questioned in the Supreme Soviet on the 14th neither the Defence Minister, Marshal Yazov, nor the Minister of Internal Affairs, B. K. Pugo, seemed to see anything untoward about such an initiative or the committee's access to the army.[42] Only after several days and perhaps in response to the massive outcry did Moscow television allow the Committee of National Salvation to fade away, along with talk of a change of government in Lithuania. A few things seem clear. It was an attempt to use force against an elected government, and to establish the precedent that some political organisations but not others had access to armed force. It was thus an attempt to reverse the CPSU disestablishment of March 1990. And the attempt was known in advance to some in Moscow, and came as no surprise to Yazov and Pugo.

At the same time there would seem to have been little coordinated strategy behind it.[43] Both in Vilnius and a week later in Riga, objectives were chosen without foresight and tactics were incoherent and hesitant. Other players were acting independently of the army. The first death (and the only death on the army side in Vilnius) seems to have been that of a KGB officer not connected with Uskhopchik's troops (and who singled **him** out for a target?). In Riga a shooting apparently from the Latvian side turned out to have been stage-managed by friends of the KGB – and Colonel Alksnis was in the car concerned![44]

Gorbachev and Yazov were of course blamed, either for sanctioning unconstitutional orders, or for presiding over an army in which such insubordination could go unchecked.[45] This is to my mind somewhat formalistic and overlooks both the scale and complexity of the army and its rising political involvement over previous months. A process whereby orders acquired increasing permissiveness and 'deniability' as they were transmitted downwards seems a more plausible reconstruction. There is unlikely to have been a direct or coordinated plot to reimpose pro-Soviet governments in the Baltic; rather a climate of fear and confusion was encouraged, in which, it may have been hoped, supporters of non-communist governments would be cowed (or provoked), opposition to them strengthened, and freebooters could seize their chance. Gorbachev would seem to have been consenting to this process – and among the freebooters were figures who reappeared in the August coup.

And Gorbachev's behaviour in the Supreme Soviet was lamentable.[46] He spoke of the tragedy of 'social polarisation' leading to violence: an evasion, as far as one can tell, and one all too reminiscent of official excuses for the invasion of Czechoslovakia. He failed completely to identify this as a constitutional crisis or to discipline those formally or in fact responsible. He went so far as to suggest in parliament that the Law *On the Press* . . . be amended.[47] His performance dissipated virtually all his remaining support among radicals, who went over to Yeltsin, and many moderate conservatives also dissociated themselves from the action.[48] It was also, as this book has argued, completely out of character; he failed to defend his most important achievements and it suggested to society that those achievements were not to be counted on. A precarious constitutionality was undermined and Yeltsin was lent considerable new strength; the latter now began to call for Gorbachev's resignation and to speak of the need for a separate Russian army.[49] All this was an extravagant price to pay for holding the army at bay – and it did nothing to hold the Union together.

## NOVO-OGAREVO

Gorbachev was caught among three contesting forces: the military, Yeltsin's Russian administration, and the leaders of the increasingly self-willed non-Russian Union-Republics. Vilnius had compromised the armed forces and shown they had nothing serious to offer civilian politics; but during February and March Yeltsin seemed to overreach himself, and the results of the Union Treaty referendum showed that, while his policies were popular in Russia, so too was the Union whose government he was opposing. These shifts in the balance of forces enabled Gorbachev to escape from the pressure of the 'Imperial Superstructure'.

At his country house at Novo-Ogarevo, outside Moscow, Gorbachev signed on 23 April 1991 the so-called '9 + 1' Agreement with the leaders of the nine Union-Republics, including Yeltsin, still involved in Union Treaty negotiations. As published the Agreement committed its signatories – without the Autonomous Republics![50] – to cooperate over speedy conclusion of the Treaty; to let 'the Six' other Union-Republics[51] decide their relations with the Union for themselves; and to hold new elections for all Union positions six months after the Treaty was signed. Implicit in this was recognition by the Union administration of the sovereignty of the Union-Republics; and that the federation inaugurated by the Union Treaty should be a very weak one in which the Centre would retain only a minimum of power.[52] It was after this that the headline 'Will Gorbachev become Queen of England?' appeared.[53]

What Gorbachev gained from the Novo-Ogarevo Agreement was the support and cooperation of the republican leaders, and above all of Yeltsin, against the military; what he conceded was the strength of the Central government after federation, and of course his own position, since there was no assurance that he could win a popular election for the Presidency. The Agreement gave the Union of the Nine four months stable government, and (unlike previous arrangements for a coalition at the top) it showed signs of lasting. But it is clear in retrospect that the army and KGB found it unforgivable and that many of their leaders turned away from civilian politics at this point.

'A SORT OF TRAITORS'

After the coup of 19 August 1991 failed,[54] sixteen people were arrested by the Union authorities and one, B. K. Pugo, Minister of Internal Affairs, killed himself before arrest.[55] Of the sixteen G. I. Yanaev was Vice-President, V. S. Pavlov the Premier, A. I. Luk'yanov Speaker of the Supreme Soviet and V. I. Boldin head of the Presidential Secretariat. From the armed forces were the Minister of Defence, Marshal D. T. Yazov, the Deputy Minister responsible for emergencies, Colonel-General V. A. Achalov, and Army General V. I. Varennikov, Commander-in-Chief of Ground Forces. No less than five were from the KGB: its Chairman, V. A. Kryuchkov, two Deputy Chairmen, V. F. Grushko and G. E. Ageev, and the head of the Presidential security guard and his deputy, Yu. S. Plekhanov and V. V. Generalov. O. S. Shenin was a CPSU Politburo member and Central Committee Secretary. O. D. Baklanov was Deputy Chairman of the President's Defence Council and A. I. Tizyakov head of an association of state-owned heavy industrial enterprises; both of these were industrialists from the defence sector and Baklanov had spent his career in rocket production. Finally, V. A. Starodubtsev was Chairman of the 'Peasants' Union', in practice an association of collective farm managers. Of these, eight were to form the State Committee for the Emergency announced on 19 August: Baklanov, Kryuchkov, Pavlov, Pugo, Starodubtsev, Tizyakov, Yanaev and Yazov. Five of them were on the USSR Security Council,[56] and four on the President's Defence Council.[57] Three had signed the reactionary manifesto *A Word to the People* in late July, a call to action addressed, *inter alios*, to the army.[58]

Four things are striking about this list. First is the number of figures it contains from the very apex of politics: the administration's malaise had gone deep. These were people who met regularly in the course of their work, something which made joint planning easier. Second, Gorbachev had appointed or recommended eight of them, four since November 1990 and four earlier; his association with Luk'yanov went back to the 1950s and with Boldin to 1981. He had been very trusting – and the conservatives of the previous winter had done their work well. Eleven or twelve of the seventeen can be identified with military, security or defence industry interests.[59] This was a different conservatism to that of the *Soyuz* group; if they had ever set up a government it is likely that it would have favoured state-run industry and had less time than Colonel Alksnis for the market. Finally only one of them was a CPSU official. The Party Secretariat met on the morning of the coup and distributed instructions to communists to support it, and someone must have convened and prepared documents for this meeting during the night of 18–19 August.[60] At the time of writing, nevertheless, the only clear evidence of official CPSU involvement in planning the coup concerns Shenin: he was present at the meeting on Saturday 17 August at which it was decided to send a delegation to Gorbachev, and he was part of this delegation.[61]

The conspirators were mostly well known to each other and they seem to have begun during the previous winter, if not before, to prepare the ground for an eventuality like the coup. But it seems that they were a loose network of like-minded malcontents, rather than an organisation with definite membership, and the specific operation of 19 August did not apparently begin to be planned until three weeks before it was launched. In Yazov's words:[62]

> We had met earlier too in various places, we often talked about it, and most often comrades Kryuchkov, Baklanov and Boldin were there . . . Involuntarily we came to the conclusion that the blame should fall on the President . . . On 20 August the Union Treaty was to be signed. For me personally and for many other comrades with whom I talked, **it suddenly became clear** that the collapse of the Union was bearing inexorably down on us.

What probably concentrated Yazov's mind was Gorbachev's announcement on 2 August, after the Union Treaty negotiations had been deadlocked for some time, that the ceremonial signing of the Treaty would take place on the 20th.[63]

Yet we need to be cautious with the conspirators' later testimony: it was in their interests to portray the operation as amateurish and improvised, and to minimise the degree of planning. Severing the President's communications with the outside world was not a task that could be undertaken without some days preparation by KGB officers.[64] The proclamations of the 'State Committee for the Emergency' were doubtless finalised in the night of 18-19 August, but they must have been drafted beforehand, and that required office facilities, which it is possible were provided by Boldin.[65] In both cases the conspirators would have had to make sure of their subordinates before bringing them into the preparations. There was to be considerable speculation later about the real ringleaders of the plot:[66] it is logical to look for these in particular among the ones who took practical steps to prepare the ground.

The picture becomes somewhat clearer on Saturday 17 August when a group met at Kryuchkov's initiative in military premises in south-west Moscow. Gorbachev was on holiday in the Crimea and it was decided to send a delegation to him next day consisting of Baklanov, Boldin, Plekhanov, Shenin and Varennikov. Plekhanov was to have Gorbachev's personal guard changed with a view to controlling his activities and the delegation was to present him with an ultimatum: either declare a state of emergency while remaining in the Crimea, or hand over his powers to the Vice-President, Yanaev.[67] They were confident that he would fall in with their wishes. The group were already calling themselves the 'committee' (for the state of emergency *vel sim.*).[68]

Parts of the KGB (but not the armed forces) were put on a state of alert at 10 a.m. on Sunday 18 August[69] and the delegates arrived at the President's Crimean villa about 5 p.m.; his external communications were cut before they went in to meet him. The intention to intimidate rather than negotiate is clear; but it alerted Gorbachev and gave him some time to prepare for trouble. He refused the committee's demands and was left incommunicado and under house arrest when the delegation returned to Moscow; in Yazov's words, their 'first plan had collapsed'. Why were the conspirators so confident, and where did they go wrong? From their point of view (and not only theirs) Gorbachev's devotion to compromise looked like capitulation to whichever pressure was the strongest. But when one looks closely at his compromises – even that of November 1990 – they were always such as to keep intact his self-image as an orchestrator or initiator. In this case – quite apart from the matter of the Union Treaty of which he was clearly proud – to cut his telephones before presenting him with a meaningless choice may have been an error of judgement on the part of the conspirators; for Gorbachev any 'compromise' on his part would forfeit a future role for himself and place him in dependence on the cabal. We saw in Chapter 4 that he is sensitive on such matters.

About 9 p.m. the delegates reported back (Boldin as their spokesman) to the main body of conspirators meeting in Pavlov's office in the Kremlin, and the mechanics of the coup were settled between then and midnight.[70] That it **was** launched early on Monday 19 August confirms that most of the tactical preparations had already been completed – but it suggests also that decisions of strategic significance may have been taken in haste.

The conspirators now had two immediate purposes. They had to ensure a speedy transfer of state power to themselves, if possible without trouble or challenge. And they had to assume emergency powers – to halt the Union Treaty ceremonies, release food into the shops and restore 'discipline' to the economy and the media. The decision was taken or finalised: the coup should look as constitutional as possible. Gorbachev was to be pronounced ill, and the Vice-President was to take over, as provided for in the Constitution; it will be remembered (p. 122) that no procedure had been established for determining a President's incapacity. The Acting-President was to declare a partial state of emergency; again this was within the law, provided that the Supreme Soviet confirmed it within a short (but unspecified) time. Under emergency powers the media were to be muzzled, the Treaty postponed, retail supplies brought into Moscow – and also troops, but not many, apparently to act as a warning to the population. The KGB and Army heads and the Premier were each to give the necessary orders in his own sector; there seems to have been no attempt to impose overall coordination.

Before dawn on Monday 19 August the Moscow television centre had been taken over by KGB units and at 6 a.m. the assumption of power by Yanaev, the latter's formation of a State Committee for the Emergency and his declaration of a partial state of emergency began to be broadcast.[71] Public meetings, demonstrations and strikes were forbidden, as were the activities of political parties 'that hinder the normalisation of the situation'. Censors re-entered media offices and the publication of all but nine trusted Central newspapers was suspended. Columns of tanks began to move towards the city centre (in rush hour). Luk'yanov convened the Supreme Soviet for 26 August and made a formal announcement that the Union Treaty was unacceptable in its current form and a 'danger to the legal system'. In the afternoon Yanaev and four other members of the State Committee gave a press conference for Soviet and foreign journalists, and Pavlov, the Premier, got the support of his Cabinet of Ministers for the state of emergency.[72] More mysteriously, General Varennikov turned up in Kiev where he tried to intimidate L. M. Kravchuk, the Speaker of the Ukrainian Supreme Soviet.[73]

Implicit in the constitutionalist approach were two major strategic choices. So long as this was no more than a legal transfer of power within the Union administration it did not touch Yeltsin's quite distinct government of the RSFSR, located in the 'Russian White House' a mile or two from the Kremlin. Whether the conspirators had plans for the arrest of Yeltsin or storming of the White House is disputed; but if they had, it would seem they did not form part of the immediate measures that unfolded on the morning of the 19th.[74] Second, it could be no part of a constitutional succession to sever internal and external communications, as the martial law regime had done in Poland in December 1981. This had fatal consequences for the coup. The orders not only of the State Committee and the CPSU but also of Yeltsin's government continued to be transmitted to the provinces; foreign and Soviet reporters continued to file stories with the outside world; the foreign minister of Russia, A. V. Kozyrev, boarded a plane for Paris to tell the world, and if necessary to found a government in exile;[75] and Radio Liberty could record programmes inside the Russian White House for broadcasting to the entire USSR, including its President!

The attempt to give the coup a veneer of constitutionality could have worked – so long as it **looked** normal and above board. But suspicion was aroused by several things. The show of troops in the streets and the criticism of *perestroika* in the Committee's proclamations seemed to point to something more than an incapacitated President.[76] Deaths of VIPs had usually been accompanied (even under Stalin) by publication of a death certificate with the names of signatory doctors; this was not a death, but people may well have asked themselves why such documentation was absent in Gorbachev's case. Suspicions were enhanced by the press conference: the new leaders seemed nervous and shifty and were not word-perfect in their story.

## THE COUP CONFOUNDED

Yeltsin's reaction was immediate and famous. At 11 a.m. on 19 August he pronounced the coup illegal and its orders invalid in Russia and at 1.00 p.m. he addressed a crowd from an armoured personnel carrier outside the White House, calling for a general strike. But he was not alone. At 11.30 a.m. five members of the Committee of Constitutional Supervision held that the coup raised serious legal questions – in particular that the Law *On . . . a State of Emergency* did not foresee any new institution taking power throughout the country.[77] The Patriarch of the Russian Orthodox Church, Aleksii II, spoke for millions when he asked that Gorbachev's own voice be heard.[78] *Izvestiya* did not publish on the 19th but published two editions on the 20th, one reproducing the Committee's news and the other in clear support of Yeltsin. Some banned newspapers appeared only in facsimile or xerox, whilst others clubbed together to publish a *Common Newspaper* outside the capital; Moldavia and Estonia were eager to print for the Central media.[79] Independent radio stations in Moscow and Leningrad were taken off the air but never for long and television readers subverted the intention of their material.[80] In Leningrad the local KGB informed the mayor, A. A. Sobchak, that they repudiated the coup, and Sobchak negotiated with the local military commander to keep troops out of the city.[81]

Outside Moscow and Leningrad responses were more confused. In the republics the governments of the Baltic, Moldavia and Kirghizia opposed the coup from the first, and they were soon joined by the Kazakhstani President, Nazarbaev. Others equivocated and in one, Azerbaidzhan, the leadership seems to have welcomed it.[82] It was a similar story in the Russian provinces: many Party organisations and some Autonomous Republics supported the Committee, whilst some cities and a few *oblast'* administrations declared for Yeltsin; but most played for time.[83] As often in Russian history this was a struggle that was to be lost or won in the capitals.

During the days of 19 and 20 August the attention of both army and people was focused increasingly on the Russian White House; this was now surrounded by barricades and tens of thousands of supporters, but they in turn were ringed with tanks. Well known figures – Shevardnadze, A. N. Yakovlev, Elena Bonner, Primakov, Yevtushenko – had joined the defenders. Late on the 19th some tank crews with their vehicles went over too, and there were persistent rumours of other officers refusing to follow orders. Women taunted the besieging troops – or fed the bewildered conscripts. The crisis came on the night of the 20th: a curfew was imposed and not obeyed, and the defenders waited for the attack that never came; civilians with Molotov cocktails took on tanks in a nearby underpass and it was here that three people – the only casualties – were killed. At 8 a.m. on 21 August a meeting of the collegium (senior staff) of the Ministry of Defence resolved to withdraw troops from Moscow – almost certainly under massive pressure from officers.[84] The Committee then had no option but to flee.

The August coup collapsed for three reasons. First were human virtues: the bravery of Yeltsin and his colleagues, the ingenuity of journalists, the conscience of officers and the resolution of hundreds of thousands of ordinary residents of the capital.[85] But in similar situations in the past people had failed to stand up, or they had tried and been butchered. Second, pluralist institutions were the condition of this new bravery: the most frightened servant of the Russian government could remember that he was technically beyond the Committee's jurisdiction; journalists knew something about the practicalities of impromptu publishing and broadcasting; there was no network of Party cells to coordinate and inform. Third were the mistaken assumptions of the conspirators: apart from minor trouble in the capitals they had expected that the people would be passive and unconcerned about legalities.[86] That they should rally to defend an elected parliament, independent newspapers or an unpopular but legal President took them by surprise. The plotters had absorbed nothing from the past six years – or the past twenty-six; their mental world was that of the dismissal of Khrushchev. The coup wrecked the very institutions and ideals whose purpose it had been to preserve. The Party was suspended and later banned (see p. 149). The Cabinet was dismissed and never replaced. The popular Bakatin became head of the KGB, with a brief to dismantle it, hiving off its components such as foreign and domestic intelligence, frontier protection and government communications to separate institutions.[87] The Union-Republics had seen through the fragility of Central power; the Baltic states seized their independence immediately and for the others the Union Treaty had been damaged beyond repair.[88]

It also spelled the end to Gorbachev's career. He returned from the Crimea declaring himself still a supporter of the 'socialist idea' and of Party reform. Despite the shock caused by Boldin, Luk'yanov, Shenin *et al.* he was reluctant to believe how many others had betrayed him. It was testimony to his principles but those who had stayed loyal were appalled; more than anything else his attempt to take up politics as if nothing had changed convinced friends and foes that he had had his day. The realities were otherwise: 'Gorbachev had returned to a different country; but did he understand it?'.[89] The people wanted simply to be rid of Party, KGB and the very names of socialism and communism; the republics did not want to share the same government; and Yeltsin meant to exploit the advantage that he had won, and won deservedly.

# 11  The Union Treaty

'Enough! We're fed up. We want to be Europeans. We're tired of models and incantations in the name of all the "isms".'
(V. K. Emel'yanov, editor, *Soviet Lithuania*, January 1990)[1]

## THE PLAN FOR A RENEWED UNION

The Soviet Union was one of the last of the world's land-based empires. We have seen how the communists adopted the tradition of Russian imperialism virtually unchanged, how this compounded the problems that ethnic diversity would in any case have caused, and how the 'federalism' of the 1936 and 1977 Constitutions was a sham. Reforms like those of 1986–9 could not but have a significant ethnic dimension, and the ethnic revival led inevitably to demands for a new apportionment of power among the nations that made up the Union. But we have also seen that the mainly Russian CPSU leadership, Gorbachev included, lacked experience of, and insight into ethnic problems;[2] they were ill prepared for the ethnic revival and political issues like federalism took them into uncharted territory. Their response was grudging and confused, as the Central Committee Plenum of September 1989 revealed,[3] and this fuelled non-Russian impatience, arousing the suspicion that Russian reformers were at heart unreconstructed centralists. But the charge that Gorbachev could have saved the Union if he had moved earlier than he did towards federalism seems unfair: neither federalism nor any authentic local politics could have co-existed with the centralised CPSU monopoly; here as elsewhere Party disestablishment was the precondition for progress.

The Party's *Nationalities Policy* . . . of September 1989 had raised, only to reject without argument, the idea of renewing the almost forgotten Union Treaty of 1922. This had associated four Union-Republics – the RSFSR (at that time including Kazakhstan and Central Asia), Ukraine, Belorussia and Transcaucasia (comprising Georgia, Azerbaidzhan and Armenia) – but it had not been a genuinely federal treaty, its provisions had been flouted under Stalin and the Baltic states and Moldavia had never acceded to it.[4] When

Gorbachev became President in March 1990 he seized upon the idea of rewriting the Union Treaty.[5]

He may have hoped at first that the new Union Treaty could be based on the April 1990 Law *On the Delimitation* . . . ,[6] but the Supreme Soviet insisted that it be negotiated with its potential signatories. In June the Council of the Federation commissioned the drafting of a working document, and representatives of the Supreme Soviets of the republics were summoned to consultations about this during August. These Supreme Soviets began to debate an agreed text in November, after which negotiations began again and the project was approved in principle at a general referendum.[7] Four drafts of the Treaty were published, in November 1990 and March, June and August 1991,[8] and its changing provisions reveal a shift in the balance of power towards the republics; it was the fourth version that was to have been signed on 20 August.

The Union Treaty negotiations were the first attempt to work out some kind of voluntary political association among the peoples of the centralised Russian-dominated Union. They were kept confidential in the main but were plainly troubled.[9] Two of their features should be singled out here. First, the President's Union administration was a party to the negotiations and played an organising and supervising role throughout. His opponents in the republics were able to present this as evidence of the 'Centre's' bad faith; they proposed that a distinct 'New Centre' should be allowed to evolve on the basis of bilateral agreements among the republics, a process from which the discredited 'Old Centre' should be excluded.[10] The Union's reply was a reasonable one: conclusion of the Treaty would mean no break in continuity for the state, and the existing Union – with its armed forces, nuclear weapons and international obligations – was an interested party that would and could not simply be wished away; there was thus no analogy with, say, the situation of the United States' Founding Fathers in 1777.

Second, those who negotiated for the republics were generally from a bureaucratic or professional background and many seem to have been sympathetic to Gorbachev's aims. But few of them had had experience of this kind of negotiation – simply to verbalise the interests of their nation or republic had been punishable a few years earlier! – and many knew that their own political position was insecure.[11] They were thus very sensitive to the mood of their mass supporters, typically the non-Russian 'titular' majority in their republic. But in assessing this mood we should recall how the Soviet experience had promoted the emotional and symbolic side of politics; the implications of 'federalism', for instance, or even of 'economies of scale' seem to have been little understood. As negotiations proceeded the participants seemed less and less to be writing a new constitution and increasingly to be concerned with short-term deals between the Union administration and republican elites.[12]


## ASPIRATIONS AND OPTIONS

Before examining the contents of the Union Treaty let us survey the interests and options of the principal groups concerned and assess the possible shapes a voluntary Union could have taken.

Clearest perhaps was the conservative position of the 'Imperial Superstructure'. At stake for it was loss of power, status and in many cases livelihood; though not directly represented at the negotiations, its implicit threat of military intervention if its interests were unduly harmed cast a shadow over the politics of 1990–1. It could argue cogently that a 'domino effect' would result from even a single secession, one that would strip the state of the territorial gains of four centuries and leave it as exposed to foreign intervention as in the Time of Troubles. This was a case that appealed to Russians living outside the RSFSR and to some other ethnic minorities.[13] The 'Imperial Superstructure', while preferring the existing unitary state, was prepared to stomach some devolution of power provided that a strong central administration was retained.

The President's Union administration was presented by its opponents as indistinguishable from the 'Imperial Superstructure' and this came close to the truth between November 1990 and April 1991. But its platform of 'a strong Centre and strong republics'[14] was distinct and more flexible. The old unitarism was finished and must be replaced by a distribution of powers between Union and republics. Gorbachev's administration was under pressure to decentralise power, but he also thought it would make for a polity more stable and legitimate than its predecessor. He was equally determined that the apportionment be thought out carefully and that certain state powers – above all over the armed forces and the nuclear arsenal – stay under central control, both because this was the most efficient and orderly arrangement and because the Union had to reckon with pressure from international opinion and its own employees.

Most important among the Union-Republican negotiators was the RSFSR. Its dominant share in the Union's population and resources (see p. 157) meant that Russian interests and personnel must loom large in any new Union, and Yeltsin's conduct of negotiations seems to have been correspondingly tough. The prevalent mood in Russia in 1990–1 was anti-Central: people had easily thrown off the notion of Russia's 'special relationship' with the Centre and attempts like the formation of the Communist Party of the RSFSR did not succeed in restoring it.

But beyond that Russian attitudes to the rest of the Empire were complex. For some, anti-Centralism entailed anti-imperialism: Yeltsin's government recognised the Declarations of Sovereignty of other Union-Republics and signed treaties with them, earning considerable goodwill from non-Russians thereby. But Russians are a people with an imperial tradition and the RSFSR itself was an ethnically diverse federation; there were still millions of Russians who took it for granted that they had earned political leadership and its perquisites through great sacrifice; for some the downfall of the Centre might allow Russia to resume the imperial mission that had been interrupted in 1917.[15] There was support for Solzhenitsyn's idea of a Slavic Union of Russians, Ukrainians and Belorussians that would abandon the rest of the Empire.[16] There was also considerable concern about Russian minorities outside Russia proper: 25 million Russians – almost a fifth – lived in other republics, and no government of Russia could afford to neglect their security and rights.

Almost any of these motives might be blended with isolationism. Russia was the main exporter of raw materials and resented a pricing system that seemed to exploit it and subsidise other republics (see p. 158). It was calculated that, if inter-republican trade were expressed in world prices, the RSFSR stood to gain 45 billion roubles per annum, the equivalent of a third of its budget. V. I. Vorotnikov, Chairman of the Presidium of the RSFSR Supreme Soviet before May 1990, was not slow to point out to manufacturing republics that the price of association might be high.[17] Such considerations gained a new importance once western republics, in particular the Ukraine, showed doubts about the Treaty; few Russians could see purpose or prospects in a state that linked them only with Muslim Central Asia.

This points up Russia's bargaining position. There was no question that Russia, meaning the RSFSR approximately in its current boundaries, could manage as a state without the fourteen other Union-Republics. It had ample resources and manpower, an all-round industrial base, adequate agriculture, a society used to cohesion and obedience, and a developed tradition of statehood. Provided it could solve the problem of the army and come to terms with the loss of empire (and it would help if it were seen to have no responsibility for this) it could take the Union Treaty or leave it. At the negotiations it could exercise what amounted to a veto and within a new Union it could dictate its terms. Yeltsin fought hard and successfully to reduce the powers of the Centre to a minimum – presumably he discerned where this would leave Russia.

When we turn to the non-Russian nations and republics it is still more difficult to generalise. For most of them there were good reasons why some kind of political relationship with Russia should be maintained. First economic: the advantages of a common market; the economies of scale arising from common research, development and investment; and the difficulties in breaking up current commercial patterns, quite apart from those of converting them to the market. The Baltic was the region of highest productivity in the Soviet Union, yet it was doubtful whether its manufactures could succeed on world markets and especially in the European Community; if they did not, the Baltic was dependent on Russia for fuel and raw materials. Balts faced the choice between a common market with the neighbour which had annexed them in 1940 – or an independence under which they might be little better than suppliers of guest workers to Germany. Central Asians, for all their opposition to the cotton monoculture, had to consider how they could break out of it without close association with a developed economy.

The advantages in common defence, especially given the cost of effective conventional defence in the late twentieth century, formed a second argument. It was an unfashionable one in the western republics (before the Yugoslav Civil War) but real enough on the southern frontier. Armenians had kept fresh their memories of attempted genocide at the hands of the Turks during the First World War, and the Georgian capital had been sacked by the Persians as recently as 1795. Independent states of Georgia and Armenia would be Christian enclaves in the Middle East, nearly as offensive as is Israel to its neighbours, and (outside a defence alliance) more vulnerable. The republics of Central Asia, even together with Kazakhstan, were smaller and weaker than their southern neighbour Iran. Iraq's annexation of Kuwait must have brought home what could happen to such states and hence the advantages of a defence pact with the North.

And a final argument sprang from the sheer size of Russia and the number and distribution of Russians: since the facts of geography could not be undone and Russia would always be the powerful neighbour, might it not be preferable to deal with her, not as an independent foreign country, but as an associate bound by some common political rules?

But set against these arguments the flood tide of autonomist sentiment, released among people who had been excluded for seventy years from control over their own affairs, cultural, economic, political, spiritual. It was a simple insistence on doing things for oneself whether they were done well or ill, on making one's own mistakes, and arguments about economies of scale, international obligations, even historical experience made little impact. Indeed everyday experience confirmed the lesson of communal self-defence: whether over shopping, conscription or dealing with the bureaucracy, the police or the Party, it was every man – every household, factory, village, region, republic – for itself! Non-Russians shared with Russians their hatred of the Centre and anything that smacked of centralisation, and it was an alliance of Russian anti-Centralists with the elites of the other republics that formed one of the political coalitions of 1990–1 (see p. 163). But even here motives were mixed. For many non-Russians the new autarky went beyond hostility to the Centre and to communism and included an element of settling scores with the Russians – for their record in ruling others, and not merely during the past seventy years.

We know that opinion was divided in many republics.[18] The view that prevailed was determined in the end less by the above considerations than by questions of size and resources, experience or traditions of distinct statehood, and relations with near neighbours in conditions of a near-paralysed Union government: in general by a republic's **need** for a Union or its ability to go it alone. Estonia, Latvia and Lithuania had been independent states between the wars; Georgia and Armenia had had a few years of independence after 1917 and much longer traditions of a separate church, script and culture. For Moldavians, whose language is Romanian, the small size of their republic did not matter; they could always rejoin Romania.[19] Above all the Ukraine, with a population of 52 million and a reasonable balance of agricultural, raw material and manufacturing resources would have little difficulty becoming a viable independent state – or even the nucleus of a non-Russian alliance.[20]

For some smaller nationalities, on the other hand, the relaxation of central control had exposed them to the petty imperialism of their near neighbours. This was the case with the Ossetes and Abkhaz of Georgia and the Gagauz of Moldavia: hardly in a position to form their own states, they preferred to be governed from distant Moscow and adopted a Unionist position, as did some of the Autonomous Republics within Russia. The Union-Republics of Central Asia needed the support of developed economies but did not intend to become clients of Iran.[21] The shrewd leader of Kazakhstan, N. A. Nazarbaev, knew that he must carry the support of both Kazakhs and Russians, respectively 40 and 38 per cent of Kazakhstan's population. There were thus two broad attitudes towards the Treaty among its potential signatories. Kazakhstan, Central Asia, most Autonomous Republics and many local minorities, Russian and non-Russian, preferred a renewed Union along the lines advocated by Gorbachev; Belorussia seems to have inclined to this position too. The Ukraine, Moldavia, the Baltic and Transcaucasian republics, and – for quite different reasons – Russia, did not mind if there was no Union and they pressed for the weakest Union they could get.[22]

## THE SHAPE OF NEGOTIATIONS

In terms of formal structure the Soviet Union could have moved in one of four directions. It could have broken up or gone into voluntary liquidation (as urged by Solzhenitsyn and the Estonian communist J. Allik), to be replaced by independent states among which new alignments might emerge. There could have been a return to the old Russian-dominated unitary structure. It could, third, have become a loose association of independent states, for which arrangement it is useful to reserve the term 'confederation'. Or finally it could have developed a truly federal system. The Union Treaty negotiations excluded the first two options by definition (which does not mean they lacked support) and they turned into a prolonged struggle over federalism and confederalism.

A federal system is one in which communities are 'united under a single independent general government for some purposes and . . . organised under independent regional governments for others'.[23] Its defining characteristic is thus the coordinate existence of two types of government, general and regional, each having powers independent of the other and neither being subordinate to the other. Central to a federal constitution is the distribution of powers between general and regional authorities and its provisions for settlement of disputes about this demarcation. In a confederation by contrast states agree to cooperate over matters of their own choosing, but without setting up an independent state or institutions for the fulfilment of joint tasks. Examples are the European Community or the United Nations Organisation, the joint institutions of which function at the will (and purse strings) of the association's members.

A move to federalism would have preserved an independent Union government and would in general have involved a minimum of disruption to existing 'pseudo-federal' institutions. But confederation also had a good deal to offer the nations of the Soviet Union. Here was a group of communities apparently condemned by geography and history into dealings of some sort, yet many of them reluctant to cooperate with each other. This would seem to suggest an association of the loosest and least demanding kind, and cooperation over no more than the necessary minimum. Its obligations could be confined to needs acknowledged by all parties, reflecting that degree of cooperation that members could realistically undertake at present. Such caution might serve to retain republics that would otherwise secede, but it would not preclude closer ties in the future.

Gorbachev always favoured federalism, but when he first broached the Union Treaty he painted a flexible picture which need not have excluded confederal elements – perhaps a two-tiered association in which, say, the Baltic and Transcaucasia could have been confederal allies of an inner federal polity.[24] In the course of 1990 however these ideas were dropped from the Union's negotiating position and the texts of the Treaty envisaged common federal arrangements for all signatories. We can assume that conservative and military pressures were important in this hardening of the Union's stance, but it would seem also that its thinking evolved, perhaps in reaction to what was met in the negotiations.

At the heart of confederalism is the subordination of general (confederal) institutions to regional ones. A confederation can achieve only so much as its members agree to implement jointly, and this may mean that, *qua* confederation, it does not achieve very much; indeed, a desire for weak government is one of the reasons for preferring confederalism to federalism. Many confederations have been set up, not so much for the purpose of joint government, but for some narrower purpose, such as defence or free trade, that can be kept distinct from the general tasks of government. Confederalism may thus associate regions with very different social or economic orders. It is features such as these that have tended to link confederalism with pre-industrial society. But since the Industrial Revolution more and more products and operations have come to depend on large-scale organisation and economy, and their increasing complexity and interdependence have imparted an organised character to new aspects of life. The range of tasks with which governments expect to be concerned has become wider and not only by their own design. Genuinely decentralised government, such as confederation, sits uneasily with the modern economy.

Let us illustrate this with an example that was surely influential in the Soviet case, that of state defence. In modern states this requires access to expensive and complex hardware, and also that soldiers be trained to use it; it is advantageous that such equipment be standard among units that will work together. A commander cannot afford contingents that do not turn up (as confederal levies have been known to do), nor contingents that are unfamiliar with, or have not maintained their weaponry. If such a commander could choose his political system, he might well favour one which allows standardised military training, or which has powers to promote manufacturing and research, or health and skills among recruits. He might look for general powers in the fields of currency and credit, of transport and science, of industrial standards and training. He would rather that such matters not be left to the varied and particularistic interests of communities. They are powers that typically rest with federal, but not with confederal authorities.

In his advocacy of federation Gorbachev repeatedly stressed the disadvantages of severing economic ties among different parts of the Union. Behind this lay the fear of a state that had lost its capacities for large scale organisation, one in which regional levels of prosperity and skill diverged and compliance with general policy declined. Such a polity would not be able to manage the complex, large-scale tasks – defence, nuclear and space science, ecological protection – without which the Union could not hope to be a world power. The outcome would be increasing polarisation of interests and finally divorce. He recognised an inherent instability in confederation,[25] and asked people (in terms reminiscent of the original communist case) to make up their minds whether they preferred sovereign autarky or the modern economy. For him the case for federalism was more than a matter of minimising change or pleasing his own constituency; federalism suited his preference for compromise, middle-of-the-road policies, and it appealed to the professional as the rational and efficient solution to a problem.

There's the rub. The definition of federalism quoted above begins with reference to communities that '**desire** to be united . . . '; federalism presupposes a greater harmony of interests and goals than does confederalism. But when we turn to the interested parties in this case what is striking is that the two strongest of them shared no common ground: the 'Imperial Superstructure' preferred a unitary state but would have settled for a strong federation; the RSFSR, supported by half the other Union-Republics, preferred to put an end to the Union but would have accepted a loose association of the confederal type. It was a dispute over the independent existence of a government at the centre,[26] and in the end it came down to a dispute over how the Union government should be financed. This was the issue hardest fought and the negotiators did not finally resolve it until three weeks before the Union Treaty was scheduled for signing, on 20 August.[27]

No government can be independent without an independent source of revenue. The Treaty's Paragraph 9 on 'Union Taxes and Dues' began: 'To finance the expenses of the Union budget . . . standard Union taxes and dues are established, **at rates determined by agreement with the republics . . .** '. Now this was the equivalent of states in the USA agreeing to federal income tax rates! And in the Soviet economic crisis it would have been next to impossible to gain the consent of all republics, and predictable that some would obstruct collection of revenue or its transfer to the federation. If the RSFSR objected, this would paralyse federal operations at one blow. This would not in fact have been federal government at all, because the general government would not have been assured of independence; it would have been confederal government, functioning at the pleasure of the republics.

It was Yeltsin, leader of the largest republic, who held out longest for this clause. For the 'Imperial Superstructure' this conjured up the nightmare of a Yeltsin, not merely running Russia, but in a position to cut off their own funds and reverse what they saw as the gains of four centuries of Russian history. This was why the plotters struck when they did, about thirty hours before the Union Treaty was due to be signed.

## THE UNION TREATY

Under the Union Treaty its signatory republics were to form a 'Union of Soviet Sovereign Republics' to succeed the 'Union of Soviet Socialist Republics'. (Both titles could be abbreviated to 'USSR' but there was no mention of 'socialism' in any text of the Treaty.) If the coup had not intervened, could this Treaty have met the needs of its signatories and formed the basis of a stable state? In judging this we should pay particular attention to the clarity of its distribution of powers, the provisions for resolution of disputes, and the possibility of disputes that might have been unforeseen or hard to resolve. We should also ask how much it addressed specific Soviet problems: fears, for instance, of discrimination against minorities, of an over-mighty Centre, or of undue Russian influence.[28]

## Distribution of Powers

The USSR was to be a 'federative democratic state': its signatory republics undertook to consign to the Union a list of powers which would make it an independent subject of international law. Once established it would have its own revenues and property, and the Treaty might not be altered except with the agreement of all the signatories. A Constitutional Court (an upgrading of the existing Committee of Constitutional Supervision) was to be set up to resolve contradictions between the 'normative acts' of Union and republics, and also to arbitrate disputes among republics or between republics and the Union.[29] In another feature characteristic of federalism, members of the Union subscribed to a number of common rules and purposes, including human rights as recognised in the Universal Declaration, representative democracy, national self-determination, the rule of law and a 'free choice of forms of property'.

The definition of the spheres of competence of the Union and the republics was of course central to the Treaty, and it was thorough and far from simple. The republics handed over to the Union powers of two types, 'exclusive' and 'joint'.

Reserved exclusively to the Union were: adoption and amendment of the Union Constitution;[30] declaration of war, conclusion of peace, the conduct of the Union's external defence and state security policies and leadership of its armed forces; conduct of the Union's foreign and external economic policies; confirmation and management of the Union budget, issuing of currency, and custody of the Union's gold, diamond and foreign currency reserves; 'organisation' of military research and production, leadership of space research and the management of air traffic and atomic energy; leadership of federal law-enforcement agencies and management of federal communications, cartographic, standards and meteorological systems.

The restrictive effect of words like 'Union', 'conduct' or 'management' is important here. 'Management of atomic energy', for instance, may have included the manufacture of nuclear weapons but it specifically excluded the mining and storage of fissile materials. Foreign and military **policy-making** were not exclusive rights of the Union (they had been in the November 1990 draft), and republics might conduct their own foreign relations, provided they did not damage the interests of other members or breach international obligations of the Union. They might also (by implication) raise their own armed forces for internal purposes; but they undertook to recognise the borders existing among themselves and not to combine or use force against the Union or other members. As the Treaty developed, a provision against republics allowing foreign troops on their soil was struck out, and one introduced prohibiting the use of the Union's armed forces for internal purposes except in cases of disaster or emergency.[31]

A longer list of powers was to be exercised 'jointly' by Union and republican organs. This included: determination of military, security and foreign policy; management of military enterprises; determination and conduct of financial, monetary, customs, credit and tax policy; determination and conduct of policy in respect of resources, the environment, energy, transport, communications and statistics; determination of the principles of social, labour, migration, education, health and welfare policy; promotion of science, technology and culture; and development of All-Union programmes for regional development and emergency relief. It was specified that there should be a single currency, credit and tax policy, customs and conscription system.

Such 'concurrent' powers, whereby both general and regional authorities may legislate in the same area, are common in federal systems, and they are usually linked to a provision for the supremacy of general law in the event of a clash. In the Soviet case Union legislation was to be supreme and could override that of the republics 'on questions within [the Union's] competence'. But the implications (for example) of international treaties can affect any area of domestic legislation and most federations have preferred an unqualified supremacy clause;[32] the Soviet provision may have been inserted to mollify republican opinion but it could have given rise to frequent complaints to the Constitutional Court. And what was to prevent the Union authorities from legislating in so detailed a fashion that republican rights were reduced to trivia? Something like this had happened under Stalin, and republican politicians were particularly suspicious of the concurrent powers.

Property 'necessary for the exercise of its powers' was to be assigned by member republics to the Union for use 'in their common interests'. This property would evidently have included military installations, but we are not told how it would have been determined nor whether it would have been liable to republican taxation.[33] The Union was to manage its own budget, raise Union taxes and receive other financial grants from the republics; but tax and grant rates were, as we have seen, subject to agreement with the republics.

This demarcation left the republics with considerably increased powers;[34] they gained exclusive control of such matters as citizenship, the organisation of local government, the courts, criminal and civil law, trade and the micro-economy. Republics might now raise their own taxes and they became the owners of all land and natural resources on their territory (except for that allocated to the Union). An earlier grant of all property on their territory was mysteriously dropped – leaving legal problems in relation to enterprises of All-Union subordination, often the most prosperous. Nevertheless the republics' financial independence and right to veto Union tax rates were substantial guarantees against an over-mighty Centre. Particularly striking were republican powers over citizenship; the text of the Treaty suggests that a republican regime could deprive people of citizenship (something that had been suggested in some republics)[35] and that they would then lose their citizenship of the Union. Republics might transfer additional powers to the Union by bilateral agreement; but the Union might not hand over any of its powers to a republic without the consent of all the others.

How clear was this distribution of powers, and what difficulties could be foreseen? It was a clearer and more thorough demarcation than any previous Soviet attempt, even that of April 1990, and it lacked the rhetoric and legal trickery of its 1936 and 1977 predecessors; yet it left some areas of potential conflict. Imprecision about concurrent powers and the distribution of property have been mentioned, nor do we know the process by which Union tax rates were to be agreed with the republics; could any republic veto them? In 1991 there were already republics refusing to transfer their contribution to federal revenue. Obscurities on such points suggest an over-burdened Constitutional Court.

**Membership of the Union**

A surprise in the November 1990 draft of the Treaty was that members might join the Union either 'directly or within the composition of other republics'. The implication was that both Union-Republics and Autonomous Republics might join, and that differences in their political status were being abolished. There were thus up to 35 members available to join the Union. Autonomous Republics had lobbied hard for this and there was some rationale to it: four of them exceeded the smallest Union-Republic in population and/or economic power. But this was outweighed by the difficulties the scheme created, in particular in those federal institutions (like the Council of the Federation) where each republic had equal representation: the Ukraine with 52 million inhabitants would have the same voice as Tuva with 300,000 and the sixteen Autonomous Republics of the RSFSR could outvote, not just the RSFSR but all the Union-Republics together! The scheme seems to have been a political manoeuvre by the Union administration, and a counter-productive one. The larger Union-Republics worked to get it overthrown and the outcome (see pp. 169, 175) was that, while the Autonomous Republics would sign the Treaty as member states, they lost their equal voice in all Union procedures except the election of the President.

New members might enter the Union with the consent of the Supreme Soviet. Members might also secede 'according to the procedure laid down by the Treaty's participants and enshrined in the Constitution and laws'. This provision was introduced in the March draft and seemed designed to signal that the Union would no longer insist on the harsh provisions of the April 1990 *Law on Secession*.[36] A similar flexibility was introduced in March 1991 in regard to a more serious problem: those republics that had announced that they would not sign the Treaty. In December 1990 official spokesmen had said that non-signatories would be held to the terms of the 1922 Union Treaty – which the Baltic republics and Moldavia had not signed![37] To have done this would have been to create a category of second-class, quasi-colonial Union membership. But in the final wording the position of non-signatories was simply to be settled 'on the basis of Union legislation, mutual obligations and agreements'.

**Union Institutions**

Even the earliest draft of the Treaty foresaw great changes to central political institutions, and these had become radical by August 1991. In the end the Cabinet of Ministers introduced in December 1990 was retained but the Council of the Federation was done away with,[38] a casualty of the row over Autonomous Republics. Its functions were transferred to a reformed Supreme Soviet.

This was to keep its existing size but its two chambers acquired for the first time clearly distinguished purposes. The Soviet of the Union, to be elected from territorial constituencies of equal size, became a lower house; most legislation would have originated there but was subject to the approval of the new upper chamber, the Soviet of Republics. The latter was to be formed on the same principle as the former Soviet of Nationalities (quotas of different size for Union-Republics, Autonomous Republics, etc.) but its deputies were to be **delegated** by the legislatures of the republics they represented, and all delegates from the same **Union Republic** (including, apparently, those from its Autonomous Republics) must vote as one bloc.[39] Besides being a house of review the Soviet of Republics was to legislate in relation to Union organs and relations among republics (i.e. on affairs of the Union *qua* Union), to ratify international treaties and approve the President's nominations to the Cabinet of Ministers. Both houses were to sit jointly to amend the Constitution, to accept new members into the Union, to approve Union budgets and 'basic internal and external policies', and to declare war and make peace. Obscure is how delegations to the Soviet of Republics might have decided their bloc vote and what their voting strength in joint sittings might have been.

And finally the Presidency. As of March 1990 a President was to be elected by an overall majority plus a majority in a majority of Union-Republics. The latter provision was now altered to a majority 'in a majority of Union **states**' and **that** of course, given that the Autonomous Republics were Union states, could be obtained entirely within the confines of the RSFSR. It was a deft stroke to make Russia *primus inter pares*.

### Assessment

The Union Treaty contained a number of obscurities and sources of conflict. Its authors attempted to marry the large-scale, coordinated management of a modern economy with maximum concessions to centrifugal autarky and the results were not entirely consistent: whilst the concurrent powers were typical of federations, the republics' control of taxes, citizenship or resources, and their representation on Union institutions came close to confederalism. Nevertheless it was a serious attempt to devolve power to a voluntary association of peoples. If it had worked it would have deflected considerable political pressure from the hard-pressed Union authorities and the President. Perhaps one's strongest impression in retrospect is the contrast between the wealth of hard thought and hard bargaining in its details and the fragility and hollowness of the scheme as a whole. It all hinged on the tax provisions: when Gorbachev compromised on these it set the coup in train, and the coup brought the entire Union edifice down.[40]

But for Yeltsin's intransigence and Gorbachev's penchant for compromise, things might have been different? No. A renewed Union would not have worked because hardly anyone wanted it to work. The coup removed people's fear of the army and let the republics do what they wanted to do; it thus accelerated a process that would in any case have been decisive sooner or later. The abstract arguments were (in my opinion) in favour of federalism; but arguments are not politics, and politics is the art of the possible. As a politician Gorbachev should either have mobilised a Unionist party much earlier, moved to dissolve the Union – or settled for confederal arrangements that commanded some consent; that he did not reflects on his weaknesses and the weakness of his position – but also on a stubbornness and principle that have been little recognised.


AFTERMATH

With the collapse of the coup the Baltic republics broke away from the Soviet Union, and the Union recognised their independence.[41] The Russian administration was now the power in the land: its President was replacing officials of the Union government, and it was astonishing how soon it asserted itself in relation to the other republics. Yeltsin's press office announced that declarations of independence among Russia's neighbours would call the mutual borders into question, whilst the mayor of Moscow, G. Kh. Popov, specified areas of the Ukraine that could be in dispute.[42] These could hardly have been chance remarks. Most other Union-Republics upgraded their declarations of sovereignty to declarations of independence over the next few weeks, whilst avoiding precision about their relations with the Union; but it was clear that they no longer thought there were any prospects of a supra-republican regime to which Russia would be subordinate.

Two interim bodies, a State Council and an Inter-republican Economic Committee, each made up of an equal number of members from each Union-Republic, were appointed to replace the Cabinet of Ministers.[43] Gorbachev meanwhile was indefatigable in trying to salvage the Union Treaty. A good idea, far too late, was to separate economic from political agreement and a *Treaty on an Economic Community* was in fact signed by eight republics in October 1991;[44] the evolution of its drafts over the previous weeks shows the familiar dilemma over central institutions. In November a fifth version of the Union Treaty was published.[45] It was highly provisional, with budgetary and military arrangements postponed to later agreement, but, such as it was, unambiguously confederal. Its central authorities would have been little more than committees of the appropriate officials from the member states; the Union would still however have constituted a state in its own right.

Seven republics sent their leaders to a meeting of the State Council on 25 November at which Gorbachev clearly hoped that the Treaty would be initialled. But they refused, opting instead to refer it back to their parliaments. The problem was essentially the same as in July: Gorbachev thought he had got agreement to the formation of a 'confederative democratic **state**', that is, to the continuation of the Union as a legal state over and above the statehood of its members. Yeltsin was apparently still urging amendments that would have ended the Union as a state.[46]

The background to the dispute was the prospective membership of this Union. Both Yeltsin and Gorbachev had said that the adherence of the Ukraine was crucial to Union: without the Ukraine there would be merely a link between Russia and Central Asia, and Russians could not see that the Central Asian component would be self-supporting or add anything but instability to their own prospects. But on 1 December Ukrainians voted overwhelmingly for independence; the majority was over 50 per cent in the mainly Russian Crimea and over 80 per cent in the Russianised Donbass.[47] There was one more factor that scuppered the Unionist cause. On 28 November the Supreme Soviet could not muster a quorum to pass the budget for the fourth quarter, and this left the Union on the edge of bankruptcy. Yeltsin immediately announced that Russia would take over responsibility for the Union budget – and thus became the Union's paymaster.[48]

Yeltsin was also taking other steps. After a meeting on 7–8 December with the leaders of the Ukraine and Belorussia in Minsk the formation of a 'Commonwealth of Independent States' (initially dubbed a 'Slavic Union') was announced. The three members agreed to maintain strategic armed forces and nuclear weapons under joint command but set up no permanent joint institutions; further, 'the application of the norms of third-party states, including those of the former USSR, [was] not permitted on the territory of the states signing this agreement'.[49] A brief attempt was made in Moscow to oppose this on the grounds that three republics could not unilaterally bring the Union to an end; but the adherence of a further eight members (Kazakhstan, the four Central Asian republics, Armenia, Azerbaidzhan and Moldavia) on 21 December, plus the Union's insolvency made resistance pointless. Gorbachev and Yeltsin agreed that the Soviet Union would cease to exist on 1 January 1992, and Gorbachev resigned on 25 December. A handful of Supreme Soviet deputies dissolved that institution the following day.[50]

# 12 Reflections: Gorbachev, Communism and Reform

'He did not know how to give us sausage, but he knew how to give us freedom. Whoever thinks the first is more important will probably end up without either the one or the other.'

(*Komsomol'skaya pravda*, December 1991)[1]

## THE LEGACY OF COMMUNISM

The 'communism' that collapsed in Eastern Europe in 1989 and in the Soviet Union in 1991 was Leninism. The word 'communism' has little analytical content and we should distinguish Lenin and his legacy firmly from both Marxism and socialism. Lenin had a revolutionary impact on the Marxism and socialism of late nineteenth-century Europe; he changed them into something hardly recognisable from a European point of view yet familiar in the context of native Russian radicalism. Some people in Lenin's own time, Rosa Luxemburg for example, saw this;[2] yet it is astonishing that today the words 'communism', 'socialism' and 'Marxism' may still be treated as interchangeable. Marxism and the European social democracy that evolved from it and other ancestors are traditions quite distinct from Leninism; they may or may not have something to offer, but that is unaffected by the collapse of Leninism.

Leninism's characteristic features lie not in policy programmes or output, but in principles of organisation, those principles that enabled CPSU leaders to construct and maintain the mono-organisational state and its state-party. Such principles as the leading role of the Party, democratic centralism, the ban on faction are what distinguish Leninism from social democracy and what give it an affinity with fascism and military government. A famous economist described the Soviet economy as a '*sui generis* war economy'; he might have gone further and called Soviet government '*sui generis* martial law'.[3] By the 1980s the officer corps of this martial administration had turned into something familiar in history: an arrogant and besieged ruling class that thought only of hanging on to power and alienated even its closest lieutenants, the technicians who ran its industry.

Why did this happen? The device of the state-party, by injecting fresh personnel and ideas into administration, had been designed to avoid such degeneration. It sounds shrewd, but there is a confusion at its heart: the Party as an agent of rejuvenation could not be effective unless it retained some independence of the state administration that was to be renewed. But as early as 1921 the leaders of the state-party began to impose centralised discipline and curb independent thinking. With time this discipline supplanted thinking itself. Leninism lost its internal coherence and adaptability; people who chanted its litanies could no longer apply it to real circumstances. This had two specific consequences. The first was that the new bureaucracy was absorbed into the conservative and imperialist traditions of the Russian state. Party 'saturation' of the bureaucracy had been meant to keep it Leninist; in fact *apparat* Leninism ended up little more than a twentieth-century Slavophilism, a claim of the special mission and destiny of Russia. Second, the specialists and technicians who were the products of Soviet industrialisation (and in a Marxian scenario the natural successors of the Bolsheviks) were impeded in the articulation and expression of their distinct interests. They remained second-class auxiliaries to the *apparat*, never strong or confident enough to compel entry into the ruling class, whilst the latter became too stupid to save itself by co-optation and evolution.

There is a double irony in this blindness. Ever since Lenin (in exile in Siberia) read Eduard Bernstein's *Evolutionary Socialism* he and his successors heaped invective on 'revisionism'. Bernstein was thoughtful and scrupulous about the relationship between theory and practice. One of the things that prompted him to revise Marxism was the observation of emergent groups of technically skilled workers who were no longer dirt-poor and who, in both aspiration and fact, were upwardly mobile. Such people are now the typical members of social-democratic parties in the West. It was their defection more than anything else that brought down Soviet Leninism – but Leninism managed to frustrate their definite emergence into politics.

Where did the Soviet experiment leave society? Two main points should be made. Society is different in its composition, in particular because of the emergence of this professional middle class. I have used 'professionals' to denote qualified persons who provide specialised services outside the bureaucracy, typically in large-scale, state-organised enterprises. They represent about 25 per cent of the workforce and were about forty per cent of the CPSU. In them society gained its first substantial group of people familiar with the rational norms and impersonal dealings of *Gesellschaft*, and hence capable of making political pluralism or a market economy work. They are western in orientation and look back with contempt on Stalin's Russian nationalism and his mystical attempts to concoct a distinctly Soviet 'science'. And because of the nature of their work they are interested in stability, evolutionary change and law and incline to the political centre.[4] Yet it is a middle class distinct from familiar Western models. Its origins do not lie in enterprise or commerce and it has no history of independence of the state. The CPSU, the state bureaucracy and the intelligentsia have all sought to speak in its name and it has hardly developed a clear sense of its own identity nor organised itself so that its interests are clearly advanced. It is easily distracted by populism or nationalism.

And society's temper and attitudes have been affected. Seventy years of state-party rule have left a bitter allergic reaction against political mobilisation and intrusion into private life, against the political use of police and political messianism. The mood of exhausted withdrawal from public life must resemble that of Central Europe at the end of the era of religious wars. The now 'private' pursuits of religion and culture have won a new trust. Above all the Soviet legacy is one of paralysis and arrested development in public life: the skills of rule-governed social interaction have been horribly damaged; in an atomised society there is an aggressive individualism that brings Hobbes to mind, combined with resentment at the West's seemingly effortless prosperity and cohesion.[5] Development not only of political culture but of structures was arrested; Leninism held back the dissolution of an empire and the spontaneous evolution of its parts which could and should have happened many decades earlier.

## PERESTROIKA: A BALANCE SHEET

With 'revolution from above', Russian autocrats thought they had a solution to the problem of modernising society whilst holding on to power. They started such revolutions but did not have to face their cyclical consequences: after revolutionary upheaval came exhaustion, stagnation, perceptions of backwardness and calls for more revolution; and society in the meantime was kept dependent on the state. The Soviet revolution turned out to be no different. I have argued that

Gorbachev perceived this and was inspired by a vision of freeing society from its dependence and breaking out of history's vicious circle. The focus of *perestroika* was the new middle class to which he belonged and which he rightly saw as the new and key element in Soviet society; in Marxist terms his aim was the 'bourgeois democratic revolution' that Russia had never experienced. At the outset he had no other means than those of revolution from above to initiate processes that he hoped would become spontaneous. From 1990 this policy changed: unilateral administrative action was replaced by legislation and a policy of social conciliation and *laissez-faire*.

Leaving aside the Cold War and the emancipation of the Soviet dependencies in Central and Eastern Europe – with which this book has not been concerned – the principal achievements of *perestroika* were in three main fields: the neutralisation and elimination of the totalitarian Party, virtually without violence; the planting and vigorous growth of media freedom and freedom of association; and the inauguration of constitutional and parliamentary politics.

Judged simply by the difference these measures made to political and intellectual life in the space of six years they are remarkable achievements. But caution is in order: effective civil rights and constitutional politics are not made but grow; how can we tell that these will not wither or be cut short like those of Russia between 1905 and 1917? We cannot be sure of course. The resistance to the coup showed people in the capital cities using the new civic freedoms to defend a constitutional order; but capital cities, though important, do not represent the majority. How strong might support for civic freedoms be outside them? Again we cannot know, but the evidence of lively local politics and the diffusion of do-it-yourself communications technology give grounds for cautious optimism. When the coup is compared with the fall of Khrushchev we see a new assertiveness and lack of deference to self-proclaimed authority.

As for the end of the CPSU, this can already be seen as a major political accomplishment. The problem Gorbachev faced was a peculiarly intractable one, and one without close historical precedent, for two reasons. The CPSU possessed means of organisation and control well beyond those of the absolutist monarchies, of France, say, or pre-revolutionary Russia. And, unlike most other twentieth century societies that have faced dictatorship – the fascist regimes of Germany and Southern Europe, the Leninist ones of Eastern Europe – most of Soviet society had had no experience of alternative forms of politics. But the mono-organisational Party has been broken and there seems little chance of such a power being reimposed. Its former agents seem incapable of anything but conspiracy, and society is now more complex than it was in the 1920s and 1930s; it would be difficult to reconstruct a network of controls as effective and comprehensive as that the CPSU used. This was surely Gorbachev's finest achievement. Nevertheless *perestroika* failed to reach its objectives in three ways. Little progress was made towards the rule of law in everyday life and society did not acquire legal personnel or procedures that it trusted. Attempts to dismantle the state-run economy were a disaster; there is little sign of the spirit of enterprise or market that were meant to take its place. The attempt to transform a unitary empire into a federation failed and politics thus lost one of the few devices that seem to help in the control of ethnic conflict.

Has the progress been enough to allow Russian and other post-Soviet societies to break out of the vicious circle? Several factors work in favour of this outcome. The middle class, while still not as effectively organised as it might be, is confident, has gained a taste for civil rights and pluralist politics and has the defeat of the coup to its credit. The loss of the empire has lifted a burden from Russian politics and the imperialist and Slavophile traditions are, for the moment, discredited. There is a new watchfulness against the power-hungry.

What may cheat them of this outcome is the failure to entrench a widespread legal or market consciousness. In conditions of material privation and national humiliation this could be fertile soil for reactionary ideas. Russia has lost most of her easy geographical access to the west and in time this could work to attenuate contacts with western ideas and experience. The state is still the employer of the overwhelming majority and the outlook for privatisation is uncertain; it is ominous that it shows no signs of relinquishing the 'temporarily' confiscated property of the CPSU.[6] Both these factors could weaken middle class independence in future years. Neither the mono-organisational Party nor military intervention is the only threat to democracy; Stalinism and fascism received little serious analysis in the Soviet period,[7] and it will be a challenge for the Union's successors to defend themselves against charismatic or demagogic usurpers. We should not be surprised if neo-feudalist or corporatist tendencies – akin to those in Japan – emerge; or if, reminiscent of Peronist Argentina or republican Iran, the state seeks to mobilise or manipulate the masses against middle class elites. The continued role of the state and the widespread frustration at arrested development make it unlikely that post-Soviet societies will follow the developmental path of North-West Europe or the United States.


GORBACHEV'S ACHIEVEMENT

How much of the *perestroika* revolution was Gorbachev's work? Might it not have happened anyway or, as many Russians put it, did not 'the people compel' it? It is certainly likely that the pressure for free media and association would have mounted under any regime. A competent but unimaginative General Secretary could have handled it in the way Janos Kádár did twenty years earlier in Hungary: by tolerating ever more diversity in private on condition of public conformity. Gorbachev was unusual in that he saw and accepted the logic of human rights dissent, that it falsified the central assumptions of the regime he commanded. This 'New Thinking' of course, as we saw in Chapter four, was not his work alone. His contribution was to bring together the isolated and alienated intellectuals who originated it, to turn a dissident subculture into a policy and to work out a strategy for realising it.

It is much less obvious that the other gains of *perestroika* would have come about as a result of social pressure. Even among the dissidents of the 1970s constitutional government was not a dominant theme;[8] it took leadership to adopt this un-Russian and un-Leninist prescription, and Gorbachev seems to have derived it from western (or possibly Czechoslovak) sources. And Party disestablishment – the voluntary and peaceful renunciation of its monopoly by a totalitarian party – was so radical and daring a solution that five years earlier few would have conceived of a communist leader recommending it, let alone of a Party being persuaded to accept it.

Could another politician have done what Gorbachev did? It required a combination of three things: intellectual ability, energy and determination, and tactical experience and skill – certainly not a unique combination of qualities, but an unusual one, and especially rare among the graduates of *nomenklatura*. Even when it was legal to disseminate them there was a remarkable lack of social analyses or prescriptions alternative to the New Thinking and none I have encountered matched the latter's scope, coherence and realism. Many were persuaded by it without being able to develop and apply it by themselves; or they lacked the independence to pursue it once it became clear that it threatened elite or their own interests. A. N. Yakovlev was perhaps the most attractive of the *perestroika* politicians, but it is doubtful whether he had the assertiveness to make a General Secretary. Yeltsin (and possibly Shevardnadze) would have lacked the necessary patience and resilience, and specialists like Ryzhkov, Shatalin or Alekseev the necessary overview. Closest to the required combination of radicalism with diplomacy are politicians like Sobchak, Bakatin or Nazarbaev – people not unlike Gorbachev in fact. The alternative of a charismatic populist would have defeated the ends of reform.

Much trickier is the question, could Gorbachev – or a reformist politician like him – have managed *perestroika* more successfully? Could the coup or the break-up of the Union have been avoided by someone without his personal failings? The reference is not to tactical mistakes; his failure to stand for general election in March 1990, his criticism of Yeltsin in May, his confused response to the Vilnius killings, the choice of Pavlov – such blunders are usually symptomatic of some deeper feature of character, but hardly altered history of themselves. This book has questioned Gorbachev's strategy on several issues after March 1990: his autumn 1990 rapprochement with the conservatives; his failure to found a new party or to let the empire go; the postponed depoliticisation of the armed forces; the pursuit of federalism against all reading of the social mood; the entire *laissez-faire* course. But one cannot know what the circumstances were really like. If these strategic choices were wrong it was a fine-run thing; different decisions **might** have made a difference to long term outcomes, but it is by no means clear.

Was *perestroika* adversely affected by failings in Gorbachev's character, failings that another politician in his place might not have shared?

I sense three main reasons for what was unsuccessful in *perestroika*. The first is failures of analysis. Gorbachev overestimated the confidence and enterprise of the middle class, the dutifulness of the *apparat* and senior officers,[9] and the cohesiveness and rationality of society in general. He understood little of ethnicity or economics; but instead of delegating he persisted in taking the initiative in these areas, initiative based seemingly on incorrect assumptions. He glossed over the distinction between legal acts and social change: the former can be introduced at the stroke of a pen whilst it takes not years but generations before the rule of law or an enterprise culture can take root in a society unused to them. He let it be suggested that progress towards the latter goals could be quite rapid and, to judge from some statements, did not himself appreciate how unrealistic this was.[10]

Linked with this was undue optimism and ambition. The problems of democracy, law, the market and empire were tackled simultaneously. They were certainly interconnected, but Migranyan's argument is impressive that priorities should have been imposed and problems tackled in a planned sequence: since democracy (for example) cannot thrive without the confidence that people derive from legal and economic security, the emphasis should have been on law and privatisation first, and democracy second.[11] It was fatally ambitious, as Solzhenitsyn saw, not to abandon the empire as a prerequisite to everything else.

The charges of unrealistic analysis and over-confidence are both telling, but they apply not just to Gorbachev but to the New Thinking in general and more or less to all the *perestroika* politicians. And they can be readily associated with Marxist optimism about social cohesion, with the maximalism and grandiosity of much Russian social thinking, and with the narrow focus and rationalism of middle-class professionals – especially in the compartmentalised and unchallenging mental world of the Soviet Union before 1985. The third reason points more specifically at Gorbachev.

He was a poor team-worker. He alienated some of his ablest allies, failed to develop Presidential institutions, held on to the initiative in areas such as economics or ethnicity that he understood poorly – and all the time neglected to cultivate or protect his political base. He took on a superhuman load. Might not a team of reform politicians have done better than one man: Yeltsin, say, as Vice-President with special responsibility for Russia, Yakovlev as leader of the governing party, Sobchak or Bakatin as Prime Minister, Nazarbaev as deputy Prime Minister in charge of decolonisation, Shatalin (or Mrs Prunskiene) at economic reform, Rutskoi (or even Gromov!) at defence?[12] . . . Suppose that soon after March 1990 Gorbachev had founded a social democratic and federalist party from CPSU reformists and then an administration along the above lines. Suppose it had announced the depoliticisation of the armed forces and bureaucracy, a network of Presidential prefects to ensure compliance with government policy and a referendum on independence in all republics . . .

The weak points in this speculation are the administration's relations with the armed forces, with Russian opinion (and Yeltsin was already ambitious) and especially with the angry and armed subculture of the *apparatchiki* and political officers; such an administration might easily have had to suspend constitutional rights in order to put down subversion from this last source. Too much would have depended on getting every facet of policy just right. It would have been a very paternalist administration, uncomfortably like the *perestroika* team of 1986–9; it might have had the effect of overawing public opinion or lulling it back to sleep – or it might have foundered, as the real-life administration did, because people insisted on doing things for themselves.

What sort of politician was M. S. Gorbachev? He will be remembered in twentieth century history as the man whose initiative brought an end to the Cold War and freedom to Central and Eastern Europe. But what sort of domestic politician? Above all he was 'a man between the past and the future . . . [He] accomplished the nearly impossible, squeezing out of himself every drop of the habits and manners of a communist boss . . . [But] simply physically he could not become different in everything.'[13]

He oversaw revolutionary changes but was a most reluctant revolutionary; he left Russia a more democratic place than it had ever been but was uncomfortable as a democrat.[14] In his centrist views and their origins he resembles the moderate Protestants who restored Charles II and introduced William III. One can imagine him as a shrewd and skilful player in one of the stable civilised oligarchies, Whig England, perhaps, or Metternich's Austria. But he was born into 'interesting' times. He is one of those figures who, coming from a ruling elite and espousing continuity and stability, nevertheless transform a system from within;[15] but they are too much bound to the old order to consolidate the new, and their successors are often more clearly remembered by history. Examples are Julius Caesar, Diocletian, the Great Elector Friedrich Wilhelm or the first Chinese Emperor Qin Shi Huang. His legacy to Russia and the Soviet Union's other successor states is the clearing of obstacles and the opening up of opportunities.

# Notes and References

Monographs and articles are referred to by author's name only, plus, where necessary, an abbreviated title or date of publication; for full details of publication, as for abbreviations of Soviet sources, see Bibliography, pp. 237–46.

## 1 An Outline of the Soviet System

1. See 'The Liberation Syndrome', *Nezavisimaya gazeta* 23 May 1991.
2. V. Kirillov, 'Beregites' lzheprorokov' (Beware of False Prophets), *Sovetskaya Rossiya* 15 August 1986. It is difficult to convey to readers unfamiliar with this kind of writing the Stalinist combination of arch sentimentality, folksy deference to authority, and sheer menace. The style is to be found in a few other documents used in this book, e.g. those by Andreeva and Bondarev & Blokhin.
3. The victim was Mr Nicholas Daniloff of *US News and World Report*; see English language newspapers of the first fortnight of September 1986.
4. V. Vasil'ev in *Literaturnaya gazeta* 38/86; *Radio Liberty Research Bulletin* 380/86 (3 October 1986) p. 2.
5. Yu. P. Vlasov in *Izvestiya* 2 June 1989 pp. 4–5.
6. The books by Pipes and Sumner are excellent introductory works on the forces that shaped the Russian state, whilst White, Brown and Gray, and Brown (1984) study aspects of its twentieth century 'political culture'. For an up-to-date history of the Soviet period see Hosking 1985.
7. Aristotle, *Politics* Book IV, 1296 a–b.
8. A. S. Pushkin, *The Captain's Daughter*, ch. 8.
9. See *Leviathan* Part I ch. 13 and Part II ch. 17.
10. On the cyclical nature of revolution from above see chapter eight of Rigby's *The Changing Soviet System.* . . .
11. *What is to be Done?*, p. 63 of Utechin's edition; and for Lenin's debt to earlier Russian radicals see Utechin's Introduction ibid., pp. 27–33.
12. *The Soviet Political Mind*, ch. 5, pp. 91–121.
13. Tiersky, pp. 14–91 explores the notion of a political party writ large.
14. It was naturally difficult for people in Soviet public life to entertain the idea that their institutions had been flawed from the outset, but by 1990 this was beginning. See, for example, S. S. Alekseev *Pr* 9 February 1990, p. 3; Yu. N. Afanas'ev *Iz* 14 March 1990, p. 2, col. 2; I. M. Klyamkin *Koms Pr* 24 June 1990; R. I. Khasbulatov *AiF* 28/90 p. 2.
15. The title CPSU was not adopted until 1952. For an introduction to the Party, see Hill and Frank, and for more detailed treatments, Schapiro 1960 and Rigby 1968. The word 'mono-organisational' is Rigby's; see *The Changing Soviet System . . . passim*. On the logical implications of single party rule see my remarks in Brown and Kaser 1982 pp. 1–6.

16. On *nomenklatura* see in particular Rigby *Political Elites* . . . , Rigby & Harasymiw, Löwenhardt, and Nove 'Is there a ruling class . . . ?'.
17. The term 'Central Committee' is sometimes confusing: it stood strictly for the Party's 'parliament' of some 300 people (a meeting of which was a Central Committee 'Plenum'), but was also used as shorthand for the Party's head-quarters staff (the '*apparat*' employed by the Central Committee Secretariat); see further pp. 49–50. The Politburo, with 12–15 members and half a dozen non-voting 'candidate members' was a subcommittee of the Central Committee.
18. One estimate in vogue in the late 1980s put the state bureaucracy at 18 million employees; that of the Party by contrast probably did not exceed 200,000.
19. Paragraph 19 of the *Rules of the CPSU* (in versions before 1990).
20. For the text of the ban on faction see Matthews pp. 149–51.
21. See paragraph 12 of the Party Rules; the phrase 'sentenced by a court' was in draft rules published in *Pr* 28 March 1990, but the whole topic was dropped from later versions.
22. Berman pp. 76–7, 84–5.
23. We make a mistake if we use the word 'ideology' as a synonym for morality or philosophy. It is not the equivalent of the sort of principles that might lead a progressive person to refrain from buying shares or goods in plastic packaging. Nor is it just a systematic account of the world, but rather that, plus normative material that serves to order other people's behaviour. Thus a doctrine that 'explains' poverty or sickness by reference to sins committed in a previous incarnation is ideological because the explanation serves also to justify status. Where a group uses ideas politically in this way, these ideas turn into ideology; typically such operations need to be organised and where we encounter ideology we should expect to find its priesthood.
24. *Pr* 4 November 1967, p. 6.

## 2 What went Wrong under Brezhnev?

1. General references on the Khrushchev and Brezhnev periods are Hosking 1985 and Brown & Kaser 1975, 1982. The chapter will make some use of Soviet administrative terms; these are listed in the Glossary.
2. Khrushchev used the term 'Presidium' for Politburo, and called himself 'First', not 'General' Secretary.
3. The romantic enthusiasm soon burnt itself out, especially as the experiment came close to creating a dust bowl.
4. The 'Secret Speech' is translated in Wolfe and in Rigby, *The Stalin Dictatorship*; it was not published inside the Soviet Union until 1989 in *Iz TsK* 3/89 pp. 128–70.
5. See R. V. Daniels in Dallin and Westin pp. 4–5, Brown 1989 pp. 109–14.
6. See *XXIII S"ezd* . . . , vol. I, p. 90.
7. See Brown & Kaser 1975 p. 10.
8. 'Sochi town council has made a number of attempts to come to power in its own town' (*Koms Pr* 7 June 1991).

9. Unless specifically sourced, statistical material in the rest of the chapter is drawn from annual editions of *Narodnoe khozyaistvo* (*The National Economy*) for the USSR and the RSFSR. On housing waiting lists see *RLRB* 376/88 (17 August 1988). On *limitchiki*, see Zaslavsky pp. 144–6, Yu. M. Luzhkov in *Iz* 21 July 1990.
10. See Hosking 1985 pp. 388–90 and Haynes & Semyonova, pp. 76–81; examples of recent newspaper coverage are *SR* 1 February 1991, *Iz* 18 May 1991, *Pr* 3 June 1991.
11. See *MN* 43/89 (22 October 1989) p. 8. For echoes of the same theme, compare A. I. Luk'yanov on the susceptibility of certain social groups to 'primitive manipulation' (*Iz* 13 March 1990), or A. N. Yakovlev on the corrosive effect on rationality of 'departmental feudalism' (ibid. 31 May 1990).
12. See Perkin pp. xi–xvi, 1–9 (quotations from p. xiii). The distinction between professional and bureaucratic employment is akin to Perkin's distinction between private and public sector professionals, ibid. pp. 11–16, 399–402.
13. My figure for competition in tertiary entry is anecdotal, but see Gorbei pp. 229–30 for further figures. For specialists in the Party see *P zh* 1/62 p. 48, 14/86 p. 23, and, for Party personnel in white-collar employment, *Iz TsK* 4/90 p. 113, *MN* 27/90 p. 6.
14. See Zaslavsky pp. 147–51, Hosking 1985 pp. 403–4.
15. See *Nar khoz* 1988 pp. 52–3.
16. See Zaslavsky pp. 13–14, 33–5, 56–9, 140–7.
17. See in general Lewin; Lapidus in chapter 4 of Bialer; and Ruble in chapter V of Breslauer 1990. T. I. Zaslavskaya's *Novosibirsk Report* was published in *Survey*, Spring 1984, pp. 88–108.
18. See Löwenhardt for the relationship between *nomenklatura*, corruption, and public distrust.
19. See *Pr* 23 January 1988, translated in *CDSP* vol. XL (1988) no. 3.
20. See *RLRB* 438/87 (29 October 1987), 352/88 (4 August 1988), *ROTU* 29/89, pp. 37–8, *Iz* 1 June 1989, pp. 5 & 9. Isupov pp. 473–6 gives data on infant mortality (on which statistics resumed in the mid 1980s); a reference on unemployment is *MN* 25/89 (18 June 1989) p. 13.
21. See *RLRB* 30/88 (22 January 1988) p. 11, 146/88 (22 March 1988). Where did the funds for the scam come from? Ultimately – I think – from diversified agriculture.
22. See *RLRB* 80/78 (16 April), 81/78 (18 April), 97/78 (3 May), 125/78 (1 June), 141/78 (26 June 1978).
23. See *RLRB* 91/88 (29 February), 95/88 (8 March), 101/88 (15 March 1988).
24. Gorbachev spoke of 'powerless centralism' in *Pr* 26 November 1989 p. 2 col. 7.
25. Possibly, for instance, A. N. Yakovlev, in view of his remarks about the 'Russian paradigm' in *Iz* 16 March 1990, p. 5 col. 2.

## 3 Events since Brezhnev

1. Quoted by A. Plutnik in *Iz* 23 December 1991.
2. Matters of historical record and matters discussed in detail in later chapters are not referenced in this chapter. For more detail see in

particular Hosking *A History* . . . , White 1990 and *Radio Liberty Research Bulletin (RLRB)* with its successor publication *Report on the USSR (ROTU)* from 1989. Recent official documents and speeches by Gorbachev are listed in sections III and IV of the Bibliography.

3. See Brown 1983.
4. See A. I. Vol'skii in *Nedelya* 36/90 pp. 6–7.
5. See Brown 1985 pp. 7–9, 14–15.
6. The playwright M. F. Shatrov claimed (*Ogonek* 4/87 pp. 4–5, and see *RLRB* 103/87 (13 March 1987) p. 12) that the Politburo was evenly divided 4:4 between supporters of Gorbachev and of a rival (Grishin or Romanov), and that Gromyko exercised a casting vote. But there were ten people in the Politburo, and Shcherbitskii was an old ally of Brezhnev; to proceed in his absence if the margin was so narrow would have been to invite trouble for the new General Secretary.
7. For Gorbachev's speech see *Komm* 7/85 pp. 4–20.
8. For more details see chapters 1 and 3 of Miller, Miller and Rigby.
9. Important sources on Yakovlev are the interview in *Koms Pr* 5 June 1990 and Tretyakov's essay in *MN* 26/90. He had been an exchange student at Columbia University in 1959. He became increasingly at odds with the CPSU and then with Marxism, and resigned from the Party in August 1991; see *SR* 3 August, *Iz* 16 August 1991.
10. See Miller, Miller and Rigby, pp. 80–4.
11. See *Pr* 13 November 1987, *Iz TsK* 2/89 pp. 239–43, 279–81.
12. T. Samolis, 'Ochishchenie', *Pr* 13 February 1986.
13. Notably by the appointment of Yu. P. Voronov as Head of the Central Committee Department of Culture; Voronov had been eclipsed since the fall of Khrushchev.
14. See Löwenhardt & van den Berg, 'Disaster at the Chernobyl Nuclear Power Plant: A Study of Crisis Decision Making in the Soviet Union', pp. 37–65 of Rosenthal, Charles & 't Hart.
15. 'Dumy o Chernobyle', *Pr* 3 June 1986. I am indebted to T. H. Rigby for pointing out the echoes of Pushkin's *Anchar*.
16. See Chapter 6 for more on *glasnost'* and the *neformaly*.
17. See *RLRB* 399/86 (23 October 1986) and Hosking, *The Awakening* . . . p. 142.
18. The business of a Conference was exclusively policy, whilst a Congress could also replace senior personnel; however no Conference had been held since 1941! Gorbachev seems to have unearthed this ancient device in order to sooth suspicions in the Central Committee.
19. See *Pr* 28–29 January 1987 and *RLRB* 42/87 (29 January 1987); Gorbachev refers to the postponements in *Pr* 26 February 1987.
20. Speech to media representatives on 10 July 1987, published in *Pr* 15 July 1987; cf *RLRB* 280/87 (29 July 1987). P. N. Fedoseev sneered at the origins of pluralism in *Pr* 27 April 1989 p. 4 col. 1.
21. See *Pr* 15 May 88.
22. See *MN* 33/87 (16 August 87) p. 12, and in general Chapter 6.
23. *Pr* 1 and 2 July 1987. The earliest case of such legislation was the Law *On Individual Labour Activity*, *Pr* 21 November 1986.
24. See *Ved SSSR* 22/88 articles 355–356 (26 May 1988), and *RLRB* 224/88 (31 May 1988).

25. *Pr* 25 June 1987.
26. See Alekseeva, and below p. 102.
27. *Le Monde* 4 December 1987.
28. *SR* 13 March 1988.
29. Proceedings: *Pr* 29 June–5 July 1988.
30. See in general Chapter 7.
31. See *Pr* 26 April 1989. Central Committee structure was somewhat complex: in addition to its full membership (307 in 1986), the candidate members (170) and the members of the Central Auditing Commission (83) formed two junior and probationary tiers. The 110 consisted of 74 full members, 24 candidates and 12 members of the CAC.
32. *Pr* 15 October 1989.
33. See *Sotsialisticheskaya ideya i revolyutsionnaya perestroika*, *Pr* 26 November 1989.
34. See Chapter 8.
35. See Chapters 8 and 9.
36. In Uzbekistan and Kazakhstan (June 1989), Azerbaidzhan and Tadzhikistan (January 1990) and on the Uzbek-Kirghiz border (June and August 1990).
37. See *SR* 25, 27, 30 May 1990.
38. See Chapter 10.
39. See Chapter 11.

## 4 The Making of Gorbachev

1. Bernstein to August Bebel quoted in Gay p. 73.
2. My starting points for Gorbachev's life have been Medvedev and Brown 1985, with further details drawn from Gorbachev in *Iz TsK* 5/89 pp. 57–60, *Pr* 12 April 1990, *Iz* 26 September 1990, *Iz* 1 December 1990 and *Koms Pr* 24 December 1991; the December 1990 speech is important because it shows signs of being delivered not only impromptu but also under stress. For interpretation, Breslauer 1989 and Gooding 1990, 1992 are recommended. Plutnik is an excellent Soviet attempt at a political portrait and I have drawn useful points from Allik, Orlov and Piyasheva. Sections II and V–VI are based on Miller 1990.
3. See *Perestroika* . . . (English edition) pp. 69–70; significantly the phrase 'stone-faced sphinxes' was left out of p. 67 of the Soviet text. See the discussion by Gooding 1990 p. 219.
4. See *Dep Verkh Sov RSFSR* (1987), p. 197, *Komm* 14/90 pp. 47–58 and Van Atta 1989; Nikonov mentions his connection with the rehabilitation of Chayanov in *Iz* 24 November 1987.
5. Mlynář's account of his friendship with Gorbachev is in *L'Unità* 9 April 1985, and extracts from his 1968 report 'Our Political System and the Division of Power' in Remington pp. 42–7.
6. For Gorbachev on leadership see *Perestroika* . . . pp. 72, 104 and *Izbrannye rechi* . . . vol. 2, pp. 77, 81–4 (a speech significantly entitled 'The Living Creativity of the People'). On earned authority see also *Pr* 21 July 1989 p. 1, cols 2–3.

7. See *Pr* 12 April 1990, and, for Shchelokov's death, *Russkaya mysl'* 20 December 1984 p. 3, and *RLRB* 6/85 (9 January 1985).
8. See Medvedev pp. 87–90.
9. *Pr* 21 January 1982.
10. In 1989 a Central Committee official, V. M. Legostaev, was to denounce Brezhnev's personnel policies for their promotion of technical rather than managerial flair, of dogmatism over imagination and of obedience over leadership; he was naturally not so crass as to refer to Gorbachev's character and career! See further *Pr* 2–3 May 1989 and Chapter five.
11. See Brown 1983 especially p. 23.
12. *RLRB* 221/85 (3 July 1985); *SR* 8 February 1986 p. 2 col. 1.
13. *RLRB* 399/86, 23 October 1986 (a closed meeting with writers held in June); *Pr* 15 July 1987 (see also Chapter 3); *Pr* 26 December 1989, p. 2, col. 5.
14. See his speeches of 10 December 1984, 'Zhivoe tvorchestvo naroda' (The Living Creativity of the People) in the full version in *Izbrannye rechi . . .* vol. 2, pp. 96–7; to the April 1985 Plenum, *Komm* 7/85 p. 9; *Political Report . . .* to the 1986 Congress, pp. 51, 57–9.
15. *Pr* 2 August 1986, p. 2, col. 2. Before 1986 Gorbachev's usual word for dependence is *tuneyadstvo*. As his target shifts, so does his label: during 1986 that word is replaced by *izhdivenchestvo* (*izhdiventsy* are 'dependants' as opposed to 'breadwinners'). His earliest use of the latter that I have traced is in February 1986 (*Political Report . . .* p. 57), where however the reference is still to economic individualism.
16. See, eg, Brown 1985 and 1989 pp. 185ff and Åslund pp. 26–34. My own views are closer to Rigby's in chapter nine of *The Changing Soviet System. . . .*
17. See, for example, Ligachev quoted in *RG* 23 April 1991, *Trud* 7 May 1991 or the opening of the August coup 'Appeal to the Soviet People' *Pr, Iz* 20 August 1991.
18. On 'thinking aloud' note his claim in *Iz* 1 December 1990 p. 4 to be discarding his prepared text. He called himself a 'centrist' in *Iz* 1 and 2 March 1991; see Shakhnazarov for a similar usage in January. Autumn 1989: speech and interview, *Pr* 16–17 November 1989; essay *The Socialist Idea and Revolutionary Perestroika*, ibid. 26 November 1989; speeches to Central Committee Plenums, ibid. 10 and 26 December 1989.
19. On Shevardnadze see *Iz* 1 December 1990 p. 4 col. 2; on planning see Shakhnazarov.
20. *Pr* 15 May 1986.
21. See *Pr* and the *Age* (Melbourne) 6 June 1989; *bezobrazie* (roughly: 'disgraceful confusion') is also an exclamation equivalent to 'outrageous!'.
22. *Pr* 29 June 1988, p. 4, col. 1.
23. See Gooding 1990 pp. 200–4.
24. Let me stress again that professionals are *not* the 'intelligentsia'; indeed, some of Gorbachev's unpopularity can be traced to intelligentsia jealousy of him as a rival for their authority.
25. On the role of compromise in Gorbachev's thinking see Plutnik p. 3 col. 5, Tretyakov 1989, Piyasheva and Reddaway 1987 (for links with

traditional Russian ideas of consensus). On 'the art of the possible' see Chebrikov in *Pr* 15 November 1988.
26. See Barber pp. 11–14, 17, 210–11, 246; I am indebted to A. P. McIntyre for referring me to this work.
27. For 'planful opportunism' see Breslauer 1989 who is himself quoting other writing on F. D. Roosevelt.
28. *Pr* 19 July 1989 p. 2 col. 1.
29. See Plutnik, p. 3 col. 1.
30. See Chapter 10.
31. See *Iz* 1 December 1990 p. 4 col. 5.
32. See, for instance, his chairing of the constitutional amendments of March 1990, *Iz* 15 March 1990, pp. 4–5, 16 March p. 3.
33. Compare Plutnik p. 3 col. 1.
34. Barber p. 12.
35. See, for example, Piyasheva and Orlik.
36. For his criticism of Yeltsin see *Pr* 13 November 1987, pp. 1–2 and *SR* 25 May 1990. There is an emotional quality to Gorbachev's attitude that suggests that Yeltsin's behaviour in 1987 amounted for him to disloyalty by a favourite son. If so, he was distracted from a danger that, for instance, Bismarck in a similar situation did not miss (see p. 160). See Plutnik for a different interpretation of Gorbachev's dealings with Yeltsin but one which stresses their significance.
37. On Armenians: *RLRB* 101/88 (15 March 1988) pp. 3–4; in Lithuania: Soviet media of 11–15 January 1990; 'in our genes' comes from *Iz* 1 December 1990 p. 4 col. 6, a meeting of which Allik gives an independent account, portraying Gorbachev as an over-possessive parent.

## 5  Objectives, Agenda, Strategy

1. Comenius is quoted at the head of Skilling, *Czechoslovakia's Interrupted Revolution*.
2. Breslauer 1989, Gooding 1990, Rigby *The Changing Soviet System* . . . (chapter 9) and (for its later stages) Migranyan 1989 are recommended on the strategy of reform.
3. Kagalovskii is a good discussion of what was wrong with *uskorenie*.
4. Quotations from *Political Report* . . . p. 58, *Perestroika* . . . p. 100, *Komm* 7/85 pp. 9 and 12, and see note 14 to Chapter 4.
5. See *RLRB* 399/86 (23 October 1986) and Hosking, *The Awakening* . . . p. 142.
6. *Political Report* . . . p. 120 is the first of many occasions when Gorbachev refused to contemplate a purge of the Party.
7. See further Tretyakov, *MN* 48/89.
8. On the salience of the media see Breslauer 1989 pp. 317–22.
9. On the evolution of Gorbachev's views on public diversity compare Reddaway 1987 pp. 23–4, interpreting a speech of February 1987, with Gooding 1990 p. 209 on one of June 1988.
10. Compare V. A. Medvedev on regime thinking 'one-and-a-half to two years' earlier in *Pr* 8 February p. 4 and *Iz* 14 March 1990 p. 4.

11. See *Pr* 14 October 1987 and BBC Monitoring Service, *Summary of World Broadcasts* SWB SU/8699/C (15 Oct 87) pp. 13–14.
12. *Pr* 15 November 1988.
13. *Pr* 17 November 1989, p. 2 col. 2.
14. See *Pr* 27 April 1989 p. 5 col. 5 (this secretary is I K Polozkov!) and *Pr* 9 October 1989 p. 2 col. 5.
15. Note who in the 1989 Politburo had arts training: Gorbachev, Yakovlev, Shevardnadze, Luk'yanov, Medvedev. . . .
16. *Koms Pr* 24 December 1991.
17. See *The Socialist Idea* . . . (*Pr* 26 November 1989) p. 2 col. 2, *Iz* 1 December 1990 p. 4 col. 5, and compare A. N. Yakovlev *Iz* 2 July 1991, Shevardnadze quoted in *ROTU* 48/91 p. 14. The word 'civilised' in reference to Soviet aspirations – and to foreign countries contrasted with Soviet reality – was given wide currency by Gorbachev at this time. Bunyan ('The way is the way . . . ') is quoted from *The Pilgrim's Progress: The Second Part* (London: Lutterworth, 1961) p. 235.
18. Machiavelli, *The Discourses* (ed Bernard Crick, Penguin 1978) p. 175.
19. See *Pr* 1 July 1988 p. 3 and 7 February 1990 p. 2.
20. See *Pr* 26 December 1989 p. 2 col. 7.
21. The critique is a synthesis of arguments from Bonner, Klyamkin, Migranyan, Popov, Shevtsova and Yeltsin *inter alios*, and (outside the Soviet Union) from Malia, Sestanovich and Reddaway 1989. Points 'for the defence' are drawn from Batkin, Kiva, Orlov and Piyasheva. 'Lover of half-measures' is Yeltsin's phrase eg pp. 105, 115, 118, 203. On lost opportunities see, for example, Shevtsova, Tsipko 1991, V. Dashichev in *Der Spiegel* 4/1991 pp. 142–3, Shevardnadze on BBC TV as reported in RFE/RL *Daily Report* 26 March 1991. Gorbachev seems to defend himself in *Pr* 26 December 1989 p. 2 col. 5 (on 'strength' in politics) or ibid. 10 December 1989 p. 1 col. 7, *Iz* 29 May 1990 p. 2, col. 1 (on timing).
22. See *Iz* 1 December 1990, p. 4 col. 5.
23. See *Iz* 16 March 1990, p. 5 col. 2, and compare *Iz* 2 July 1991. To judge from Hosking *The Awakening* . . . there may be an allusion to the author V. Grossman.
24. See in particular Migranyan, *Novyi mir* 7/89.

## 6 *Glasnost'* and Interest Groups

1. See *A Man for All Seasons* (London: Heinemann, 1963) p. 39.
2. Most, but not all, television viewers received some locally made programmes in addition to two channels of Central (Moscow) Television.
3. The legal basis of censorship seems to have been a statute of 6 June 1931, the text of which I have been unable to trace; see Brown *et al.*, *The Cambridge Encyclopedia* . . . p. 411.
4. See Illesh & Rudnev, *Iz* 9 October 1990.
5. See Party Rules (before 1990) paragraphs 3b and 3c.
6. From interview with Yakovlev in *RLRB* 487/87 (1 December 1987).
7. See *Pr* 3 March 1990 pp. 3–4.

8. P. K. Romanov, Director of the Main Administration for the Protection of State Secrets in the Press since 1966 was replaced by V. A. Boldyrev; unlike his predecessor Boldyrev gave interviews.

9. See Boldyrev 1988, 1989 and 1990, Glazatov, Illesh & Rudnev plus M. Fedotov in *MN* 43/88 (23 October 1988) p. 12–13.

10. These were G. Ya. Baklanov (*Znamya*), V. A. Korotich (*Ogonek*), E. V. Yakovlev (*Moscow News*) and S. P. Zalygin (*Novyi mir*).

11. Compare Latsis, *Iz* 28 August 1991.

12. See *Pr* 14 February 1987 p. 1 col. 7, and M. S. Solomentsev in *Pr* 19 August 1988.

13. See *Iz TsK* 3/89 pp. 128–70.

14. For rehabilitations of public figures see *Pr* 6 February 1988 (Bukharin, Rykov); ibid. 27 March 1988 (Voznesenskii, Tukhachevskii); ibid. 10 July 1988 (Bukharin and Rykov reinstated in CPSU); ibid. 5 August 1988 (Zinov'ev, Kamenev). Statistics on rehabilitations: *Iz* 13, *KZ* 14 February 1990, *Prav vest* 7/90 p. 11. Of the 3.8 million 786,000 were said to have been shot and 740,000 secretly rehabilitated in 1954–61.

15. And one cultivated by the Gorbachevs: see K. S. Karol, *Le Nouvel Observateur* 24 September 1985, 8 May 1987.

16. See The Socialist Idea . . . p. 1 cols 5–6.

17. See *Pr* 21 April, 8 November 1990, *Iz* 1 March 1991 p. 2 cols 6–7. Compare Shakhnazarov's remarks on revolutionaries at the head of Chapter 9.

18. *Iz* 16 March 1990, p. 5 col. 2.

19. See *Iz* 14 August 1990.

20. Important documents are Burtin, Kudryavtsev 1988, Selivanov.

21. See, for example, *Iz* 21 February 1990, *MN* 8–9/90 (4 March 1990) p. 27, Albats in *MN* 10/90.

22. Note, for example, how the announcement of the Party's withdrawal from *nomenklatura* was followed immediately by Boikov's and Toshchenko's survey of public opinion on the Party; see *Pr* 15 and 16 October 1989.

23. See *Sov Lit* 1, 2, 7, 13 March 1990. The first election in which full lists of candidates with political affiliations were published in advance seems to have been that in Georgia in October 1990; see *ZV* 13–18 October 1990.

24. See *SR* 13 March 1988, *Pr* 5 April 1988 (translated in *CDSP* vol. XL (1988) nos 13 and 14). In *Koms Pr* 5 June 1990 A. N. Yakovlev refused to confirm or deny authorship of the *Pravda* editorial.

25. Such an investigation would have revealed that Central Committee Secretary Medvedev had more obvious contacts with Andreeva than did Ligachev: the former had once worked at Andreeva's institute. Andreeva continued to be active on the neo-Stalinist fringe of Russian politics (see, eg, *Rossiya* 19/91 p. 7) and after the August coup became leader of her own party.

26. See *Ved SSSR* 15/89 (12 April 1989) article 106 and (in a new series) 9/89 (9 August 1989) article 203.

27. See *MN* 36/90 (16–23 September 1990) p. 4, 43/90 (4–11 November 1990) p. 14.

28. Compare, for instance, 'Perestroika i vlast' ' in *Pr* 31 January 1990 with Tsipko in *MN* 22/90 and 24/90, the call for the resignation of Gen. A. M.

Makashov in *Iz* 20 June 1990, Migranyan in *MN* 26/90 or Khasbulatov in *AiF* 28/90; and compare **all** these with Plutnik's political portrait of Gorbachev.

29. See P. Gutiontov in *Iz* 12 July 1990.
30. For text see *Iz* 20 June 1990 with draft ibid. 4 December 1989; compare *ROTU* 45/90 pp. 4–11.
31. Laws defining such secrets were not passed immediately, and this enabled the censors to stage a temporary comeback under a new name; see Boldyrev 1990, Glazatov, Illesh & Rudnev. Competition among the new media soon dealt with them more effectively, at least in big cities.
32. See *Iz* 23 August 1990 p. 3, 2 September 1990 p. 2, *MN* 41/90 (21–28 October 1990) p. 3, *AiF* 41/90 (October 1990) p. 3.
33. See *MN* 38/90 (30 September–7 October 1990) p. 5, *SR* 16 October 1990. *SR* had been a joint publication of the All-Union Central Committee and the RSFSR state bodies; it became an organ of the Central Committee 'for the communists of the Russian Federation'.
34. See *MN* 36/90 (16–23 September 1990) p. 4 for a proposal to limit media ownership to 30 per cent in the RSFSR.
35. The legislative basis of this (as of censorship) is obscure. *Prav vestnik* 11/90 p. 8 cites a decree of 1930, and B. Eliseev, *Pr* 11 August 1989, another of 1932.
36. Party Rules paragraph 68 or (1986–90) paragraph 61.
37. For general accounts of the *neformaly* see Brovkin; V. E. Bonnell in chapter IV of Breslauer 1990; Hosking, *The Awakening* . . . chapters 4 and 8, and in *ROTU* 44/91 pp. 5–8; A. Jones & W. Moskoff, *PC* November–December 1989, pp. 27–39; and Rigby, *The Changing Soviet System* . . . pp. 216–19.
38. See Kagarlitsky, pp. vii–ix, 322–5, 334, 341–3, 353, 359–60, and compare *RLRB* 341/82 (23 August 1982), 380/87 (23 September 1987).
39. A. N. Yakovlev's term as head of the CPSU Propaganda Department.
40. For statistics see *Pr* 27 December 1987, 11 November 1988 and 10 February 1989.
41. See *RFER Situation Reports*, Baltic Area, October to December 1988.
42. See Alekseeva '*O proekte zakona* . . . '.
43. See *Iz* 4 June (draft), 16 October 1990 (text) and *ROTU* 46/90 pp. 1–3.
44. See O. S. Shenin in *Pr* 2 February 1991 p. 2.
45. See *Ved SSSR* 22/88 articles 355–356 (26 May 1988), and *RLRB* 224/88 (31 May 1988). It was argument about the tax provisions that led to late sittings and postponed voting for the first time in the (old) Supreme Soviet.
46. See *ROTU* 5/89 pp. 31–2, 13/89 pp. 9–12, 34/89 pp. 12–16, 41/89 pp. 3–5, and for statistics *Prav vest* 19/89 p. 11, *ROTU* 37/90 p. 10.
47. See 'Status – "oboronke"' in *Pr* 6 September 1990, Lemaev in *Iz* 1 October 1990.
48. See *Pr* 15 May 1988 and *ROTU* 28/89 pp. 10–12.
49. See Van Atta 1991 p. 22; this was after Yeltsin had begun a distinct programme of land privatisation there.
50. See *Iz* 21 July, 15 August 1990, *ROTU* 39/90 pp. 10–12. My thanks to Thane Gustafson for background in SOVSET' messages 2184 and 3021 (26 April 1989 and 1 July 1990).

51. Text in *Iz* 6 March 1990.
52. Quoted from *MN* 35/90 (9–16 September 1990) p. 10.
53. Under Gorbachev, Stolypin began to get favourable treatment in the Soviet media; see, for instance, *PU* 23 & 24 May 1990, *Nedelya* 19/91 p. 7, *Koms Pr* 1 June 1991 p. 3. It is worth noting that Stolypin did not rely on law alone but arranged financial credits for those who made use of his scheme.
54. See Ershov and Kiva *Iz* 24 January 1991 for examples of recent Soviet writing on the political role of the middle class.
55. *Pr* 12 May 1988.
56. For the background of deputies see *Iz* 6, 26 May 1989, *MN* 24/89 (11 June 1989) p. 8, *SR* 18 May 1990, *PU* 18 May 1990; I am grateful to Dr Marko Pavlyshyn for the data on *Rukh*.
57. See, for instance, Yanaev in *Pr* 16 May 1990. An interview with A. I. Vol'skii (then chairman of an employers' association) in *Trud* 8 May 1991 is remarkable for its assumptions of trade union cooperativeness, whilst Yeltsin's ban on political organisations in the workplace (*SR* 23 July, *Iz* 29 July 1991 p. 2) treats unions almost as an afterthought.
58. The organisation of populist mass movements in middle-class interests (such as V. A. Yarin's 'United Front of Russian Workers' in 1989–90, or of Yeltsin's supporters against Gorbachev in early 1991) is a sub-category of this.
59. See *ROTU* 32/89 pp. 1–4 and *SR* 29 August 1989 p. 2.

## 7 Perestroika and Political Institutions

1. Vaculík is quoted from Hamšík, p. 182.
2. See Miller 1988; Burtin and Selivanov are items from this time, and see note 9 below.
3. See Mann 1988 and Miller 1988; the analysis draws in particular on the Conference Resolutions 'On Democratisation of Soviet Society and Reform of the Political System' and 'On Legal Reform', *Pr* 5 July 1988.
4. See clause 9 of 'On Democratisation . . . ', ibid.
5. An exception was made in 1989 in favour of **Prime** ministers and **chairmen** of *ispolkomy*.
6. See Law *On the Status of People's Deputies*, *Iz* 9 June 1990, article 37.
7. The phrase *sotsialisticheskoe pravovoe gosudarstvo* draws on the German *Rechtsstaat* and might be better translated 'socialist constitutional state' or 'socialist rule of law'. The idea goes back to a Gorbachev speech (see *Pr* 19 February 1988 p. 2 col. 3) but the phrase seems to originate in the *Pravda* editorial 12 May 1988.
8. See *Ved SSSR* 6/88 article 94.
9. See V. N. Kudryavtsev *Pr* 3 May and V. Savitskii ibid. 19 May 1988; also 'Demokratizatsiya i zakonnost'' ibid. 14 March, V. Stepnov ibid. 6 May, V. Polyakov ibid. 14 May and B. M. Lazarev ibid. 23 June 1988.
10. See, concerning the police, 'Professionaly i apparatchiki', *Iz* 31 July 1989, with reply ibid 1 August 1990.
11. *Pr* 26 December 1989.
12. See for example the speech of the future Deputy Prime Minister, L. I. Abalkin, *Pr* 30 June 1988 pp. 3–4, especially p. 4 cols 2–3.

13. *Iz* 3 December 1988.
14. See Constitution, Article 113, point 14, and, on the Afghanistan decision, *Iz* 22 March 1989 p. 5, *ROTU* 17/89 pp. 11–12, 50/89 pp. 4–8.
15. *Iz* 4 December 1988.
16. On procedures and conduct of the elections see Mote; Mann, Monyak & Teague pp. 13–22; and *ROTU* 10/89 pp. 5–7, 22/89 pp. 3–5.
17. See for example G. V. Barabashev (member of the Central Electoral Commission) in *Iz* 14 March 1989.
18. The election is sometimes called 'semi-democratic' etc for the distinct reason that one third of the deputies were chosen by the 'public organisations'. This gave some people two votes, but not all of the public organisations conducted undemocratic elections among their members, and some elected excellent deputies.
19. Election results: *Iz* 19 March 1989 (reserved CPSU seats), ibid. 29 March, 5, 15 April, 20, 24 May 1989.
20. *Iz* 29 April 1988, translated in *CDSP* vol. XL (1988) no. 18.
21. For the social composition of deputies see *Iz* 6, 26 May 1989, *MN* 24/89 (11 June 1989) p. 8, *Pr* 6 October 1989, *AiF* 4/90 (27 January 1990) p. 8, *ROTU* 18/89 pp. 1–6, Mann, Monyak & Teague pp. 31–2.
22. See *Iz* 29 May 1989, p. 1, col. 2.
23. For membership of the Congress, the Supreme Soviet and the latter's commissions and committees see *Narodnye deputaty SSSR*. Membership of the Supreme Soviet and its organs is also in *Iz* 1 June and 13 July 1989.
24. See, for example, *Iz* 1 August 1989 p. 2 col. 2, *Ved SSSR* 9/89 article 203 (on 'anti-Soviet agitation and propaganda'); *Iz* 15 February 1990 (Gorbachev's appeal for an emergency Congress session); ibid. 16 June 1990 (Ryzhkov's marketisation proposals).
25. See *Iz* 21–24 June, 4 July, *Pr* 6, 11 July 1989.
26. The failure of others to nominate suggests a conscious decision to adopt a low profile – and **that** suggests Gorbachev's continued domination of the Politburo. V. I. Vorotnikov was perhaps expected to become Speaker of the RSFSR Supreme Soviet.
27. This is to omit figures from the Baltic like I. O. Bishers, M. I. Lauristin or K. S. Khallik who left the Supreme Soviet during 1990 but became public figures in their own republics.
28. See *ROTU* 32/89 p. 33; a year later Sobchak was calling it the 'parliamentary opposition' in *Iz* 10, *Pr* 11 September 1990.
29. See *ROTU* 11/90 p. 36, 20/91 pp. 16–21.
30. See *Iz* 26 September 1989.
31. See *Pr* 19 July 1989 p. 2 cols 2–3.
32. Compare the alignments of December 1990 in *Iz* 26 December 1990 p. 6 cols 1–2.
33. Deputies were arranged by region not political complexion. To form a Supreme Soviet the entire Congress voted *seriatim* on lists put forward by and from republican blocs of deputies. See Mann, Monyak & Teague pp. 23–7.
34. See especially Klyamkin's and Migranyan's writing of this period.
35. See *Iz, Pr* 29 November 1989, *ROTU* 49/89 p. 25, 52/89 p. 17, 23/90 pp. 19–20.

36. See *Iz* 23 October 1989 p. 1 cols 6–7, Yakovlev in *Koms Pr* 13 March 1990.
37. The precedents set by General Jaruzelski of Poland may have been influential. There a post of president was approved in April 1989; Jaruzelski, the Party first secretary, was elected president, having promised to resign from all Party office, in July; and in August he designated a non-communist to form a government, effectively ending the Party monopoly. In late January 1990, after the break-up and renaming of the Polish United Workers' Party, he declined to join either of its offshoots or any other party, saying that 'he wanted to remain a spokesman for the people'.
38. Gorbachev is said to have cancelled meetings with foreigners on 4 January; see *ROTU* 2/90 pp. 33–4.
39. See *Pr* 13 February 1990 p. 2 col. 3, *Iz* 16 March 1990.
40. The Presidency was written into Articles 127–127[10] of the Constitution, see *Iz* 16 March 1990. Note that its Russian title was the neologism *Prezident*, not the usual *predsedatel'* (chairman or president) which I have translated as 'Speaker' for the period December 1988–March 1990.
41. See Article 113, point 14.
42. Because it would have obliged Russian candidates to seek coalition with voters from other republics in order to win.
43. See Articles 127[4] and 127[5], and, for a discussion of the Presidential Council, E. V. Yakovlev, *MN* 33/90 (26 August–2 September 1990) pp. 8–9.
44. See *SR* 22 June 1990 p. 3 col. 3.
45. *Pr* 16 May 1990.
46. See *SR* 18 May 1990.
47. For Burlatskii see *Iz* 28 June 1989 p. 2, and, for Ryzhkov's anxiety about the weakening of the Council of Ministers, E. V. Yakovlev 1990. The separation of the 'domestic' from the 'national security' arm of government, and the removal of the latter from direct parliamentary control are reminiscent of Bismarck's Germany; see Koch, especially p. 125.
48. For the Committee's formation and terms of reference see the Law *On Constitutional Supervision* . . . , *Pr* 26 December 1989, and Constitution, Articles 110 (point 9) and 125; for its membership: *Pr* loc. cit. and *Ved SSSR* 18/90 article 314.
49. See *Iz* 18 January 1991.
50. See *Iz* 15 September, 27 October, 30 November 1990 and 15 February, 4 April, 14 October 1991, and, for discussion of the Committee's role, Alekseev *passim*, Feofanov, Kudryavtsev 1991 and Piskotin.
51. The device of 'a majority in a majority of republics' might usefully have been adopted here.
52. See Chapter 10.

## 8   Gorbachev and the CPSU

1. Quoted from *The Discourses*, ed. Bernard Crick (Penguin 1978) p. 175, emphasis mine.
2. See documents in *Pr* 31 July 1988, *P zh* 16/88 pp. 30–4, *Iz TsK* 1/89 pp. 81–8.

3. Told to a *raikom* secretary by his grandson and recounted by I. K. Polozkov in *Pr* 18 October 1989.
4. See *Pr* 26–27 April 1989.
5. Proceedings in *Pr* 19 & 21 July 1989. This was not a Central Committee Plenum, but a meeting of regional first secretaries who, in less hectic times, would expect automatically to be part of the Central Committee.
6. *Pr* 21 July 1989 p. 3 col. 7.
7. Ibid. p. 1 cols 3–4.
8. Ibid. 19 July p. 2 col. 1.
9. General Jaruzelski, imposing martial law at a time when he was both General Secretary and Commander-in-Chief, would perhaps have been a more relevant comparison for Gorbachev.
10. See, for instance, *Pr* 19 February 1988 p. 3 col. 3, and clause 1 of the Conference Resolution 'On Democratisation . . . ' *Pr* 5 July 1988. The Party had always criticised *podmena* of course; it was a mark of Gorbachev's seriousness that interventionist institutions were actually closed down.
11. See Rahr in *ROTU* 15/89 (14 April 1989) pp. 19–24 and 52/89 (29 December 1989) pp. 3–4.
12. See *Iz* 26 July 1990 p. 3.
13. See *Pr* 15 October 1989. The 'registration' (*uchetno-kontrol'naya*) *nomenklatura* was the list of posts, incumbents of which were not formally determined by the Party, but who still required Party ratification; see Shvets pp. 156–7. It is uncertain what the precise scope of this list was, but it almost certainly included elected deputies and the office-bearers of public organisations other than the Party.
14. See *Iz* 4 December 1989; Gorbachev, to be sure, was not its author – but he had devoted much energy to building an unconstrained working environment for the Supreme Soviet Commissions that drafted it.
15. See: 'Vedushchaya ili rukovodyashchaya?' *Pr* 30 April 1989 p. 4; Gorbachev to Hungarian leaders in TASS 25 July 1989, quoted by *ROTU* 31/89 p. 37; G. Kh. Shakhnazarov to *Yomiuri Shimbun* 27 September 1989, quoted by ROTU 40/89 p. 32; *The Socialist Idea* . . . p. 2.
16. See *Pr* 26 December 1989 p. 2 col. 7.
17. See *Rebuilding Russia* p. 84.
18. The stimulus seems to have been the Estonian Declaration of Sovereignty in November 1988; note the title of V. M. Chebrikov's speech in *Iz* 14 November 1988. The influence of Yugoslav experience is not impossible: earlier than the other communist parties the League of Communists of Yugoslavia lost its clear identification with Leninist organisation and policies, but kept, especially between 1967 and 1980, a stronger commitment than most Yugoslav institutions to the idea of Yugoslav ('South Slav') unity.
19. See *Pr* 9 December 1989; other examples: *Pr* 17 November 1989 p. 2 col. 5, 10 December 1989 p. 1 col. 4, 26 December 1989 p. 2 col. 8 (Gorbachev). Once the cause of Article six was lost, it became an argument for the Presidency: see *Iz* 13 March 1990 p. 2 col. 2 (Luk'yanov) or 14 March 1990 p. 2 col. 6 (Vorotnikov).

20. It is striking, for instance, that for all their stress on leadership and solidarity communist parties never developed an equivalent of the priest in his or her pastoral role.
21. See Schneider p. 11, quoting 'high-ranking Party officials'.
22. See *Pr* 11 July 1990 p. 2 cols 6–7 or Piyasheva's account. I have heard it said privately that he referred to the CPSU in 1990 as a 'monster' (*chudovishche*) that could not be left to its own devices, but have been unable to trace a source; it sounds perhaps more like A. N. Yakovlev.
23. Contrast his serious defence of the Union Treaty, which he called a 'last bulwark' (*Iz* 1 December 1990 p. 4) and which cost him his career.
24. See *Iz* 13 December 1989 p. 4 col. 4.
25. See especially the call by Elena Bonner (Sakharov's widow) for the Party to be 'disbanded by a decree of the Congress of USSR People's Deputies rather than of the Party Congress. Its property must be nationalised.' (*MN* 30/90 (5–12 August 1990) p. 5.)
26. See *Iz* 8 February 1990 p. 2 with *ROTU* 7/90 p. 32.
27. On bureaucracy see *MN* 36/89 (3 September 1989) p. 5, 42/89 (15 October 1989) p. 3 and *Pr* 16 October 1989 p. 1; on opposition: R. A. Medvedev quoted in *ROTU* 47/89 p. 2 and Yu. A. Prokof'ev in *MN* 36/89 p. 5.
28. See *Iz* 23 May 1990.
29. For proceedings see *Pr* 3–15 July 1990, and for the Rules, ibid. 18 July 1990. This final text is worth comparing with the drafts in *Pr* 28 March and 28 June 1990 and Gorbachev's survey of proposed amendments ibid. 13 July p. 2.
30. Compare *Iz TsK* 7/90 p. 53 with 8/90 p. 162.
31. See Rule 34, and compare Rule 35 in the June draft and Gorbachev's comments in *Pr* 13 July 1990 p. 2 col. 5.
32. Note the implication: they had not had such access formerly! *Apparatchiki* – in an obscure provision – were also subjected to labour law; this probably means 'subject to no *nomenklatura* than that of their formal employers'; as Löwenhardt 1984 shows, one of the few public manifestations of *nomenklatura* was a list of jobs, holders of which could not sue their employers!
33. For background see *ROTU* 19/90 (11 May 1990) pp. 1–3, 27/90 (6 July 1990) pp. 1–6, and, for proceedings of the party's inaugural congress, *SR* 20–26 June, 21 August–7 September 1990. Alone of the Union-Republics the RSFSR had had no CPSU institutions at the republican level but had shared All-Union facilities.
34. These phrases seem to have been borrowed from the revised Rules of the Czechoslovak Communist Party of 1968: see Remington p. 268.
35. See *ROTU* 5/90 (2 February) pp. 7–9, 26/90 (29 June) pp. 1–3, 48/90 (30 November 1990) p. 22 and Schneider p. 14.
36. See *MN* 19/91 (12–19 May 1991) p. 5. For other material on internal disunity see A. N. Yakovlev in *Iz* 2 July 1991, I. D. Laptev in *AiF* 40/91 pp. 4–5, and D. Mann in *ROTU* 30/91 pp. 1–9.
37. See Latsis *Iz* 16 July 1990 for an example of the arguments.
38. In August 1991 A. N. Yakovlev resigned to pre-empt expulsion for 'actions contradicting the Rules **and** directed at splitting the Party' (my

emphasis); see *Iz, SR* 16 August 1991. It illustrates both *apparat* confidence and its sense of law.

39. See *P zh* 14/90 pp. 26–31.
40. Three quarters of the Central Committee were nominees of provincial organisations voted on by Congress at large; see *Pr* 13 July p. 3 cols 2 & 4, 14 July p. 3 col. 8.
41. See, for instance, the RSFSR attempt to ban simultaneous holding of party and state offices: *SR* 22 June 1990 with the report of the Committee of Constitutional Supervision, *Iz* 27 October 1990; or the decree banning party organisation at the workplace discussed below.
42. See *NG* 29 January 1991 as quoted in *ROTU* 8/91 (22 February 1991) p. 1. Note that the Law *On Public Associations* prohibited interference of this kind, but it did not come into effect until January 1991.
43. See Rule 37 (and compare Rule 38 in the June draft).
44. Examples in *ROTU* 33/91 p. 25.
45. Examples in *Iz* 10 July 1990 p. 2, *MN* 26/90 (8 July 1990) p. 2, *ROTU* 33/90 p. 22.
46. See *SR* 23 July, *Iz* 29 July 1991 p. 2 and *ROTU* 33/91 (16 August 1991) pp. 21–5 – where it is suggested that the Committee of Constitutional Supervision would have upheld the decree.
47. See N. E. Kruchina, *Pr* 12 March, 5 July 1990, *ROTU* 47/91 p. 6.
48. See *Iz TsK* 8/90 p. 94 and RFE/RL *Daily Report* no. 233 (10 December 1990).
49. See *MN* 43/90 (4–11 November 1990) p. 14.
50. For the settlement see General Lizichev in *Pr* 19 March 1990; Marshal Yazov, *KZ* 3 June 1990; Gorbachev, *Pr* 3 July p. 2 col. 3, 13 July 1990 p. 2 col. 5; the draft CPSU Rules of March; and its draft Programme, *Pr* 27 June 1990. Stages in its implementation are in *Iz* 5 September 1990, *KZ* 12 January, 30 March, 2 April 1991. It is worth comparing the process in the Polish Army, which was 'departisanised' (its phrase) in November 1989 and depoliticised in February 1990; see *ROEE* 13/90 pp. 31–5.
51. See *Iz* 15 February 1991 p. 2, 14 November 1990 p. 2 col. 3. The appointment of the conservative Colonel-General N. I. Shlyaga as head of the new Main Political Administration will have confirmed the same message: see *Iz* 18 July p. 2, *KZ* 20 July 1990 p. 1.
52. This was no longer an MPA duty, whilst the new secretary of the All-Army Party Committee (*KZ* 2 April 1991) was an elected representative, not an appointment from above.
53. Compiled from data in *Iz TsK* 4/90 pp. 113–5; cf. *MN* 27/90 p. 6.
54. See *Pr* 26 July 1991 p. 2 col. 3, *RG* 25 April 1991.
55. See *Iz TsK* 8/90 pp. 91–8, 5/91 pp. 71–3, *Pr* 5 February 1991 p. 4, *ROTU* 33/91 p. 43. In its final year the CPSU did not publish the 'central' portion of its budget, amounting in previous years to about 10 per cent of membership dues and about two thirds of publishing income.
56. Compiled from *P zh* 11/91 p. 31, *Iz TsK* 2/89 p. 139; compare Teague & Tolz p. 4.
57. See *Iz* 2 March 1991 p. 2 col. 5.
58. I owe this phrase to the Ukrainian politician Levko Lukyanenko.

59. Like the groups that clung to paganism after the Roman Empire adopted Christianity! But its systemic nature is confirmed by the occurrence of similar coalitions in Rumania, Bulgaria and Albania during the same period.
60. Foreseen clearly, for instance, by Tretyakov in *MN* 26/90 p. 9.
61. See Migranyan *MN* 26/90 p. 6 and A. N. Yakovlev *Iz* 2 July 1991; Brown 1991 claims that Yakovlev was advising this in mid-1990. Such a realignment of forces had been one of the successes of Polish Solidarity in 1980–1, when it reduced the PUWP virtually to a party of the *apparat*; perhaps the memory of this served to inhibit Gorbachev?
62. See *Pr*, *Iz* 26 April, *NG* 27 April, *Pr* 29 April 1991.
63. See *SR* 12 April 1991. Under the name People's Party of Free Russia this is at the time of writing the largest party in Russia; see Schneider pp. 11 and 14.
64. See *ROTU* 28/90 (12 July 1991) pp. 1–4, 30/91 (26 July 1991) pp. 7–8, 11. Despite the evidence of Gorbachev's benevolence towards the Movement, it seems clear that he pressed for it not to become a party in direct competition with the CPSU.
65. See *Pr* 23 August 1991 p. 2 col. 5.
66. Examples concerning military regulations, defence councils, directives to the judiciary and customs exemption have been cited; for others see Teague & Wishnevsky pp. 24–5, Teague & Tolz pp. 5–8 (the latter quoting claims that the Party had been preparing to go underground since 1987!).
67. A. N. Yakovlev in *Iz* 2 July 1991 p. 2.
68. *Iz TsK* 12/90 pp. 20–3.
69. See Chapter 10.
70. See *SR* 22 August 1991, *ROTU* 35/91 p. 52.
71. See *Iz* 26 and 30 August, *KZ* 27 August 1991.
72. See *RG* 9 November 1991.
73. See C. Thorson, *ROTU* 40/91 pp. 4–8, Schneider p. 18. Reprisals against former CPSU members or neo-communist foundations seem however to have been avoided.

## 9 Society and Politics under the Presidency

1. *Der Spiegel* 4/1991 p. 134.
2. See B. V. Gidaspov *Pr* 6 July 1990, p. 4 cols 1–2 or Yu. Boldyrev *Koms Pr* 11 July 1990. Yet even the Moscow staff of the Presidential Council had not been organised by August 1990; see E. V. Yakovlev, *MN* 33/90.
3. See *Iz* 26 August, *Koms Pr* 6 September, *RG* 5 November 1991.
4. See *Iz* 17 November 1990.
5. See above pp. 147–8, and compare the letter of A. Efimov in *Koms Pr* 20 July 1991 p. 4.
6. *Iz* 14 November 1990 p. 2.
7. See *SR* 25 May, *Pr* 29 May 1990.
8. See *Pr* 8 November 1990.
9. See *Kommersant* 17/91 (22–29 April 1991) p. 30.

10. See Reddaway 1989 for one of the earliest analyses.
11. See *ROTU* 21/90 p. 11.
12. Against this 'war of laws' there was even a law passed enjoining obedience to the law! See *Iz* 26 October 1990.
13. For recent treatment of Soviet ethnic issues see Goble, Karklins, Graham Smith and Zaslavsky pp. 91–129.
14. See, in respect of the Baltic, *RFER* 'Baltic Area Situation Report' 11/88 (5 October 1988) p. 3, *RLRB* 445/88 (7 October 1988) pp. 11 and 13.
15. But note the views of Khallik op cit.: the lack of civil rights and institutions perforce put a heavier duty on ethnic structures.
16. See *SE* 18 November 1988 and Sheehy, *ROTU* 27/90 p. 14.
17. See *Pr* 22 September 1989, p. 1, col. 5, and ibid. 26 December 1989, p. 2 col. 7.
18. For Plenum proceedings see *Pr* 20–22 September 1989, and for *The Nationalities Policy* . . . , *Pr* 17 August 1989 (draft) and *Pr* 24 September 1989 (as adopted); compare *ROTU* 35/89, 39/89 pp. 1–4.
19. See Sheehy, *ROTU* 45/90 pp. 23–5. An Autonomous Republic (or ASSR) was a province-sized ethnic territory within a Union-Republic; 16 out of 20 of them were in the RSFSR.
20. See Kudryavtsev & Topornin.
21. See *Iz* 6 April (Secession), 3 May (*On the Delimitation* . . . ), and 4 May *On the Languages* . . . ). Sheehy comments on the first in *ROTU* 17/90 pp. 2–5.
22. See *Sov Lit* 13–15 March 1990.
23. On the new republican administrations see *ROTU* 1/91 pp. 20–54.
24. The popular mood was summed up to Gorbachev, pointedly and courageously, by the Russian editor of the Russian-language newspaper of Lithuania in January 1990: see heading to Chapter 11.
25. See *Iz* 19 December 1989 p. 4 col. 3, *Prav vest* 5/90 pp. 6–7.
26. See in particular the Treaty between the RSFSR and Ukraine, *PU* 21 November 1990.
27. See *Pr* 9 August 1990 p. 2 with *New York Times International* 3 September 1990 p. 2.
28. See *Pr* 8 July 1990 p. 4; I am indebted to Peter Reddaway for this observation.
29. See *ROTU* 9/91 pp. 40–2, 12/91 p. 25.
30. For analysis of the alignments among RSFSR deputies see *AiF* 17/90 p. 2, 26/90 pp. 4–6, 29/90 p. 2, 37/90 p. 4.
31. See Koch p. 126.
32. See above pp. 142–3. Party membership in the armed forces was kept out of the Soviet media until 1990, but it had long been known; see Miller, *Sov Stud*, July 1988, *Iz TsK* 4/90 p. 113 (the jobs of 1.2 million are unaccounted for), *Pr* 7 July 1990 p. 2 col. 6, *MN* 27/90 p. 6. According to *Pr* 27 November 1991 there were about 30,000 primary CPSU organisations in the armed forces.
33. See *ROTU* 43/90 pp. 12–14, 2/91 p. 4, 5/91 p. 30.
34. For material on plans for army reform see Yazov, *KZ* 18 November 1990, *Prav vest* 48/90 pp. 5–12, *ROTU* 15/90 pp. 8–10, 43/90 pp. 6–8, 27/91 pp. 9–14.

35. Some senior commanders evidently tried to encourage such attitudes: in mid 1989 the commander of the Internal Forces, Yu. V. Shatalin, offered himself as a hostage to Azeri insurgents and gave interviews about it afterwards; see *MN* 40/89 p. 5.
36. See further *ROTU* 1/91 pp. 11–12, 5/91 pp. 29–30, 23/91 p. 6.
37. See *ROTU* 51–52/91 pp. 25–6.
38. See *Koms Pr* 25 November 1990 p. 1.
39. See *SE, Iz* 15 January 1991, RFE/RL *Daily Report* no. 15 (22 January 1991).
40. Notably a former deputy chief of General Staff, K. I. Kobets, a former deputy head of the MPA, D. A. Volkogonov, the future head of the Russian KGB, V. V. Ivanenko and Colonel A. V. Rutskoi, his future Vice-President. See Gryaznevich, *ROTU* 15/91 p. 18, *AiF* 14/91 p. 4.
41. See, for example, their attempts to interest Yeltsin when he was first secretary in Moscow, *RLRB* 187/87 (14 May 1987) p. 13.
42. For surveys see Schneider in particular; further: *ROTU* 34/90 pp. 8–16, 47/90 pp. 3–6, 1/91 pp. 12–15; *MN* 21/90 p. 6, 28/90 pp. 8–9; *Iz TsK* 8/90 pp. 145–61, 9/90 pp. 87–9, 2/91 pp. 61–8.
43. For example the Inter-regional Group and *Soyuz* at the Union level, 'Democratic Russia' and 'Communists of Russia' in the RSFSR, or *Rukh* and the 'Group of 239' in the Ukraine; these were often more important than the newly founded parties.
44. See *ROTU* 18/91 pp. 1–3; Kiva, *Iz* 26 February 1991, on the democrats' attitudes to the CPSU; and, on the 'lumpenisation' of the left, Tsipko 1991, Kiva loc. cit. and B. Kagarlitsky as quoted in Australian Broadcasting Commission *Correspondents Report* 17 March 1991.
45. See *Iz* 26 December 1990 p. 6 col. 1; ibid. 21 December 1990 p. 5 col. 8.
46. On Ligachev see the interviews in *Iz* 14 September and *ZV* 22 December 1990; in the former he makes Delphic utterances about a new False Dmitrii (a pretender from the Time of Troubles – Yeltsin??) but it is scarcely a rallying cry.
47. On *Soyuz* see *ROTU* 20/91 (17 May 1991) pp. 16–21. Its leaders were all Party members but did not take the CPSU whip in parliament.
48. In just over three weeks he had articles in *SR* 21 November and *KZ* 8 December 1990, as well as in the *Washington Post* 16 November, *Boston Globe* 18 November, *Los Angeles Times* 22 November, and *Observer* 9 December 1990 (these last four were unavailable to me).
49. See *SR, KZ* loc. cit. and compare Gryaznevich.
50. See p. 8.
51. Michel Tatu quoted in *ROTU* 20/91 p. 19. The strong representation of '*Volksrussen*' rather than '*Reichsrussen*' is another point of resemblance with the NSDAP.
52. See Dunlop *ROTU* 6/91 and K. Lubenchenko *MN* 1/91 (6–13 January 1991) p. 4.

## 10 The August Coup

1. See *KZ* 15 November 1990 with *ROTU* 49/90 pp. 1–3, *KZ* 8 December and *New York Times* 24 December 1990.

2. For Gorbachev's two speeches and the reaction to the first, see *Iz* 17 November 1990.
3. See *SR* 18 November 1990 p. 3.
4. See *Iz* 16 October 1990 p. 4 col. 2, *SR* 21 November 1990, *Iz* 24 November 1990 p. 1, RFE/RL *Daily Report* no. 228 (3 December 1990), *ROTU* 50/90 pp. 8, 19, 23.
5. Respectively a member of the Presidential Council and Gorbachev's personal assistant for economics. See *Koms Pr* 22 January 1991, *The Financial Times* 26 January 1991, as summarised in Rahr, *ROTU* 7/91.
6. See *AiF* 1/91 p. 1, and compare Migranyan in *MN* 4/91 (27 January–3 February 1991) p. 5, and L. Telen, ibid. p. 3.
7. It was published on 24 November (see Chapter 11) but its principal terms were already determined; see *KZ* 7 November 1990.
8. See *Pr* 13, 23 December, *Iz* 26 December 1990; *Iz* 13 February 1991.
9. See *KZ* 8 December 1990, the *Age* (Melbourne) 19 January 1991.
10. See *Iz* 1 December 1990 p. 4, quotation from col. 8.
11. Some of the fiercest attacks on *perestroika* came at a Central Committee Plenum at the end of January 1991: see *Pr* 1–2, 4–5 February 1991.
12. Akhromeev killed himself after the August coup and Shlyaga was dismissed, but not arrested as a participant.
13. See Shakhnazarov; Allik had spoken in similar terms in December.
14. For the revised Constitution see *Iz* 27 December 1990, and compare the new institutions with those discussed on pp. 120–6 above.
15. Composition in *Iz* 8 March 1991, and see p. 176 below.
16. Ministers were now quite clearly public servants and could not be questioned in parliament. For Cabinet membership see *Iz* 2, 4 March 1991.
17. The 16 Autonomous Republics within the RSFSR could outvote not just Russia but all the Union-Republics together! For the conservatism of Autonomous Republics see the voting patterns in *AiF* 15/91 pp. 4–5.
18. Both Council of the Federation and Cabinet resembled the equivalent institutions of Bismarck's Germany; see Koch pp. 121–34.
19. Constitutional amendments had to be passed by two-thirds of the total Congress membership. Many deputies from the Baltic, Transcaucasia and Moldavia were boycotting proceedings and hence even quite small lobbies could thwart a two-thirds majority. This affected results every bit as much as the balance of conservative and radical forces.
20. As observed by Sobakin, *Iz* 9 March 1991.
21. See *Iz* 27–29 December 1990. The succession rules discussed on p. 122 were amended in favour of the Vice-President.
22. One of their stipulations may have been the holding of the March 1991 referendum on the Union Treaty. For outsiders this seemed to serve no purpose: its results were entirely predictable, and it polarised many communities, making a negotiated settlement more difficult. But from the conservatives' standpoint it documented the (mainly Russian) majority for Unionism, a majority which, in their view, should be binding on all republics. A.I. Luk'yanov was to claim during the August coup (*Pr* 20 August 1991) that Gorbachev had broken faith with the referendum results.
23. The decree on joint patrols was signed by the Defence and Interior Ministers in late December (see Rahr *ROTU* 7/91, Kudryavtsev 1991),

but by Gorbachev not until *Iz* 30 January 1991. For the Law *On the Legal Regime of a State of Emergency* see ibid. 9 April 1990.

24. See *ROTU* 36/91 pp. 7–8, 13–14.
25. See *Iz* 15 November 1990.
26. See *Iz* 3 December, with Gromov interviewed in *SR* 5 December 1990. Bakatin was disliked by conservatives for encouraging depoliticisation of the police force.
27. For appointment see *Iz* 14–15 January 1991; on his insubordination, *ROTU* 27/91 pp. 1–6.
28. See *Iz* 21 December 1990 p. 5 cols 7–8, with Alksnis's and Gorbachev's responses ibid. pp. 7–8.
29. See *ROTU* 2/91 p. 31.
30. He had been Chairman of the Committee of Youth Organisations (1968–80), a body which handled the foreign relations of the Soviet youth movement, and Deputy Chairman of the Union for Friendship and Cultural Relations with Foreign Countries (1980–6); these appointments would have required KGB approval and the work would have involved cooperation with security.
31. See Orlik, *Iz* 23 August, with *Pr* 2 September 1991. A related incident: in August 1990 Shevardnadze whilst in the USA was told by a 'competent authority' that the Americans had attacked Baghdad – and had to ask James Baker for the truth (*ROTU* 48/91 p. 14); 'competent authority' was an accepted euphemism for the KGB.
32. See *EL* 9 October 1990, with Presidential annulment in *Iz* 28 November 1990.
33. See *Sov Lat* 11 August 1990, *Iz TsK* 12/90 pp. 21–3, *SR* 21 November 1990. The Committee of Constitutional Supervision (it will be remembered) could not deal with republican acts.
34. See, for example, *ROTU* 12/91 pp. 21–4.
35. See *Iz* 28 November 1990; on the risk of vigilante action see *ROTU* 1/91 pp. 57–8, 2/91 p. 21.
36. See *Iz* 8 January 1991, *ROTU* 3/91 pp. 7–9. The situation was further complicated by issues of CPSU property, often, as we have seen, media premises. It would seem to be legitimate to ask for police assistance in restoring property pronounced legally one's own; but in the case of the Riga Press Building, the pro-CPSU wing of the Latvian Communist Party asked, not the local police, but military units of the All-Union MVD, to overturn a decision of the Latvian parliament! See *ROTU* 2/91 p. 19 and Latsis *Iz* 22 January 1991.
37. See *ZV* 12 December 1990 (Presidential annulment *Iz* 8 January 1991) and *ROTU* 51/90 pp. 8–9.
38. *Iz* 2 January 1991 p. 4.
39. See *Iz* 10 January 1991.
40. See *ROTU* 4/91 pp. 6–15, 28–30, 5/91 pp. 6–9, 16–24.
41. See Latsis *Iz* 15 January.
42. See *Iz* 14 January 1991.
43. See Kusín, *ROTU* 4/91 and Latsis *Iz* 22 January.
44. See *Iz* 15, 17, 18 January 1991; *ROTU* 7/91 p. 27, 10/91 pp. 8–9, *KZ* 5 February 1991 p. 3.

45. See Alekseev, Kudryavtsev, Latsis, Piskotin and Shatalin (for January and February 1991); also Patriarch Aleksii in *Iz* 15 January, Alekseev in *Koms Pr* 15 January, *Iz* 18 January, Bakatin in *Koms Pr* 16 January. For parliamentary reactions see *Iz* 14–16 January.
46. See *Iz* 15, 16, 23 January 1991 and *ROTU* 4/91 pp. 1–3.
47. See *MN* 4/91 p. 6.
48. For instance R. N. Nishanov (*Iz* 8 February) or G. S. Tarazevich (*ROTU* 6/91 p. 2).
49. See *SE*, *Iz* 15 January, *Pr*, *Iz* 20 February 1991, *ROTU* 9/91 pp. 40–2.
50. See pp. 169–70 above.
51. The three Baltic republics, Moldavia, Georgia and Armenia.
52. Text in *Pr* 24 April 1991. One newspaper, *Kommersant*, thought there was a secret codicil to the Agreement (17/91 (22–29 April 1991) pp. 1–3); correct or not, its interpretation of the overt and implicit meaning of the Agreement rings true. See also *Iz* 26 April, *Koms Pr* 30 April 1991.
53. *Kommersant* 17/91 p. 30.
54. This reconstruction of the coup was written on the basis of sources available in 1991 and before the conspirators were brought to trial. *ROTU* 35/91 and 36/91 provided valuable chronology and analysis, and Elliot's eyewitness impressions are recommended. The following Russian sources were useful: Gorbachev's press conference, *Pr* 23 August 1991 p. 2; documents in *Koms Pr* 27 and 29 August 1991; statements under questioning of Yazov, Kryuchkov and Pavlov (the 'coup tapes'), *Iz* 10 October 1991 p. 7; statements in the RSFSR Supreme Soviet, *Iz* 22–23 October 1991; interview of E. K. Lisov, RSFSR Deputy Procurator-General, *Pr* 26 October 1991; report of formal charges against the conspirators, *RG* 15 January 1992. The 'coup tapes' were leaked to *Der Spiegel* and published there on 7 October, then retranslated into Russian and published in *Izvestiya*; there seems to be no suggestion that their material was forged.
55. See *RG* 15 January 1992, and compare *SR*, *RG* 7 September 1991. A further Politburo member, Yu. A. Prokof'ev, first secretary of Moscow *gorkom* was arrested in August but is absent from the list of those charged.
56. Kryuchkov, Pavlov, Pugo, Yanaev, Yazov – a majority of the nine members of the Security Council!
57. Baklanov, Kryuchkov, Pavlov and Yazov.
58. Starodubtsev, Tizyakov and Varennikov; see Bondarev, Blokhin *et al.* Note that General Gromov who also signed this manifesto seems not to have been involved in the coup.
59. In addition to the listed affiliations Pugo and probably Yanaev had KGB connections.
60. See *Iz* 22 October 1991. L. P. Kravchenko claimed later that he was given the State Committee's orders for the media at 1.00 a.m. on the 19th, by the Central Committee Secretary Yu. A. Manaenkov and in the Central Committee building; see *ROTU* 36/91 p. 84. The first secretary of L'vov *obkom* was in Moscow on the 18th and met B. K. Pugo; a file in the L'vov *obkom* 'on the introduction of state of emergency' contained material dated 19 August, but was itself dated **18** August; see ibid. pp. 92–3 and *Postfactum News Review* 26 August 1991.

61. Shenin was also the author of the instructions to Lithuanian communists cited on p. 140.
62. See 'coup tapes' col. 1, my emphasis.
63. See *ROTU* 32/91 p. 39.
64. See A. Oleinikov, *Pr* 28 October 1991 p. 3.
65. See Lisov, loc. cit.
66. The names most often mentioned were Luk'yanov and Kryuchkov (see I. S. Silaev, *Iz* 23 August, A. N. Yakovlev quoted in *ROTU* 36/91 pp. 74–5, Gorbachev, *Iz* 20 September 1991).
67. See Yazov and Kryuchkov loc. cit. cols 1–2 and 6, Gorbachev, *Pr* 23 August p. 2 col. 1, Luk'yanov quoted in *ROTU* 35/91 p. 50. Gorbachev is the only one of these who suggests he was given any kind of choice.
68. Yazov and Pavlov (loc. cit. cols 2 and 7) claimed that the State Committee for the Emergency was not formed until late on the 18th August, but Gorbachev said the delegation that had met him earlier called itself 'the committee'. See also Lisov, loc. cit.
69. *Koms Pr* 27 August.
70. Yazov and Pavlov, loc. cit. cols 2, 4 and 8. It seems to have been at this meeting that the First Deputy Premier, V. I. Shcherbakov, revealed that the Union authorities simply did not dispose of the expected reserves of retail goods, and that the Foreign Minister, A. A. Bessmertnykh, refused to join the coup; see also *ROTU* 36/91 p. 91.
71. Details in this paragraph from *ROTU* 35/91 pp. 35–40, *Pr* 20 August.
72. *Iz* 23 August; one of the few ministers to object was the Minister for the Environment, N. N. Vorontsov, mentioned above p. 117.
73. See *ROTU* 36/91 p. 49.
74. Kryuchkov and Yazov denied such plans, loc. cit. cols 3 and 6, but for claims they existed see *Iz* 26 August p. 6, *Pr* 3 September, *AiF* 35/91 p. 6. The latter refer clearly to an operation that might have been launched on 20 August.
75. See *ROTU* 35/91 p. 46.
76. Compare the interrogator in 'coup tapes' col. 3, and Bakatin, *MN* 36/91 p. 6.
77. See *Koms Pr* 27 August; the most telling points were censored out of the version in *Pr*, *Iz* 20 August.
78. *Iz* 21 August; he had been asked by Yeltsin on the 19th to declare himself and this statement was made on the 20th (*ROTU* 35/91 p. 40).
79. See Elliot pp. 64–5, *ROTU* 36/91 pp. 24–5.
80. Some examples ibid.
81. See *Iz* 23 August.
82. The only other military actions were taken in the Baltic. In Kirghizia the President, A. Akaev, put down a local coup on the 19th. See *ROTU* 35/91 pp. 41–5, 36/91 pp. 42–5.
83. See *Postfactum News Review* 22 August 1991, *ROTU* 35/91 pp. 48–50, 44/91 pp. 31–2.
84. See *Koms Pr* 27 August, *Financial Times* 24 August as quoted in *ROTU* 36/91 p. 13.
85. As Elliot writes, 'a politically conscious section of the population – probably not the majority, but sufficiently numerous to prevail'.

86. See Yazov, Kryuchkov loc. cit. cols 3, 4, 6. Yazov's assumption of social docility was extraordinary: 'Who could have imagined that they would throw down Molotov cocktails . . . ?'
87. See Bakatin 1991, *Iz* 14 October p. 2, 7 November 1991 p. 1.
88. On these points see Chapters 8 and 11.
89. Otto Latsis, *Iz* 23 August 1991.

## 11 The Union Treaty

1. *Sov Lit* 16 January 1990; see p. 227 note 24.
2. They (and in particular A. N. Yakovlev) have been accused, to my mind plausibly, of deliberately encouraging nationalism in the Baltic; see *Pr* 11 July 1990, p. 5, *ROTU* 29/90 p. 7. One suspects that they saw in the Baltic the most westernised part of the Union, a region whose high-productivity economy and orderly politics offered a model for *perestroika*, and that they simply underrated the strength of separatist feeling.
3. See p. 156 above.
4. For its text see Vasil'ev and Gureev pp. 164–9; some comments in Kudryavtsev *Iz* 30 November 1990.
5. See *Pr* 6 February 1990 p. 2 col. 2, *Iz* 16 March 1990 p. 2 col. 2. For more detail on the evolution of the Treaty plan see Sheehy, *ROTU* 7/90 pp. 9–11, 27/90 pp. 14–17.
6. See p. 157.
7. Stages in negotiations and drafting are noted in: *Iz* 13, 14 June, *Pr* 16, 21 June, *Iz* 21, 24 July, *EL* 27 July, *Iz* 4, 7 August, 6, 26 September, 2 October, 3 November, *KZ* 7 November 1990, *Iz* 9 February, 7, 12 March, *Pr* 25 May, 4 June 1991, *RG* 11 June 1991. The referendum of 17 March 1991 solved very little: 76 per cent supported a renewed Union but it was boycotted in six republics; see above p. 229 note 22, *Iz* 18 December 1990 p. 2 cols 2–3, 18, 30 January 1991, 18, 19, 27 March 1991 with *ROTU* 7/91 pp. 5–8, 13/91 pp. 1–23.
8. See *Iz* 24 November 1990, 9 March, 27 June and 15 August 1991.
9. Rassolov is an unusually well-informed interpretation of the early stage of negotiations.
10. See Khasbulatov, *AiF* 28/90 and 30/90, for an example.
11. In Azerbaidzhan the ruling group had been dislodged by mass revolt in January 1990 and restored by the army. Note the deft evolution of L. M. Kravchuk in Ukraine from party secretary (for ideology!) to leader of a moderate nationalist coalition.
12. Those who lost out were the Autonomous Republics (see below), and still more 'non-titular', non-Russian ethnic minorities, especially the Armenians of Nagorno-Karabakh.
13. But note where it was vulnerable: Russian officers and bureaucrats could not but be influenced by the anti-Centralist currents in Russia proper.
14. See the *Nationalities Policy* . . . , section 2, point 1, and V. G. Afanas'ev in *Iz TsK* 6/89 p. 81.
15. See, for example, *ROTU* 41/91 p. 6, 47/91 pp. 20–3.
16. See Solzhenitsyn 1991 pp. 11–29. This was taken up by Yeltsin in early 1991: see *MN* 4/91 (27 January–3 February 1991) p. 1, *ROTU* 7/91 p. 36,

RFE/RL *Daily Report* 18 and 19 March 1991 and Tsipko 1991. For its first few days the Commonwealth of Independent States was also referred to as a Slavic Union.

17. See *Prav vest* 5/90 pp. 6–7, *Pr* 21 July 1989 p. 4 col. 6, *SR* 3 September 1989 p. 3 col. 5.

18. Above all in Ukraine, where the Popular Front (*Rukh*) originated and flourished in the Austrianised mainly Uniate-Catholic western provinces and extended its support only gradually into the centre and the Russianised east.

19. It is conceivable that similar considerations worked in Azerbaidzhan, in respect either of Iran with which it shares Shi'ite Islam, or of the linguistically similar Turkey.

20. Discussions were held in Minsk in November 1990 about a Baltic-Black Sea Union of the Ukraine, Belorussia and the three Baltic states; see RFE/RL *Daily Report* nos 222–223 (23 & 26 November 1990). Colonel Alksnis claimed the CIA was behind the idea, according to *Koms Pr* 20 November 1990.

21. Despite proximity few Central Asian Muslims are Shi'ite.

22. See Rassolov, speeches of republican leaders in *Iz* 17 November, 22 & 23 December 1990 and provisional Treaty signatories in *Iz* 12 & 13 March 1991.

23. See Wheare especially pp. 2–4, 29–36 (quotation from p. 36) and Kudryavtsev & Topornin.

24. See *Pr* 6 February 1990 p. 2 col. 2, *Iz* 16 March 1990 p. 2 col. 2. The idea of entry on different terms may have owed something to the special status of Finland and Poland under the Tsars; it was first raised in this context by Muksinov, *Sov gos i pravo* 10/89 pp. 3–13. See also ROTU 49/89 p. 5, 27/90 pp. 13–14.

25. See Henry Kissinger 'Gorbachev's revolution lets empire strike back', *Australian* 21 January 1991.

26. Yeltsin's attitude to this independence was encapsulated in his proposal to put its major ministers in the gift of the RSFSR parliament; see p. 152 above.

27. See RFE/RL *Daily Report* no. 144 (31 July 1991).

28. Analysis is of the fourth published text in *Iz* 15 August 1991 except where otherwise noted. I have drawn also on the following: Constitutional amendments in *Iz* 27 December 1990; R. N. Nishanov *On the General Conception* . . . ; the Law of April 1990 *On the Delimitation* . . . ; the RSFSR Decree of June 1990 *On the Delimitation of Administrative Functions* . . . ; the Ukrainian Declaration of Sovereignty of July 1990; and section 2 of *Basic Directions* . . . in *Iz* 27 October 1990. For parliamentary discussion see *Iz* 29 November, 4 December, 21–23 December 1990, 28 May 1991, *SR*, *RG* 5 June 1991. Other useful commentaries are Lazarev, Kudryavtsev 1990, *Pr* 10 December 1990, and Sheehy in *ROTU* 51/90 pp. 1–6, 12/91 pp. 1–4. I am grateful to Rudolf Plehwe for comments on a draft of this section.

29. The President and the two chambers of the Supreme Soviet would each have appointed one third of the Court's members.

30. Since the Treaty could only be amended by agreement of all the signatories this appears to create two levels of Constitution.
31. The influence of the Vilnius fiasco is plain here. There was no provision (analogous to Article 2, Section 2 of the US Constitution) allowing the Union to assume control of republican forces.
32. Compare Treaty Paragraph 11 with the US Constitution, Article 6.
33. Military installations in a place like Kazakhstan covered a lot of territory; republics had had no significant taxation powers hitherto.
34. These were not listed in the Treaty but can be deduced by comparing the Union's powers in the Treaty with those in the Law *On the Delimitation . . .* of April 1990.
35. See, for example, the ideas of Z. K. Gamsakhurdia in *Iz* 2 January 1991.
36. See p. 157 above; this had stipulated *inter alia* that two-thirds of the electorate must support secession – a provision that seemed to rule independence out for some republics.
37. See Nishanov quoted in *Iz* 4 December 1990 p. 1.
38. See pp. 123, 169 above.
39. There is a resemblance here to the German *Bundesrat* under Bismarck. But it would surely have been less cumbersome to retain a small Council of the Federation for the purpose.
40. See pp. 177, 192 above.
41. See *ROTU* 36/91 pp. 85–6, *Iz* 26 August, *Ved SSSR* 37/91 articles 1091–1093.
42. See *ROTU* 36/91 p. 81.
43. *Iz* 29 August, 6 September 1991.
44. They were Russia (subject to amendments), Belorussia, Kazakhstan, the four republics of Central Asia and Armenia; see *Iz* 4 September, 4 October, 18 October 1991.
45. *Iz* 25 & 26 November 1991.
46. They were the same republics that had signed the Economic Treaty, minus Armenia; see *Iz* 26 November 1991, *ROTU* 49/91 (6 December 1991) pp. 1–4.
47. See *PU* 7 December 1991.
48. *Iz* 29 November, 2 December 1991.
49. *Iz* 9 December 1991, cf. *ROTU* 51–52/91 pp. 1–7, 27–30, *RRR* 2/92 pp. 1–5; text ibid. pp. 4–5, *RG*, *PU* 10 December 1991.
50. See *Iz* 25–31 December 1991, *RRR* 2/92 pp. 56–8.

## 12   Reflections: Gorbachev, Communism and Reform

1. *Koms Pr* 24 December 1991.
2. See Luxemburg 1904 especially pp. 86–94, 102.
3. Oscar Lange in *The Political Economy of Socialism* (Warsaw, 1957) p. 16, as quoted in Nove 1961 p. 22. This is what Russian intellectuals mean when they speak of the persistence of elements of War Communism.
4. I disagree with the view often expressed that there was no middle ground in Soviet politics (see, for example, *The Economist* 26 January 1991 p. 37). Consider the coalition of moderate ex-communists and moderate

nationalists that the Ukrainian politician L.M. Kravchuk was able to mobilise in late 1991 (see *ROTU* 50/91 pp. 1–5). It was exactly what Gorbachev had held out as a model – but the unique pressures of Party and Union leadership on Gorbachev made it much more difficult for him to realise.

5. Sir Karl Popper foresees that '[t]he capitalism of the supermarkets – and that is what they so fervently desire – will remain beyond their reach'; see Urban, *ROTU* 22/91. This may well be correct; but the resentment that options open to others should be closed to Russian society could become a political force in itself and stimulate something very like Slavophilism.

6. See Schneider p. 18.

7. By modifying its policies in 1953–7 the CPSU managed to get Stalinism treated as something accidental and avoided a thorough social reckoning with it.

8. There were exceptions of course, in particular Academician Sakharov and the lawyer V.N. Chalidze.

9. This is to sidestep a rather different point made, for example, by Malia and Sestanovich: that Gorbachev exaggerated the danger from the *apparat* and used this as an excuse for his immobility. There is no denying the intellectual bankruptcy and demoralisation of the 'Imperial Superstructure'; but combined with its access to resources this made it more, not less, dangerous.

10. Recall Yakovlev's talk of breaking with 'the thousand-year-old Russian paradigm of unfreedom', above p. 88. The German banker Alfred Herrhausen was asked by Soviet politicians how long he thought it would take *perestroika* to be effective; he answered, apparently to their surprise, 'Two generations: one to will it and one to realise it'. (Information kindly supplied by Hans-Joachim Fliedner.)

11. See *Novyi mir* 7/89. I accept Migranyan's general point about prioritisation, but not his specific argument for a constitutional order short of democracy, on the model, say, of Hanoverian Britain or Prussia after Frederick the Great. Given twentieth century communications technology and the mobilised nature of Soviet society I doubt if there could have been an alternative to the formal trappings of mass democracy.

12. And Shevardnadze still at foreign affairs. Note that Gromov, for all his conservatism, was not accused of complicity in the coup.

13. A. Plutnik in *Iz* 23 December 1991.

14. See Plutnik and Brown 1991.

15. Gooding 1992 makes a similar point.

# Bibliography

## I  Newspapers and Journals

### A  Soviet Newspapers

|                                              | Abbreviation |
| -------------------------------------------- | ------------ |
| *Argumenty i fakty*                          | *AiF*        |
| *Izvestiya*                                  | *Iz*         |
| *Kazakhstanskaya pravda*                     | *Kaz Pr*     |
| *Kommersant*                                 |              |
| *Kommunist* (Armenia)                        | *KE*         |
| (became *Golos Armenii* August 1990)         | *GA*         |
| *Komsomol'skaya pravda*                      | *Koms Pr*    |
| *Krasnaya zvezda*                            | *KZ*         |
| *Literaturnaya gazeta*                       | *LG*         |
| *Moscow News*                                | *MN*         |
| *Nedelya*                                    |              |
| *Nezavisimaya gazeta*                        | *NG*         |
| *Pravda*                                     | *Pr*         |
| *Pravda Ukrainy*                             | *PU*         |
| *Pravitel'stvennyi vestnik*                  | *Prav vest*  |
| *Rossiiskaya gazeta*                         | *RG*         |
| *Sovetskaya Belorossiya*                     | *SB*         |
| *Sovetskaya Estoniya*                        | *SE*         |
| *Sovetskaya Latviya*                         | *Sov Lat*    |
| *Sovetskaya Litva*                           | *Sov Lit*    |
| (became *Ekho Litvy* April 1990)             | *EL*         |
| *Sovetskaya Rossiya*                         | *SR*         |
| *Trud*                                       |              |
| *Zarya vostoka* (Georgia)                    | *ZV*         |
| (became *Vestnik Gruzii* February 1991)      | *VG*         |

### B  Soviet Journals

|                                       |                   |
| ------------------------------------- | ----------------- |
| *Izvestiya TsK*                       | *Iz TsK*          |
| *Kommunist*                           | *Komm*            |
| *Narodnyi deputat*                    | *Nar dep*         |
| *Novyi mir*                           |                   |
| *Ogonek*                              |                   |
| *Partiinaya zhizn'*                   | *P zh*            |
| *Sovetskoe gosudarstvo i pravo*       | *Sov gos i pravo* |
| *Vedomosti Verkhovnogo Soveta SSSR*   | *Ved SSSR*        |

## C  Non-Soviet Journals, Translations and Abstracts

| | |
|---|---|
| *Current Digest of the Soviet Press* | *CDSP* |
| *Problems of Communism* | *PC* |
| *Radio Liberty Research Bulletin* | *RLRB* |
| *Radio Free Europe Research* | *RFER* |
| *Report on the USSR* | *ROTU* |
| *Report on Eastern Europe* | *ROEE* |
| *RFE/RL Research Report* | *RRR* |
| *Russkaya mysl'* (Paris) | |
| *Soviet Economy* | *Sov Econ* |
| *Soviet Studies* | *Sov Stud* |
| *Survey* | |

## II  Monographs and Articles

Yevgeniya Albats, 'Will there be an End to the Lubyanka?', *MN* 10/90 (11 March 1990) p. 15.

S. S. Alekseev, 'Konstitutsionnyi nadzor: pervye shagi i problemy' (Constitutional Supervision: First Steps and Problems), *Iz* 28 August 1990.

———— 'Konstitutsiya i vlast'' (The Constitution and Power), *Iz* 3 December 1990.

———— 'The Non-Legal Aspects of the Battle', *MN* 4/91 (27 January–3 February 1991) p. 10.

———— 'Tret'ya vlast'' (The Third Power), *Iz* 23 February 1991.

L. Alekseeva, 'O proekte zakona o dobrovol'nykh obshchestvakh i samodeyatel'nykh ob"edineniyakh' (On the Draft Law on Voluntary Societies and Self-Managing Associations), *RLRB* (Russian Series) 78/88 (5 September 1988).

Patriarch Aleksii II, statement on Lithuania, *Iz* 15 January 1991.

V. I. Alksnis, 'Vyiti iz nokdauna' (Coming out of a Knock-down), interviewed in *SR* 21 November 1990.

———— 'O pol'ze sporov s Prezidentom . . . ' (The Use of Quarrels with the President . . . ), interviewed in *KZ* 8 December 1990.

Jaak Allik, 'Idti vperedi mechty' (Anticipate Dreams) *SE* 8 December 1990 (and summarised in *Iz* 1 December 1990 p. 3).

Nina Andreeva, 'Ne mogu otstupat' ot printsipov' (I Cannot Renounce Principles), *SR* 13 March 1988; editorial/reply: *Pr* 5 April 1988.

Anders Åslund, *Gorbachev's Struggle for Economic Reform*, Cornell University Press, 1989.

V. V. Bakatin, 'Struktura organov gosbezopasnosti byla opasnoi dlya gosudarstva' (The Structure of the State Security Organs was a Threat to the State), *Iz* 30 August 1991 p. 3.

Yuri Bandura, 'CPSU Portrait', *MN* 27/90 (15–22 July 1990) p. 6.

James D. Barber, *The Presidential Character: Predicting Performance in the White House*, Englewood Cliffs, NJ: Prentice-Hall, 1972, 1977.

L. Batkin, 'Mertvyi khvataet zhivogo' (The Dead Seize the Living), *LG* 38/89 (28 September 1989) p. 10.

H. J. Berman, *Justice in the USSR*, revised edition, enlarged, Harvard University Press, 1950, 1963.

Eduard Bernstein, *Die Voraussetzungen des Sozialismus und die Aufgaben der Sozialdemokratie*, Stuttgart: Dietz, 1899, 1920; in English *Evolutionary Socialism*, New York: Huebsch, 1909.

Seweryn Bialer (ed), *Politics, Society and Nationality Inside Gorbachev's Russia*, London & Boulder: Westview Press, 1989.

V. Boikov & Zh. Toshchenko, 'Posmotrim pravde v glaza' (Let Us Look Truth in the Face), *Pr* 16 October 1989.

V. A. Boldyrev, interviewed, *Iz* 3 November 1988, 9 February 1989, 26 July 1990.

Yu. V. Bondarev, Yu. V. Blokhin *et al.*, 'Slovo k narodu' (A Word to the People), *SR* 23 July 1991.

Elena Bonner, 'On Gorbachev', *New York Review of Books*, 17 May 1990, pp. 14–17.

———— 'What Happened is that Nothing Happened', *MN* 30/90 (5–12 August 1990) p. 5.

George W. Breslauer, 'Evaluating Gorbachev as Leader', *Sov Econ*, vol. 5, no. 4, October-December 1989, pp. 299–340.

———— (ed), *Can Gorbachev's Reforms Succeed?*, University of California at Berkeley, 1990.

Vladimir Brovkin, 'Revolution from Below: Informal Political Associations in Russia 1988–1989', *Sov Stud*, vol. 42, no. 2, April 1990, pp. 233–57.

Archie Brown, 'Andropov, Discipline and Reform?', *PC*, vol. xxxii, no. 1, January-February 1983, pp. 18–31.

———— (ed), *Political Culture and Communist Studies*, London: Macmillan, 1984.

———— 'Gorbachev: New Man in the Kremlin', *PC*, vol. xxxiv, no. 3, May-June 1985, pp. 1–23.

———— (ed), *Political Leadership in the Soviet Union*, London: Macmillan, 1989.

———— 'The Accidental Revolutionary', *Sunday Age*, 29 December 1991, reprinted from *Los Angeles Times*, 23 December 1991 p. B5.

Archie Brown, John Fennell, Michael Kaser and H. T. Willetts (general eds), *The Cambridge Encyclopedia of Russia and the Soviet Union*, Cambridge University Press, 1982.

Archie Brown and Jack Gray (eds), *Political Culture and Political Change in Communist States*, London: Macmillan, 1977, 1979.

Archie Brown and Michael Kaser (eds), *The Soviet Union since the Fall of Khrushchev*, London: Macmillan, 1975 and 1978.

———— *Soviet Policy for the 1980s*, London: Macmillan, 1982.

Yu. Burtin, 'Svoboda vybora' (Freedom of Choice), *Iz* 29 April 1988.

Alexander Dallin and A. F. Westin (eds), *Politics in the Soviet Union: Seven Cases*, New York: Harcourt, Brace & World, 1966.

*Deputaty Verkhovnogo Soveta RSFSR 11-ogo sozyva*, Moscow: Izvestiya, 1987.

John B. Dunlop, 'The Leadership of the Centrist Bloc', *ROTU* 6/91 (8 February 1991) pp. 4–6.

Iain Elliot, 'Three Days in August: On-the-Spot Impressions', *ROTU* 36/91 (6 September 1991) pp. 63–7.

V. K. Emel'yanov, speech at Lithuanian CPSU *aktiv*, *Sov Lit* 16 January 1990.

S. Ershov, 'Middle Class: dlya sebya ili dlya vsekh?' (Middle Class: for Themselves or for All?), *LG* 26/90 (27 June 1990) p. 14.

*Ezhegodnik Bol'shoi Sovetskoi Entsiklopedii*, Moscow: Sovetskaya Entsiklopediya, annual since 1957.

Yu Feofanov, 'Ne speshite na barrikady' (Don't Rush to the Barricades), *Iz* 12 September 1990.

Peter Gay, *The Dilemma of Democratic Socialism*, Columbia University Press, 1952, 1962.

N. Glazatov, 'Bestsenzurnaya tsenzura' (Censorless Censorship), *Prav vest* 40/90, pp. 22–3.

Paul Goble, 'Ethnic Politics in the USSR', *PC*, vol. xxxviii, no. 4, July-August 1989, pp. 1–14.

John Gooding, 'Gorbachev and Democracy', *Sov Stud* vol. 42, no. 2, April 1990, pp. 195–231.

———— 'Perestroika as Revolution from Within: An Interpretation', *Russian Review*, vol. 51, no. 1, January 1992, pp. 36–57.

M. S. Gorbachev, *Political Report of the CPSU Central Committee to the 27th Party Congress*, Moscow: Novosti, 1986.

———— *Perestroika: New Thinking for Our Country and the World*, London: Collins, New York: Harper & Row, 1987.

———— *Perestroika i novoe myshlenie dlya nashei strany i dlya vsego mira*, Moscow: Politizdat, 1988 (Russian version of Gorbachev 1987).

———— *Sotsialisticheskaya ideya i revolyutsionnaya perestroika* (The Socialist Idea and Revolutionary Perestroika), *Pr* 26 November 1989.

———— *Izbrannye rechi i stat'i*, Moscow: Politizdat, 6 vols 1987–9.

G. F. Gorbei *et al.* (eds), *Narodnoe obrazovanie i kul'tura v SSSR*, Moscow: Finansy i statistika, 1989.

V. Gryaznevich, 'Neposledovatel'nost' Gorbacheva razdrazhaet pravykh. No konets perestroiki – eshche ne konets reform' (Gorbachev's Inconsistency Annoys the Right. But the End of Perestroika is still not the End of Reforms), *Chas pik* (Leningrad Union of Journalists) 8/90.

Dušan Hamšík, *Writers Against Rulers* (translated by D. Orpington), London: Hutchinson, 1971.

Viktor Haynes and Olga Semyonova, *Workers Against the Gulag: The New Opposition in the Soviet Union*, London: Pluto Press, 1979.

Ronald J. Hill and Peter Frank, *The Soviet Communist Party*, London: Allen & Unwin, 1981, 1983, 1986.

Geoffrey Hosking, *A History of the Soviet Union*, London: Fontana/Collins, 1985, 1990

———— *The Rediscovery of Politics*, The 1988 Reith Lectures, reprinted from *The Listener*, 10 November–15 December 1988, London: BBC, 1988.

———— *The Awakening of the Soviet Union*, London: Heinemann, 1990, 1991 (updated revision of Reith Lectures).

A. Illesh & V. Rudnev, 'Tsenzura otmenena, tsenzory ostayutsya' (Censorship is Over, Censors Remain), *Iz* 9 October 1990.

A. A. Isupov *et al.* (eds), *Naselenie SSSR*, Moscow: Finansy i statistika, 1989.

Konstantin Kagalovskii, 'Vperedi – epokha nestabil'nosti' (The Epoch of Instability is Ahead), *NG* 30 April 1991 p. 4.

Boris Kagarlitsky, *The Thinking Reed: Intellectuals and the Soviet State, 1917 to the Present* (translated by Brian Pearce), revised paperback edition, London and New York: Verso, 1989.

Rasma Karklins, *Ethnic Relations in the USSR: The Perspective from Below*, London and Boston: Allen & Unwin, 1986.

K. S. Khallik (Hallik), interviewed in *SE* 4 December 1990.

R. I. Khasbulatov, 'Kakim byt' Soyuznomu dogovoru? (What should the Union Agreement be like?), *AiF* 28/90, (14–20 July 1990) and 30/90 (28 June–3 August 1990).

Henry Kissinger, 'Gorbachev's revolution lets empire strike back', *Australian* 21 January 1991.

A. V. Kiva, 'Tret'ya sila' (The Third Force), *Iz* 28 September 1990.

———— 'Oktyabr' v zerkale utopii i antiutopii' (October in the Mirror of Utopias and Anti-utopias), *Iz* 5 November 1990.

———— 'V plenu maksimalizma' (Hostage to Maximalism), *Iz* 24 January 1991.

———— 'Gorbachev, El'tsin i my' (Gorbachev, Yel'tsin and Ourselves), *Iz* 26 February 1991.

I. M. Klyamkin, 'Sto dnei Prezidenta' (The President's Hundred Days), *Koms Pr* 24 June 1990.

I. M. Klyamkin & A. Migranyan, 'Nuzhna "zheleznaya ruka"?' (Is an 'Iron Hand' Necessary?), *LG* 33/89 (16 August 1989) p. 10.

H. W. Koch, *A Constitutional History of Germany in the nineteenth and twentieth centuries*, London and New York: Longman, 1984.

N. E. Kruchina, 'Byudzhet KPSS: domysly i fakty' (The CPSU Budget: Conjectures and Facts) *Pr* 12 March 1990.

———— speech to XXVIII Party Congress, *Pr* 5 July 1990.

V. A. Kryuchkov, 'Navodit' poryadok vmeste' (Establish Order Together), *Pr* 13 December 1990.

———— 'KGB protiv sabotazha' (The KGB against Sabotage), *Pr* 23 December 1990.

———— 'K staromu vernut'sya nevozmozhno' (There is No Returning to the Old Ways), *Iz* 26 December 1990 p. 8.

V. N. Kudryavtsev, 'Verit' cheloveku' (Trust in People), *Pr* 3 May 1988.

———— 'O novom Soyuznom dogovore' (On the New Union Treaty), *Iz* 30 November 1990.

———— 'Demokratiya i pravovoi poryadok' (Democracy and Legal Order), *Iz* 5 February 1991.

V. N. Kudryavtsev and B. Topornin, 'Kakim byt' novomu Soyuznomu dogovoru?' (What should the New Union Agreement be like?), *Iz* 18 June 1990.

V. V. Kusín, 'Patterns of Intervention: Budapest, Prague, Vilnius, Riga', *ROTU* 4/91 (25 January 1991) pp. 3–6.

O. R. Latsis, 'Vpechatleniya, fakty i my' (Impressions, Facts and Ourselves), *Iz* 16 July 1990.

———— 'Ya boyus' politicheskogo Chernobylya' (I Fear a Political Chernobyl'), *Iz* 15 January 1991.

———— 'Rikoshet' (Ricochet), *Iz* 22 January 1991.

———— 'Gorbachev vernulsya v druguyu stranu. Ponimaet li on eto?' (Gorbachev has Returned to a Different Country. Does He Understand this?), *Iz* 23 August 1991.

———— 'Krushenie avtoritarnoi modeli' (The Collapse of the Authoritarian Model), *Iz* 28 August 1991.

B. M. Lazarev *et al.* (eds), *Novyi Soyuznyi dogovor: poiski reshenii* (The New Union Treaty: Search for Solutions), Moscow: Institute of State and Law, USSR Academy of Sciences, 1990.

V. M. Legostaev, 'Intellektual'noe dostoinstvo partii' (The Intellectual Quality of the Party), *Pr* 2 & 3 May 1989.

V. I. Lenin, *What is to be Done?*, translated by S. V. & P. Utechin, ed. S. V. Utechin, Oxford: Clarendon, 1963.

———— *State and Revolution*, Moscow: Progress, 1969.

N. V. Lemaev, 'Kto sleduyushchii?' (Who is Next?), interview in *Iz* 1 October 1990.

Moshe Lewin, *The Gorbachev Phenomenon: A Historical Interpretation*, University of California Press and London: Radius, 1988.

E. K. Lisov, 'Sledstvie rabotaet na istinu' (The Investigation is Working on the Truth), interview in *Pr* 26 October 1991.

General A. D. Lizichev, speech to Central Committee Plenum, *Pr* 19 March 1990.

John Löwenhardt, 'Nomenklatura and the Soviet Constitution', *Review of Socialist Law* 10 (1984) 35–55.

———— 'Political reform under Gorbachev: Towards the defeudalisation of Soviet politics?', *Acta Politica* (Amsterdam), vol. xxiii, 1988, no. 1, pp. 1–20.

John Löwenhardt & G. van den Berg, 'Disaster at the Chernobyl Nuclear Power Plant: A Study of Crisis Decision Making in the Soviet Union', pp. 37–65 of Rosenthal, Charles & 't Hart (eds).

Rosa Luxemburg, *Leninism or Marxism?* 1904 and University of Michigan Press, 1961.

Yu. M. Luzhkov, '100 pervykh dnei' (A Hundred First Days), interview, *Iz* 21 July 1990.

Martin Malia, 'The August Revolution', *New York Review of Books*, 26 September 1991, pp. 22–8.

Dawn Mann, *Paradoxes of Soviet Reform: The Nineteenth Communist Party Conference*, Washington DC: The Center for Strategic and International Studies, 1988.

Dawn Mann, Robert Monyak and Elizabeth Teague, *The Supreme Soviet: A Biographical Directory*, Munich: RFE/RL and Washington DC: CSIS, 1989.

Mervyn Matthews (ed), *Soviet Government: a Selection of Official Documents on Internal Policy*, London: Jonathan Cape, 1974.

Zhores Medvedev, *Gorbachev*, Oxford: Blackwell, 1986.

A. Migranyan, 'Dolgii put' k evropeiskomu domu' (The Long Road to a European Home), *Novyi mir* 7/89 pp. 166–84.

———— 'A Situation of Dual Power', *Novyi mir* 26/90 (8–15 July 1990) p. 6.

R. F. Miller, J. H. Miller and T. H. Rigby (eds), *Gorbachev at the Helm: A New Era in Soviet Politics?*, London: Croom Helm, 1987.

John H. Miller, 'The Communist Party: Trends and Problems', chapter 1 of Brown and Kaser 1982.

———— 'The Geographical Disposition of the Soviet Armed Forces', *Sov Stud*, vol. xl, no. 3, July 1988, pp. 406–33.

———— 'The XIX Party Conference: Prospects for Political Reform', *The Age Monthly Review* (Melbourne), September 1988, p. 12.

———— 'Gorbachev the Radical', paper presented at the 1990 Annual Meeting of the American Political Science Association, San Francisco, September 1990.

Zdeněk Mlynář, 'Il mio compagno di studi Mikhail Gorbaciov', *L'Unità* (Rome) 9 April 1985.

M. E. Mote, 'Electing the USSR Congress of People's Deputies', *PC* vol. xxxviii, no. 6, November-December 1989, pp. 51–6.

I. Sh. Muksinov, 'Sovetskii federalizm i kompleksnoe ekonomicheskoe i sotsial'noe razvitie soyuznykh respublik' (Soviet Federalism and All-round Economic and Social Development of the Union-Republics), *Sov gos i pravo* 10/89 pp. 3–13.

*Narodnoe khozyaistvo RSFSR*, Moscow: Statistika, annual (with variations in title) since 1957.

Narodnoe khozyaistvo SSSR, Moscow: Statistika, annual (with variations in title) since 1956.

*Narodnye deputaty SSSR: spravochnik*, Moscow: Vneshtorgizdat, 1990.

A. A. Nikonov, 'Takim on byl' (That is How he Was), *Iz* 24 November 1987.

———— 'Polveka vmeste. Kak dal'she?' (Half a Century together. What Next?), *Komm* 14/90 pp. 47–58.

R. N. Nishanov, 'Ob obshchei kontseptsii novogo Soyuznogo dogovora i poryadke ego zaklyucheniya' (On the General Conception of the New Union Treaty and the Manner of Concluding it), *Iz* 20 December 1990 pp. 2–3.

Alec Nove, *The Soviet Economy*, London: George Allen & Unwin, first edition, 1961.

———— *Stalinism and After*, London: Allen & Unwin, 1975, 1981.

———— 'Is there a ruling class in the USSR?', *Sov Stud*, vol. xxvii, no. 4, October 1975, pp. 615–38.

Yu Orlik, 'Seryi kardinal' (The Grey Cardinal), *Iz* 23 August 1991.

Yu M. Orlov, 'Kto i za chto kritikuet Prezidenta?' (Who Criticises the President, and for What?), *AiF* 32/90 (11–17 August 1990) p. 5.

Harold Perkin, *The Rise of Professional Society: England since 1880*, London and New York: Routledge, 1989.

Richard Pipes, *Russia under the Old Regime*, London: Weidenfeld & Nicolson, 1974.

M. I. Piskotin, 'Konstitutsii nuzhna zashchita' (The Constitution Needs Defending), *Iz* 26 January 1991.

L. Piyasheva, 'Zachem Gorbachevu radikaly?' (Why does Gorbachev need the Radicals?), *SE* 24 August 1990.

Al'bert Plutnik, 'On prikhodil – eto znachitel'nee togo, chto on ukhodit' (He Happened – That is More Important than his Going'), *Iz* 23 December 1991.

G. Kh. Popov, 'The Times are Getting Tougher', *MN* 42/90 (28 October–4 November 1990) p. 7.

Alexander Rahr, 'Gorbachev and El'tsin in a Deadlock', *ROTU* 7/91 (15 February 1991) pp. 1–5.

M. M Rassolov, 'Kakim on budet, nash Soyuz?' (What Will it be Like, our Union?), *Prav vest* 37/90 pp. 1 & 4.

Peter Reddaway, 'Gorbachev the Bold', *New York Review of Books*, vol. xxxiv, no. 9, 28 May 1987, pp. 21–5.

———— 'Is the Soviet Union Drifting towards Anarchy?', *ROTU* 34/89 (25 August 1989) pp. 1–5.

R. A. Remington, *Winter in Prague: Documents on Czechoslovak Communism in Crisis*, Cambridge, Mass. & London: MIT Press, 1969.

T. H. Rigby, *Communist Party Membership in the USSR, 1917–67*, Princeton University Press, 1968.

———— (ed), *The Stalin Dictatorship*, Sydney University Press, 1968.

———— *Political Elites in the USSR: Central Leaders and Local Cadres from Lenin to Gorbachev*, Aldershot, Hants & Brookfield, Vermont: Edward Elgar & Gower Publishing Co, 1990.

———— *The Changing Soviet System: mono-organisational socialism from its origins to Gorbachev's restructuring*, Aldershot, Hants & Brookfield, Vermont: Edward Elgar & Gower Publishing Co, 1990.

T. H. Rigby and Bohdan Harasymiw (eds), *Leadership Selection and Patron-Client Relations in the USSR and Yugoslavia*, London: Allen & Unwin, 1983.

Uriel Rosenthal, M. T. Charles & Paul 't Hart (eds), *Coping with Crises. The Management of Disasters, Riots and Terrorism*, Springfield Illinois: Charles C. Thomas, 1989.

*Rules of the Communist Party of the Soviet Union*, Moscow: Foreign Languages Publishing House, numerous issues. For *Rules* . . . of 1990 see *Pr* 28 March, 28 June and 18 July 1990.

T. Samolis, 'Ochishchenie' (Purification) *Pr* 13 February 1986.

V. Savitskii, 'Vybor sud'i' (Electing a Judge), *Pr* 19 May 1988.

Leonard Schapiro, *The Communist Party of the Soviet Union*, London: Eyre & Spottiswoode, 1960, 1970.

Eberhard Schneider, 'The New Political Forces in Russia, Ukraine and Belorussia', *ROTU* 50/90 (13 December 1991) pp. 10–18.

V. Selivanov, 'O sile i avtoritete partii' (On the Power and Authority of the Party), *Pr* 2 May 1988.

Stephen Sestanovich, 'In Praise of the Liberal Demagogue', *Quadrant* (Melbourne), vol. xxxv, no. 10, October 1991, pp. 12–21. Reprinted from *The National Interest* no. 25, Fall 1991, pp. 1–15.

G. Kh. Shakhnazarov, 'Gorbatschow würde stürzen', interview in *Der Spiegel* 4/1991, 21 January 1991, pp. 131–4.

S. S. Shatalin, 'Nel'zya borot'sya so zlom pri pomoshchi zla' (You can't Fight Evil with Evil), *Koms Pr* 22 January 1991.

General Yu. V. Shatalin, 'The General's Line', interviewed *MN* 40/89 (1 October 1989) p. 5.

Ann Sheehy, 'Supreme Soviet Adopts Law on Mechanics of Secession', *ROTU* 17/90 (27 April 1990) pp. 2–5.

———— 'Moves to Draw Up New Union Treaty', *ROTU* 27/90 (6 July 1990) pp. 14–17.

———— 'Fact Sheet on Declarations of Sovereignty', *ROTU* 45/90 (9 November 1990) pp. 23–5.

———— 'The Draft Union Treaty: A Preliminary Assessment', *ROTU* 51/90 (21 December 1990) pp. 1–6.

———— 'Revised Draft of the Union Treaty', *ROTU* 12/91 (22 March 1991) pp. 1–4.

E. A. Shevardnadze, speech on resignation, *Iz* 21 December 1990 p. 5 cols 7–8.

L. F. Shevtsova, 'Krizis vlasti' (Crisis of Power), *Iz* 17 September 1990.

Yulii Shreider, 'Sindrom osvobozhdeniya' (The Liberation Syndrome), *NG* 23 May 1991 p. 5.

I. A. Shvets (ed), *Slovar' po partiinomu stroitel'stvu* (Dictionary of Party Construction), Moscow: Politizdat, 1987.

H. Gordon Skilling, *Czechoslovakia's Interrupted Revolution*, Princeton University Press, 1976.

Graham Smith (ed), *The Nationalities Question in the Soviet Union*, London & New York: Longman, 1990.

V. K. Sobakin, 'Mnogo li vlasti u Prezidenta?' (Does the President Have Much Power?), *Iz* 9 March 1991.

A. A. Sobchak, *Khozhdenie vo vlast'* (Coming to Power), Moscow: Novosti, 1991.

M. I. Solomentsev, interviewed on Politburo Commission on rehabilitations: *Pr* 19 August 1988.

A. I. Solzhenitsyn, 'Kak nam obustroit' Rossiyu?' (How Should We Rebuild Russia?), *Koms Pr, LG* 18 September 1990.

———— *Rebuilding Russia*, London: Harvill, 1991 (English version of Solzhenitsyn 1990).

B. H. Sumner, *Survey of Russian History*, London: Methuen, 1944.

Elizabeth Teague & Vera Tolz, 'CPSU R.I.P.', *ROTU* 47/91 (22 November 1991) pp. 1–8.

———— & Julia Wishnevsky, 'El'tsin Bans Organised Political Activity in State Sector', *ROTU* 33/91 (16 August 1991) pp. 21–5.

Ronald Tiersky, *Ordinary Stalinism: Democratic Centralism and the Question of Communist Political Development*, London: Allen & Unwin, 1985.

V. Tretyakov, 'Gorbachev's Enigma', *MN* 48/89 (26 November 1989) pp. 9–10.

———— 'Politburo's Nice Guy' (on A. N. Yakovlev), *MN* 26/90 (8–15 July 1990) pp. 8–9.

A. S. Tsipko, 'Someone Must Quit', *MN* 22/90 (10–17 June 1990) p. 3.

———— 'The Fate of the Socialist Idea', *MN* 24/90 (24 June–1 July 1990) p. 6.

———— 'Ukraine, Russia, and the National Question', interview in *ROTU* 33/90 pp. 19–24.

———— 'Boyus' novogo Kerenskogo' (I Fear a New Kerensky), *Koms Pr* 16 March 1991.

R. C. Tucker, *The Soviet Political Mind*, revised edition, London: Allen & Unwin, 1972.

George Urban, ' "The Best World We Have Yet Had" George Urban interviews Sir Karl Popper', *ROTU* 22/91 (31 May 1991) pp. 20–2.

*Ustav Kommunisticheskoi Partii Sovetskogo Soyuza*, Moscow: Politizdat, numerous issues; see *Rules of the CPSU*.

Don Van Atta, 'Theorists of Agrarian *Perestroyka*', *Sov Econ* vol. 5, no. 1, January–March 1989, pp. 70–99.

———— 'First Results of the "Stolypin" Land Reform in the RSFSR', *ROTU* 29/91 (19 July 1991) pp. 20–3.

V. I. Vasil'ev and P. P. Gureev, *Obrazovanie i razvitie SSSR kak Soyuznogo gosudarstva* (The Formation and Development of the USSR as a Union State), Moscow: Izvestiya, 1972.

A. I. Vol'skii, 'Smotret' otkrytymi glazami . . . ' (Look with Open Eyes . . . ), *Nedelya* 36/90 pp. 6–7.

———— 'Otkaz ot perestroiki oznachal by katastrofu' (Rejecting Reconstruction would Mean Catastrophe), *Trud* 8 May 1991.

A. A. Voznesenskii, 'Dumy o Chernobyle' (Thoughts on Chernobyl'), *Pr* 3 June 1986.

K. C. Wheare, *Federal Government*, fourth edition, RIIA, Oxford University Press, 1963.

S. L. White, *Political Culture and Soviet Politics*, London: Macmillan, 1979.

———— *Gorbachev in Power*, Cambridge University Press, 1990.

B. D. Wolfe, *Khrushchev and Stalin's Ghost*, New York: Praeger 1957.

*XIX Vsesoyuznaya Konferentsiya KPSS: Stenograficheskii otchet*, Moscow: Politizdat, 1988.

*XXIII S"ezd KPSS: Stenograficheskii otchet*, Moscow: Politizdat, 1966.

*XXVII S"ezd KPSS: Stenograficheskii otchet*, Moscow: Politizdat, 1986.

A. N. Yakovlev, 'Sotsializm: ot mechty k real'nosti' (Socialism – from Dream to Reality), *Komm* 4/90 pp. 8–21.

———— 'Rvetsya li k vlasti Gorbachev?' (Does Gorbachev seek Power?), *Koms Pr* 13 March 1990.

———— 'Na poroge krutykh peremen' (On the Threshold of Drastic Changes), *Iz* 31 May 1990.

———— 'Politika interesna v perelomnye vremena' (Politics are Interesting in Critical Times), interview in *Koms Pr* 5 June 1990.

———— 'Naiti sily i muzhestvo na deistvitel'noe obnovlenie' (Find the Strength and Courage for Real Renewal), *Pr* 23 June 1990.

———— speech to XXVIII Party Congress, *Pr* 4 July 1990, pp. 2–3.

———— 'Glavnyi itog s"ezda – razdelenie partiinoi i gosudarstvennoi vlasti' (The Main Result of the Congress – Separation of Party and State Power), *Iz* 26 July 1990.

———— 'Nuzhen novyi shag' (A New Step is Needed), *Iz* 2 July 1991 p. 2.

E. V. Yakovlev, interviewed by Radio Liberty, *RLRB* 487/87 (1 December 1987).

———— 'The Presidential Council', *MN* 33/90 (26 August–2 September 1990) pp. 8–9.

G. I. Yanaev, 'Profsoyuzy: krutoi povorot' (Trade Unions: a Sharp Turning Point), interview in *Pr* 16 May 1990.

Marshal D. T. Yazov, 'Voennaya reforma' (Military Reform), *KZ* 3 June 1990.

B. N. Yeltsin, speech to XXVIII Party Congress, *Pr* 8 July 1990 p. 4.

———— *Against the Grain: An Autobiography of Boris Yeltsin*, London: Jonathan Cape, 1990.

———— 'Soyuznyi dogovor i suverenitet Rossii' (The Union Treaty and Russian Sovereignty), *Iz* 14 November 1990.

———— press conference on his visit to the Baltic, *Iz* 15 January 1991.

T. I. Zaslavskaya, 'The Novosibirsk Report', *Survey*, vol. 28, no. 1, Spring 1984, pp. 88–108.

Victor Zaslavsky, *The Neo-Stalinist State: Class, Ethnicity & Consensus in Soviet Society*, Brighton: Harvester Press, 1982.

## III Official Communiqués, Documents and Legislation

(in chronological order of events)

### 1953–64

Khrushchev's 'Secret Speech' *On the Cult of Personality and its Consequences*: in English, in Wolfe, and Rigby, *The Stalin Dictatorship*; in Russian in *Iz TsK* 3/89 pp. 128–70.

### 1964–82

XXIII Congress of the CPSU: proceedings: *XXIII S"ezd KPSS: Stenografi-cheskii otchet*, Moscow: Politizdat, 1966.

Constitution of the USSR (the 'Brezhnev' Constitution): *Ved SSSR* 41/77 article 617.

### 1986

XXVII Congress of the CPSU: proceedings: *Pr* 26 February – 9 March 1986; or *XXVII S"ezd KPSS: Stenograficheskii otchet*, Moscow: Politizdat, 1986.

Law *On Individual Labour Activity: Pr* 21 November 1986.

### 1987

Central Committee Plenum, January 1987: resolution: *Pr* 29 January 1987.

Central Committee Plenum, June 1987: resolution: *Pr* 27 June 1987

Law *On the State Enterprise (Association)*: draft: *Pr* 8 February 1987; as adopted: ibid. 1 July 1987; amendments: *Iz* 11 August 1989.

Law *On the Manner of Appeal to a Court against Illegal Actions of Official Persons Restrictive of Citizens' Rights*: *Pr* 2 July 1987.

Rehabilitation of Chayanov and Kondrat'ev: *MN* 33/87 (16 August 1987) p. 12.

### 1988

Central Committee Plenum, February 1988: communiqués: *Pr* 18–19 February 1988; resolution: ibid. 20 February 1988.

Rehabilitation of Bukharin: *Pr* 6 February 1988; subsequent cases: ibid. 27 March 1988, 10 July 1988, 5 August 1988.

Central Committee Plenum, September 1988: communiqué: *Pr* 1 October 1988.

Declaration of Sovereignty of Estonia: *SE* 28 November 1988.

Central Committee Decree *On Commissions of the Central Committee of the CPSU*: *Pr* 29 November 1988.

Law *On Cooperation*: draft: *Pr* 6 March 1988; as adopted (26 May 1988): *Ved SSSR* 22/88 article 355; addendum: *Iz* 31 December 1988.

XIX Party Conference: theses: *Pr* 27 May 1988; proceedings: ibid. 29 June–3 July 1988; resolution: ibid. 5 July 1988; or *XIX Vsesoyuznaya Konferentsiya KPSS: Stenograficheskii otchet*, Moscow: Politizdat, 1988.

Constitutional Amendments: draft: *Pr* 22 October 1988; as adopted: *Iz* 3 December 1988.

Law *On Election of People's Deputies*: draft: *Pr* 23 October 1988; as adopted: *Iz* 4 December 1988.

## 1989

Results of General Elections to Congress of People's Deputies: *Iz* 19 March 1989 (CPSU seats); *Iz* 29 March, 5, 15 April, 20, 24 May 1989 (territorial constituencies).

Central Committee Plenum, April 1989: proceedings: *Pr* 26–27 April 1989.

Congress of People's Deputies of the USSR, First Session: proceedings: *Iz* 26 May–11 June 1989.

Supreme Soviet of the USSR: membership: *Iz* 1 June 1989; opens: *Iz* 8 June 1989; membership of Standing Committees and Commissions: *Iz* 13 July 1989.

Meeting of Regional First Secretaries, July 1989: proceedings: *Pr* 19, 21 July 1989.

Declaration of the Central Committee *On the Situation in the Republics of the Soviet Baltic*: *Pr* 27 August 1989.

Central Committee Plenum, September 1989: proceedings: *Pr* 20–22 September 1989. Platform of the CPSU *The Nationalities Policy of the Party in Contemporary Conditions*: draft: *Pr* 17 August 1989; as adopted *Pr* 24 September 1989.

Session of the Central Committee Commission on Questions of Party Construction and Cadres Policy: report: *Pr* 15 October 1989.

Central Committee Plenum, 9 December 1989: proceedings: *Pr* 10 December 1989, *Iz TsK* 4/90 pp. 25–112.

Decree of Central Committee Plenum *On the Formation of the Russian Bureau of the Central Committee*: *Pr* 10 December 1989.

Second Congress of People's Deputies: proceedings: *Iz* 13–26 December 1989.

Central Committee Plenum, 25–26 December 1989: proceedings: *Pr* 26–27 December 1989, *Iz TsK* 6/90 pp. 40–141; resolution: *Pr* 28 December 1989.

Law *On Constitutional Supervision in the USSR*: *Pr* 26 December 1989.

## 1990 (January–June)

Central Committee Plenum, February 1990: proceedings: *Pr* 6–9 February 1990.

Platform of the CPSU Central Committee for the XXVIII Party Congress, *Towards Humane, Democratic Socialism*: *Pr* 13 February 1990.

KGB Statement on Numbers of Purge Victims: *Iz* 13 February, *Pr*, *KZ* 14 February 1990, *Prav vest* 7/90 p. 11.

*Democratic Platform* for the XXVIII Party Congress: *Pr* 3 March 1990.

Results of Elections to the Lithuanian Supreme Soviet: *Sov Lit* 1, 2, 7, 13 March 1990.

*Fundamentals of Legislation of the Soviet Union and Union Republics on Land*: *Iz* 6 March 1990.

Results of Elections to the Congress of People's Deputies of the RSFSR: *SR* 14, 28 March 1990.

Law *On Property in the USSR:* Iz 10 March 1990.

Central Committee Plenum, March 1990: proceedings: *Pr* 12, 15, 17–20 March 1990.

Third Congress of People's Deputies: proceedings: *Iz* 13–17 March 1990.

Act *On the Restoration of an Independent Lithuanian State: Sov Lit* 13 March 1990; *Provisional Basic Law of the Lithuanian Republic:* ibid. 15 March 1990.

Law *On the Establishment of the Post of President of the USSR and the Amendment and Amplification of the Constitution:* draft: *Iz* 5 March 1990; as adopted: ibid. 16 March 1990.

Presidential Council: membership: *Iz* 25–26, 29 March 1990; first session: ibid. 28 March 1990.

Council of the Federation: first session: *Iz* 31 March 1990.

Law *On the Manner of Settling Questions Connected with the Withdrawal of a Union-Republic from the USSR: Pr* 7 April 1990.

Law *On the Legal Regime of a State of Emergency: Iz* 9 April 1990 or *Ved SSSR* 15/90 article 250.

Law *On the Languages of the Peoples of the USSR:* passed 24 April, published *Iz* 4 May 1990

Law *On the Delimitation of Powers between the Soviet Union and Subjects of the Federation:* passed 26 April 1990, published *Iz* 3 May 1990.

Congress of People's Deputies of the RSFSR: opens: *SR* 17 May 1990; proceedings: ibid. 19 May–24 June 1990; election of Speaker: ibid. 27, 30 May 1990; election of Supreme Soviet: ibid. 12 June 1990.

Report of N.I. Ryzhkov *On the Economic Situation of the Country and the Concept of Transition to a Regulated Market Economy: Iz* 25 May 1990.

Law *On the Status of People's Deputies of the USSR: Iz* 9 June 1990.

Declaration *Of the State Sovereignty of the RSFSR: SR* 14 June 1990.

Foundation Congress of the Communist Party of the RSFSR: proceedings: *SR* 20–26 June, 21 August–7 September 1990.

Law *On the Press and other Means of Mass Information:* draft: *Iz* 4 December 1989; as adopted: *Iz* 20 June 1990.

Decree of the Congress of People's Deputies of the RSFSR *On the Mechanism of Popular Power in the RSFSR:* unadopted draft *Decree on Power: AiF* 25/90 (23 June 1990); as adopted: *SR* 22 June 1990.

Decree of the Congress of People's Deputies of the RSFSR *On the Delimitation of Administrative Functions over Organisations on the Territory of the RSFSR (The Basis of a New Union Agreement): SR* 24 June 1990.

### 1990 (July–December)

XXVIII Congress of the CPSU: proceedings: *Pr* 3–14 July 1990; membership of Politburo, Secretariat and Central Committee: ibid. 15 July 1990.

*Programmatic Statement* of XXVIII Party Congress: drafts: *Pr* 13 February and 27 June 1990; as adopted: ibid. 15 July 1990.

*Rules of the CPSU:* drafts: *Pr* 28 March and 28 June 1990; as adopted: *Pr* 18 July 1990.

Declaration *Of the State Sovereignty of the Ukraine: PU* 17 July 1990 or *AiF* 29/90 (21–27 July 1990).

Presidential Decree *On the Restoration of the Rights of All Victims of Political Repression in the 1920s to the 1950s:* Iz 14 August 1990.

Statement of the USSR Government *On the Preparation of a Single All-Union Programme of Transition to a Regulated Market Economy and On Drawing Up Measures to Stabilise the National Economy:* Iz 11 September 1990.

Law *On Freedom of Conscience and Religious Organisations:* draft: Iz 5 June 1990; as adopted: ibid. 9 October 1990.

Lithuanian Law *On Political Parties:* draft: Sov Lit 6 February 1990; as adopted: EL 9 October 1990.

Results of elections to Georgian Supreme Soviet: ZV 13–18 October 1990.

Law *On Public Associations:* draft: Iz 4 June 1990; as adopted: ibid. 16 October 1990.

*Basic Directions of the Stabilisation of the National Economy and the Transition to a Market Economy* approved by the Supreme Soviet on 19 October 1990: Iz 27 October 1990.

Law *On Ensuring the Effectiveness of Laws and Other Legislative Acts of the USSR:* Iz 26 October 1990.

Supreme Soviet debate of 16–17 November 1990: Iz 17–18 November 1990.

*Treaty between the Ukrainian SSR and the RSFSR:* PU 21 November 1990.

Statement of Minister of Defence: Iz 28 November 1990.

*Union Treaty* (or *Treaty of the Union of Sovereign Republics*): drafts: Iz 24 November 1990, 9 March 1991, 27 June 1991, 15 August 1991.

Fourth Congress of People's Deputies: proceedings: Iz 17–29 December 1990.

Resignation of Foreign Minister, E. A. Shevardnadze: Iz 21 December 1990 p. 5.

Constitution of USSR, Amendments: Iz 27 December 1990.

Law *On the Universal Poll (Referendum of the USSR):* Iz 28 December 1990 p. 2.

### 1991

Decree of Supreme Soviet *On the Organisation and Measures for Conducting the USSR Referendum on the Question of Preserving the USSR:* Iz 18 January 1991 p. 3.

Plenum of the Central Committee of the CPSU: Pr 1–6 February 1991.

List of republics initialling Union Treaty: Iz 12 March 1991

*On the Results of the USSR Referendum of 17 March 1991:* Iz 27 March 1991.

*Collective Statement on Urgent Measures to Stabilise the Situation in the Country and Overcome its Crisis* (the 'Novo-Ogarevo Agreement'): Pr 24 April 1991.

Plenum of the Central Committee of the CPSU: Pr 25–30 April 1991.

Law of the RSFSR *On the President of the RSFSR:* RG 27 April 1991.

Law *On the Organs of State Security in the USSR:* Iz 24 May 1991.

Constitution of the RSFSR, Amendments of 24 May 1991: SR 7 June, RG 13 June 1991.

Results of Presidential Election in the RSFSR: SR 20 June 1991.

Ukase of the President of the RSFSR *On Halting the Activity of the Organisational Structures of Political Parties and Mass Social Movements in the State Organs, Establishments and Organisations of the RSFSR:* SR 23 July 1991.

Manifesto 'Slovo k narodu' (A Word to the People), signed by Yu. V. Bondarev, Yu. V. Blokhin *et al.*, *SR* 23 July 1991.

Plenum of the Central Committee of the CPSU: *Pr* 25–30 July 1991.

'Appeal to the Soviet People' of State Committee for the Emergency: *Pr, Iz* 20 August 1991.

Decree no. 1 of the State Committee for the Emergency: *Pr* 20 August 1991.

Law *On the Organs of State Power and Administration of the USSR in the Transitional Period: Iz* 6 September 1991.

*Treaty on an Economic Community: Iz* 4 October 1991; draft: ibid. 4 September 1991.

Interrogation of D. T. Yazov, V. A. Kryuchkov and V. S. Pavlov (translated from *Der Spiegel* 7 October 1991): *Iz* 10 October 1991.

Hearings in Supreme Soviet of the RSFSR on the Role of the Communist Party in the Putsch: *Iz* 22, 23 October 1991.

Decree of the President of the RSFSR *On the Activity of the CPSU and the CP RSFSR: RG* 9 November 1991.

*Treaty on a Union of Sovereign States (draft): Iz* 25 November 1991.

*Agreement on the Foundation of a Commonwealth of Independent States: RG* 10 December 1991.

Charges laid in the Case of the State Committee for the Emergency: *RG* 15 January 1992.

**IV  Speeches and Statements of Gorbachev**

(in chronological order; up to late 1988 these may be located in his *Izbrannye rechi i stat'i*)

### 1984–86

Nomination of Chernenko as Chairman of the Presidium of the Supreme Soviet: *Pr* 12 April 1984.

'Zhivoe tvorchestvo naroda' (The Living Creativity of the People), speech to ideological workers, 10 December 1984: *Pr* 11 December 1984 and *Izbrannye rechi* . . . , vol. 2 pp. 75–108.

Speech to April 1985 Central Committee Plenum: *Komm* 7/85 pp. 4–20.

Interview with *L'Humanité: SR* 8 February 1986.

*Political Report* to XXVII Party Congress: *Pr* 26 February 1986.

Television statement after Chernobyl': *Pr* 15 May 1986.

Discussion with writers on 19 June 1986: *Arkhiv samizdata* 5785, excerpted in *L'Unità* 7 October 1986 and *RLRB* 399/86 (23 October 1986)

Speeches in Vladivostok: *Pr* 27–29 July 1986; in Khabarovsk: ibid. 30 July–2 August 1986.

Speech in Krasnodar: *Pr* 20 September 1986.

Statements after Reykjavik Summit: *Pr* 14 and 15 October 1986.

### 1987

Speech to January 1987 Central Committee Plenum: *Pr* 28 January 1987.

Speech at XVIII Trade Union Congress: *Pr* 26 February 1987.

Speeches to June 1987 Central Committee Plenum: *Pr* 26–27 June 1987.

Speech to media representatives of 10 July 1987: *Pr* 15 July 1987.

Speech to representatives of the French public: *Pr* 30 September 1987.

Speech in Murmansk: *Pr* 2 October 1987.

Speech in Leningrad: *Pr* 14 October 1987, BBC Monitoring Service, *Summary of World Broadcasts* SWB SU/8699/C (15 October 87).

'Oktyabr' i perestroika: revolyutsiya prodolzhaetsya' (October and *Perestroika*: the Revolution Continues), speech on 70th anniversary of October Revolution, *Pr* 3 November 1987.

Speech to Moscow *gorkom* on dismissal of B. N. Yeltsin: *Pr* 13 November 1987.

### 1988

Speech at February 1988 Central Committee Plenum: *Pr* 19 February 1988.

'Arendnyi podryad – kratchaishii put' k prodovol'stvennomu dostatku' (The Tenant Contract – the Shortest Way to Adequate Food Supplies), address and discussion with farmers: *Pr* 15 May 1988.

XIX Party Conference: *Political Report*: *Pr* 29 June 1988; closing speech: *Pr* 2 July 1988.

### 1989

Speeches to April 1989 Central Committee Plenum: *Pr* 26–27 April 1989.

Interview with *Iz TsK* 5/89 pp. 57–60.

Speeches to July 1989 Meeting of Regional First Secretaries: *Pr* 19, 21 July 1989.

Speeches to September 1989 Central Committee Plenum: *Pr* 20, 22 September 1989.

Speech to and interview with All-Union Student Forum: *Pr* 16–17 November 1989.

Essay *Sotsialisticheskaya ideya i revolyutsionnaya perestroika* (The Socialist Idea and Revolutionary *Perestroika*): *Pr* 26 November 1989.

Speeches to December 1989 Central Committee Plenums: *Pr* 10, 26 December 1989.

### 1990

Speeches in Lithuania: *Pr* 12–14 January 1990.

Speeches to February 1990 Central Committee Plenum: *Pr* 6, 9 February 1990.

Speeches to March 1990 Central Committee Plenum: *Pr* 12, 18 March 1990.

Inaugural speech as President: *Iz* 16 March 1990.

Conversation with Komsomol delegates: *Pr* 12 April 1990.

'Slovo o Lenine' (A Word on Lenin): *Pr* 21 April 1990.

Speech to RSFSR Congress of People's Deputies: *SR* 25 May 1990.

Television statement on Regulated Market Economy: *Iz* 29 May 1990.

Report to XXVIII Party Congress: *Pr* 3 July; other speeches: ibid. 11, 13, 14 July 1990.

Speech on anniversary of Revolution: *Pr* 8 November 1990.

Speech to soldier deputies of 13 November 1990: *KZ* 15 November 1990 pp. 3–4.
Speeches to Supreme Soviet of 16 & 17 November 1990: *Iz* 17 November 1990.
Speech to representatives of culture on 28 November 1990: *Iz* 1 December 1990 p. 4.
Speech to Fourth Congress of People's Deputies: *Iz* 18 December 1990 pp. 1–2.
Statement after resignation of Shevardnadze: *Iz* 21 December 1990 p. 8.

**1991**

Appeal to Lithuanian Supreme Soviet: *Iz* 10 January 1991.
Statement on Vilnius shootings: *Iz* 23 January 1991.
Speech to Belorussian intelligentsia: *Iz* 1 March 1991.
Speech in Mogilev: *Iz* 2 March 1991.
Television speech on All-Union Referendum: *Iz* 16 March 1990.
Speeches to Central Committee Plenum: *Pr* 25, 27 April 1991.
Press conference with the President of France: *Pr* 8 May 1991
Speech in Alma-Ata: *Pr* 1 June 1991.
Nobel Lecture: *Pr* 6 June 1991.
Press conference with the Norwegian Prime Minister: *Pr* 7 June 1991.
Speech to Central Committee Plenum: *Pr* 26 July 1991.
Press conference on return to Moscow: *Pr* 23 August 1991.
Resignation from post of General Secretary: *Iz* 26 August 1991 p. 2.
'Conversation with the President over Tea': *Iz* 20 September 1991.
Interview with *Komsomol'skaya pravda: Koms Pr* 24 December 1991.

# Index